Barnes & Noble Critical Studies

General Editor: Anne Smith

Coleridge and the Literature of Sensibility

COLERIDGE AND THE LITERATURE OF SENSIBILITY

George Dekker

BARNES & NOBLE
BOOKS
10 East 53d St, New York 10022
(a division of Harper & Row Publishers, inc.)

Barnes & Noble Books
Harper & Row, Publishers, Inc.
10 East 53rd Street
New York

ISBN 0-06-491655-3

First published in the U.S.A. 1978

© 1978 by George Dekker

Printed and bound in Great Britain
MCMLXXVIII

Contents

Introduction

The Poet looks before and after, and so therefore must the literary scholar. To be sure, we have learned to be wary of several dubious models of historical contingency—such as those which teach us that certain eighteenth-century poets were essentially 'pre-romantics' or conversely, and less misleadingly, that the Romantics were essentially 'heirs' of the Enlightenment. They were essentially themselves, we are prompt to retort; and we are depressed that so much that once passed for literary history implicitly denies the historicity of Romantic and 'pre-romantic' alike. How much preferable, after all, is the alternative offered in Northrop Frye's classic essay 'Torwards Defining an Age of Sensibility' (*ELH*, June 1956, 144–52). Frye argues there for the radically different characters, the incommensurability almost, of the 'Age of Sensibility' and the 'Romantic Age'. I am one reader who gratefully accepts many of his demarcations. In particular, is he not right that the former age is especially distinguished by 'an interest in the poetic process as distinct from the product'? I think so and am confirmed in my belief by the way Frye uses this simple distinction to discover a common ground between such diverse masterpieces (or 'characteristic documents') of the age as *Ode on the Poetical Character, Tristam Shandy, Temora,* and *A Song to David.*

Yet by insisting so categorically on the special character of the literature of the mid and late eighteenth century, Frye also perpetuates the myth (which he elsewhere attacks) of a unified English Romantic Age, born full-grown in 1798 and marching off in an entirely new direction. On reflexion, many of us must wish to reaffirm that important continuities do exist and that, while it is certainly wrong to value the earlier period chiefly for 'Romantic moments' in a waste of Sensibility and decrepit Augustanism, it is no illusion that such moments (whatever we call them) are numerous and somehow historically significant. Nor, on the other hand, is it solely as inessential vestiges that the psychological preoccupations and formal discoveries of the Age of Sensibility survive in the nineteenth century: they are alive and functioning in the poetry of Wordsworth and Coleridge and continue to exert their influence in the extended lyrics of writers as remote as Whitman and Eliot. Though the term 'pre-romantic' does scant justice to the originality and daring of eighteenth-century literature, it points to an important truth.

My contention in this essay is that the early Romantics are our best (as they are also notoriously our worst) guides to what is characteristic and permanently interesting in the preceding age. Coleridge in particular really did know more about the literature of Sensibility than any twentieth-century scholar can hope to do. For him the issues raised by that literature were, quite literally, matters of life and death which he had finally to confront with all his great passion and intelligence. The proof that this is so is his last major poem, *Dejection: An Ode*, which in form as in theme, in imagery as in attitudes to life and art, is at once an epitome and profound criticism of the literature of Sensibility. As such it affords one of our best points of entry to, and perspective on, a wide range of antecedent traditions in creative and generic theory, iconography, metascientific speculation, literary biography and actual poetic practice.

Of course the poem *Dejection* is no mere precipitate of 'influence' but a work great in force of personal experience as in answering strength of art. It is a poem, indeed, which increasingly since World War II has been recognized as one of the pivotal masterpieces of Romantic literature. And it is precisely because *Dejection* transcends both its literary origins and its immediate personal occasion that it is still alive and largely available to readers who know little or nothing about Sensibility or the private agonies and joys of the Coleridge–Wordsworth circle. But the margin of incomprehension and error implied by my 'largely' is wider than appears at first sight, or even after many readings of the poem. For in spite or because of his apparent modernity, we know less about the rhetoric of Coleridge's poetry or the meaning of his key terms than we do about those of Pope, say, or Donne. So effective is the spell of his rhetoric that usually we are not even conscious that it is there. But there it certainly is, and if we fail to perceive how it works—or, for the twentieth-century reader, how occasionally it does not work—we must often misconstrue the poem as seriously as when we fail to register the exact meaning of his words. Nor can we truly appreciate just how great a personal and artistic triumph it is.

This essay takes its bearings from *Dejection: An Ode*, then, and is equally an interpretation of that poem and a contribution to eighteenth-century studies. In my first chapter I try to reconstruct the story of the genesis of *Dejection* in relation to Coleridge's own experience and writings. The story as I tell it differs widely from all previous accounts, and I believe it makes better sense both of the poem and of the biographical evidence. My second chapter takes its departure from those lines in *Resolution and Independence* which appear to be an 'answer' to *Dejection*. I seek to explain why Wordsworth

> thought of Chatterton, the Marvellous Boy,
> The sleepless soul who perish'd in his pride:
> Of him who walk'd in glory and in joy
> Behind his plough upon the mountain side. . . .

and I show how the imagery and psychological analysis in Coleridge's ode develop out of the eighteenth-century literature of Genius, Sensibility and Suicide. Chapter Three places the central figure of the Aeolian Lute-Poet in the context of previous usage in English literature. Chapter Four is a study of the complex connexions between creativity and what Coleridge and Wordsworth called 'Joy' as this was described not merely in their own writings but in works by (among others) Addison, Edward Young and Boehme. In Chapter Five I examine the generic background of *Dejection* and discover elements of theme, form and structure in the eighteenth-century 'greater' ode which are central not merely to Coleridge's odes but also to his Conversation poems, to the 'greater Romantic lyrics' of later English poets, and even to the symbolist lyrics of the American poetic tradition. The last and briefest chapter is a stanza-by-stanza commentary. This is something less than a full digest of the previous chapters and more than a mere appended essay in practical criticism; it is, rather, something of both and is intended to leave the reader with a sense of the unfolding design and wholeness, rather than of the fascinating parts and aspects, of *Dejection: An Ode*.

That Wordsworth figures prominently throughout a study of young Coleridge, *Dejection* and the literature of Sensibility will surprise no-one, but my frequent references early in the book to Lamb, Southey and many other exact or elder contemporaries should perhaps be prefaced with a further note on organization and objectives. The book begins with biography, intensely intimate and local and slow-motioned in character, and moves towards the impersonality of literary form and the long perspectives of intellectual and generic history, concluding with a close reading of *Dejection* in the light of all that I have said before. This arrangement has at least two advantages. First, it brings us to grips at once with that remarkably full and yet still tantalizingly incomplete information about Coleridge's private life to which we have privileged access but which can have been known only to a few of his closest friends—friends who were able (however imperfectly and unevenly) to balance this information against letters, conversations and observations that have not come down to us. Given the confessional nature of the poem and the strange history of its successive avatars, we could scarcely avoid this treacherous biographical ground if we would. In traversing it, however, we can at least make ourselves very aware of what we do *not* know, as well as what we do, about the circumstances surrounding the composition of *Dejection*; and we can isolate for special preliminary scrutiny these matters, which are and probably must remain highly conjectural, from matters of literary history which are not or are much less so. A second advantage of the organization I have adopted is that, by shifting our attention increasingly to matters not only less conjectural but also much more firmly in the public domain of letters, we are better prepared to read the poem as it might have been by its most nearly ideal reader: which is to say, in my view, not by the poet's most intimate friends nor yet by the most resourceful practical critic today, but by such informed contemporaries as Scott, Southey or Taylor of Norwich. Coleridge's, as the last generation of the old century and the first of the new, was still deeply inward with the moods, conventions and aspirations of the Age of Sensibility, but its sympathy was tempered by political activism and the lengthening necrology of poets who had followed Burns and Chatterton down the ways of despondency and madness. It was at once sympathetic and critical, and it was probably the last generation to be fully aware of the then public meanings of major symbols, formal conventions and theories about the nature of perception and creativity which are central to *Dejection*.

Studies of the poem have sometimes been written without much awareness of the cultural gap between these writers and the next generation or even of the experiential gap between Coleridge in 1802 and Coleridge in 1817. But before complaining that other approaches are prone to error, I should acknowledge the dangers of distortion which inhere in my own. I am able to recognize two principal dangers. The first is one common to all fairly ambitious studies of 'literary convention' or 'historical context'—that by glozing a text with many examples of previous or contemporary usages of words, symbols, verse forms, etc., a scholar may direct attention to everything *except* that which is fresh and unique in the new context, hence the new usage, that a great poet gives them in a particular poem. Though doubtless real enough, this risk is scarcely commensurate with the one entailed by ignorance of such usages, and it may be greatly reduced by scrupulous attention to the uniqueness not merely of the text especially under study but also of those cited as 'parallels', 'precursors', or 'influences'. This brings me to the second, actually the reverse of the first, danger which seems to be inherent in my approach. We apprehend that the perspective on eighteenth-century literature afforded by a 'Romantic' poem must be in some respects distorting or diminishing: it creates the mirage of the 'pre-romantic'. Of the several answers to this objection, the first (and the premise of the others) is that *Dejection* is not just any Romantic poem but one which is the most deliberate and informed of judgments on Coleridge's inheritance from eighteenth-century thought and literature. Another answer is that all literary history and interpretation is written from a limiting as well as a (hopefully) revealing vantage-point, and my own is no exception. Much that would obviously have to be included in a 'comprehensive' study of the literature of Sensibility—e.g. *Clarissa*, the connexions between Sensibility and contemporary evangelical movements—is omitted here; yet much is retained and placed in a longer historical and critical perspective than is usual in eighteenth-century studies. Finally, I believe that the best safeguard against contextual obfuscation— close attention to the uniqueness both of text and contexts—is also the best safeguard against the 'pre-romantic' fallacy. There-

11

fore, although *Dejection* is my point of departure and return throughout this study and I have included nothing that seems to me irrelevant to its better understanding, I have construed 'relevance' liberally: I have permitted myself to become deeply interested in the literature of Sensibility for its own sake.

Since this is a book likely to be read by students of Coleridge in the first instance, I shall say nothing further here about eighteenth-century literature and scholarship. Something remains to be said concerning studies of Coleridge. Generally speaking, in discussing the contributions of other scholars, my policy has been to spare the admonitory *sic*! For I have wished to write, if not quite a genial book, then at least one animated by a Coleridgean awareness that progress in literary studies—especially Coleridgean studies—is necessarily a collaborative affair, subject to many individual oversights and plain blunders. There are various reasons why this should be so, but here it may suffice to point out that none of us, not even Lowes, has been or is ever likely to be as 'myriad-minded' as the subject of our researches. All the same, nearly every book worth writing has its polemical occasion, and this one was written partly in response to, and in correction of, certain distorting tendencies which I have noticed in recent studies of Coleridge's poetry.

Two of these tendencies may be identified and diagnosed very briefly; they result from faulty or at any rate unreliable methodologies and are by no means peculiar to Coleridgean studies. One is the practice of using an author's later writings to interpret his earlier ones, as if his intervening experience of life and letters were of no consequence. While the evidence afforded by Coleridge's later writings and recorded comments cannot be simply dismissed as irrelevant to interpretations of *Dejection* and the masterpieces of the *annus mirabilis*, surely it must be used with extreme caution and strict attention to chronology. How casual and incautious interpreters have sometimes been in this respect can be exemplified by the frequent misidentification of the 'one Life' passage in *The Eolian Harp* (lines 26–33), which was in fact added in 1817, as an example of Coleridge's early (1795–6) thought and style. This error is no longer made by reputable scholars, I believe, but more subtle trans- or *impositions* from his later writings are all too common in studies of his poetry.

A related problem, to which I have already alluded, is the tendency of biographers to present conjecture as fact and to do so as it were accretively until successive versions of an event build up into an elaborate structure of surmise. Just how elaborate may be shown by one of the most recent accounts of the composition of *Dejection*, in Molly Lefebure's *Samuel Taylor Coleridge: A Bondage of Opium* (1974):

On the evening of Sunday, April 4, the day before the Wordsworths were to leave, the Greta Hall folk took tea (in those days an evening ceremony) with the Calverts at Greta Bank. Here Dorothy repeated some of William's verses to the company, *including lines from the new ode* [the Immortality ode] (*which William may well already have recited himself to Coleridge on Skiddaw, the previous day*)....

When he got back to Greta Hall from Greta Bank S.T.C. withdrew to his study and his laudanum bottle. Weeping, he stayed by his window for a long time....

On that memorable Sunday, April 4, 1802, the lines of Wordsworth's new ode must have struck into Coleridge's soul like an implement of torture. He watched the sun set over the Coledale Fells and the new moon come up with the old moon in her lap, reminding him of the ancient Scots ballad of Sir Patrick Spens....

Everything that I have italicized in this passage is inference; all or none of it may be true. Now it may be objected to my use of it as an example that Ms Lefebure is not a professional scholar but rather one whose initial interest in Coleridge and the Wordsworths was that of a freelance writer in search of material for a play. However, as the reader who bears with me through the first chapter will discover, Ms Lefebure's only original contributions to the story of *Dejection* as she tells it (and as it is generally told) are the laudanum and weeping. The rest is the joint 'reconstruction' of two generations of distinguished Coleridge–Wordsworth scholars. I do not mean to suggest that we should be other than grateful for their knowledgeable and sometimes inspired guesswork; for any account of the genesis of *Dejection* has to be largely speculative and some speculations are better informed than others. But a student of the poem needs to know where fact ends and conjecture begins and also how a biographer's conjectures may spring from, as assuredly they perpetuate, debatable assumptions about the nature and meaning of the poem.

The fictions of his commentators are sometimes necessary—I

shall create one or two of my own—and they are intended to bridge the gaps in our information rather than to deceive an unwary reader. Coleridge's own fictions have often seemed quite different, which is to say quite mischievous and reprehensible, in character. From Southey to De Quincey to Wellek, readers there have been who felt that his many empty promises, plagiarisms and lies were no better than those of any other man. But not until recently, with the appearance of Norman Fruman's *Coleridge, the Damaged Archangel* (1971), has there been a full, systematic study of Coleridge's duplicity. However well-written, such books are unpleasant to read, and their authors run many scholarly risks—the chief of which is that obsessive mistrustfulness is merely the obverse of credulity, and just about as incapacitating in the end. Yet students of Coleridge have so often ignored the evidence of duplicity, or failed to bring a tempered scepticism to the subject, that we should not blame Professor Fruman for sometimes going to the opposite extreme. Indeed, I think he is often most right when he appears to be most churlish, as when he contends that Coleridge's early statements about the *extempore* composition of his poems are scarcely ever to be taken at face value. The trouble is that Professor Fruman doesn't seriously consider how contemporary literary conventions and creative theory might be adduced to qualify the moral and pathological diagnosis of such deceptions. As I read it, the evidence indicates that Coleridge *and* most of his readers were willing dupes of a vatic myth which, while it illumined certain aspects of the creative mystery, obscured many others behind a Sibylline smokescreen. Where then does literary convention end and neurotic manœuvre begin? More important, how should our reading of his poetry be affected by our answers to these questions? I believe that only by being more sceptical about the man can we start to understand the true nature, which is to say the rich artifice and wealth of inherited as well as immediately personal experience, of a *Kubla Khan* or *Dejection*. And then we may return from the art to the 'real life' of the artist in the century of Smart, Chatterton, and the 'Enchanted Hero' of Addison's Pleasures of the Imagination: we may inquire how far the fictions that poets lived by were enabling or destructive of their talents, or both, but we shall not suppose that any simple answers can be given.

As for the later Coleridge, who alleged a 'genial coincidence' between his own earlier ideas and those of the German thinkers whom he sometimes did documentably plagiarize wholesale and word for word, I have but little to say about him in this book. I do have rather a lot to offer in support of the old-fashioned view of him as a library cormorant early gathering in a vast store of facts, images and ideas, many of which were the common aliment of the European Enlightenment and nourished as well Voltaire and Erasmus Darwin, Schelling and Goethe, Shelley and Madame de Staël. Some of these found their way into Coleridge's early (and best) poetry. I see no reason to doubt that he also enjoyed occasional premonitory glimpses of the great critical and philosophical syntheses he later discovered in Schlegel and Schelling. However, I am concerned here only incidentally with the possible provenance of 'his' later ideas, but very much with the fact that as a young man he had a wonderful gift for synthesizing other men's materials, and that this gift made his poetry greater, not lesser, than it would have been otherwise.

A muck-raking book like *Coleridge, the Damaged Archangel* is perhaps an American phenomenon in kind, but ever since Humphry House's fine *Coleridge* (1953) British judgments of *Dejection* have also been troubled and confused by the problem of Coleridge's honesty. House stopped short of arguing that the private 'unexpurgated' verse letter version of *Dejection* is better, because more honest, than the published ode. But at least two subsequent British selections of Coleridge's poetry, that by James Reeves and that by William Empson and David Pirie, print only the verse letter on the grounds that the ode is a bowdlerized text. Which text to prefer, and on what grounds, are critical questions of the first and most practical importance—and not less so because the value of 'sincerity' or 'authenticity' in poetry has been voluminously and inconclusively debated on both sides of the Atlantic. Yet I submit that the general debate can be usefully side-stepped and both critical and moral satisfaction obtained in this case, if only (I repeat) we are more sceptical about the man and more attentive to his art.

The means to do so are available thanks to the labours of several generations of scholars, and especially to the recent editions of Coleridge's notebooks and letters by Kathleen Coburn and the late Earl Leslie Griggs. As for the many insightful commentators on Coleridge's poetry, I believe I have learned most from Lowes, House and M. H. Abrams. My debts to other interpreters of his poetry

15

and thought in the context of English and European Romanticism are acknowledged in my notes, though too barely, I fear, and too often absent-mindedly. A few studies of Coleridge have appeared so recently as to preclude my making full use of them, but I know of only one that publishes evidence both substantially new and relevant to my concerns. This is John Beer's *Coleridge's Poetic Intelligence* (1977) which in effect reinforces without pre-empting my findings in Chapters Three and Four. Still more recently another early manuscript of *Dejection* has come to light. Because the version given in this MS. differs from the verse letter only in comparatively minor ways, its discovery does not affect my argument. I have been able to add a brief account of it, but not unfortunately a full listing of its variants, in the textual appendix.

A book which has been in the making since 1957—albeit with prolonged interruptions—must also owe much to the advice of learned correspondents, colleagues and friends. I have been especially ruthless in exploiting the time and good nature of Linda Jo Bartholomew, Gordon Brotherston, Donald Davie, Howard Erskine-Hill, Newell Ford, John Hayden and Donald Wesling. Advice from Earl Leslie Griggs and Richard Harter Fogle came at precisely the right time, when I had completed a penultimate draft of this book and needed fresh counsel and encouragement. I am grateful too, for the help of Jane Brooks, George H. Brown, Philip Damon, Stephen Gill, Ken Fields, Janice Haney, Joseph C. Harris and Anne Mellor. They all, for their part, must be thankful that the book, now open to public criticism, is at last beyond their power and mine to improve.

It is a pleasure to acknowledge the courtesy and aid I have received from the staffs of the following libraries: the British Library, the Cambridge University Library, the Dove Cottage Library, the University of Essex Library and (not least) the Stanford University Library.

A grant from the Dean of Graduate Studies at Stanford University defrayed the expenses of preparing the final typescript and index.

The following presses have granted permission to quote from their publications: Oxford University Press for quotations from the *Collected Letters of Samuel Taylor Coleridge*, *The Poems of Samuel Taylor Coleridge*, *Journals of Dorothy Wordsworth* and *The Poetical Works of Wordsworth*; Routledge & Kegan Paul Ltd.

and the Princeton University Press for quotations from *The Note-books of Samuel Taylor Coleridge*. For permission to reproduce the text of the verse letter to Sara Hutchinson, I am indebted to the Librarian and Trustees of the Dove Cottage Library.

Wivenhoe, Essex
1977

Quotations and Abbreviations

Quotations from *Dejection: An Ode* and the verse letter to Sara Hutchinson are from the texts given in the Appendix. Except when noted otherwise, quotations from other poems by Coleridge are from E. H. Coleridge's edition of *The Poems of Samuel Taylor Coleridge* (London, 1912). Unless noted otherwise, quotations from Wordsworth's poems are from Thomas Hutchinson's edition, revised by Ernest de Selincourt, of *The Poetical Works of Wordsworth* (London, 1936). Page references to these editions are not given, since I assume that the reader of this book will know the poems and have ready access to these, the Oxford Standard Authors, editions. In references to editions of the letters, notebooks, and journals of Coleridge, William and Dorothy Wordsworth, I have used the following abbreviations:

Letters   *Collected Letters of Samuel Taylor Coleridge*, ed. Earl Leslie Griggs (Oxford, 1956–71), 6 vols.

Notebooks   *The Notebooks of Samuel Taylor Coleridge*, ed. Kathleen Coburn (London, 1957–), vols. 1–.

Journals   *Journals of Dorothy Wordsworth*, ed. Mary Moorman (London, 1971).

Quotations from works which Coleridge certainly or probably knew are usually from eighteenth-century editions, which I have compared with modern editions whenever possible. The most important of these, simply abbreviated *Anderson*, is Robert Anderson's *The Works of the British Poets* (London, 1793–1807), 14 vols.

1

The Reshaping Spirit

Good verse *most* good, and Bad verse then seems better
Receiv'd from absent friend by way of letter.
For what so sweet can labor'd lays impart
As one rude rhyme warm from a friendly heart?
—*Anon.*, epigraph to Poetical Epistles in
Poems on Various Subjects (1796)

Tho' sweet thy measures, stern must be thy thought,
Patient thy study, watchful thy mild eye!
Poetic feelings, like the stretching boughs
Of mighty oaks, pay homage to the gales,
Toss in the strong winds, drive before the gust,
Themselves one giddy storm of fluttering leaves;
Yet, all the while self-limited, remain
Equally near the fixed and solid trunk
Of Truth and Nature in the howling storm,
As in the calm that stills the aspen grove.
—Keswick, Sept. 9, 1802, S.T.C.

1

There was a time when scholars fretted over Coleridge's reasons
for addressing *Dejection: An Ode* to 'Edmund' in 1802 and to
'Lady' later on. For overwhelming internal and external evidence
proved that the real addressee of the poem was, of course, William
Wordsworth. But then Ernest de Selincourt brought to light, not
only the verse letter to Sara Hutchinson which antedated and (in
a way) subsumed all other known versions of *Dejection*, but also
the first full text of the Dorothy Wordsworth journal which told
about the doings of Coleridge, Sara Hutchinson, and the Wordsworths during the brilliant creative spring and summer of 1802.[1]
Clearly, the story of the making of *Dejection* was much more

complicated than could have been supposed before the publication of these documents. It was, also, in some measure, the story of the making of the *Immortality* ode and *Resolution and Independence*—and of the making and unmaking of many a working, living relationship within the extended Coleridge–Wordsworth–Hutchinson family group. Moreover, the basic meaning and honesty of Coleridge's ode were now called into question; for perhaps it was no more than a bowdlerized edition of the verse letter—like the Rev. William Knight's edition of Dorothy's journal. Such were the implications of these texts, and during the years following their publication many critics have joined the argument about the formal, intellectual, and moral integrity of *Dejection*,[2] while a number of scholars have joined de Selincourt in the difficult task of construing a few unambiguous facts and many cryptic phrases into a coherent account of the relationships between that poem and other poems by Coleridge and Wordsworth, and between Coleridge, his wife, and his friends during the months when those poems were mainly composed.[3] The result of these critical and biographical explorations is—beyond question—a greatly enhanced understanding of Coleridge and his poem, especially as they stand in relation to other poems and people. And yet I shall argue in the pages that follow that we are in some respects further from an understanding of *Dejection* than were the happy readers who simply supposed that the ode was an ode but that 'Edmund' or 'Lady' was William. To say so is not to plead for a return to New Critical innocence; it is to stress the danger of falling into thinking that we know much more than we really do. What do we know and what do we think we know about the making of *Dejection*?

For this episode as for the rest of his story, Coleridge's letters and notebooks have to be consulted; I believe they can tell us more about the genesis of *Dejection* than is usually supposed. Yet they certainly say very little about the actual writing of the poem, and what they do say is retrospective, guarded, and in some instances deliberately misleading. Other normally helpful sources, such as William Wordsworth's or Charles Lamb's correspondence, are silent on this subject. In fact, as I have already suggested, speculations about the composition of *Dejection* are based largely on a few entries in Dorothy's journal and on internal evidence provided by the verse letter to Sara.

What does this occasional poem tell us about its own occasion?

To begin with, it is dated 'April 4, 1802.—Sunday Evening,' and this information agrees with the evening scene described in the body of the poem. Not only does the 'action' of the poem take place between sunset and midnight, but, as an almanac for 1802 will confirm, the new moon described so unforgettably in the opening stanza would actually have appeared in the night sky on 4 April. This dating is further corroborated by echoes of the *Immortality* ode, which was begun on 27 March and could not have been shown to Coleridge before 28 March at the earliest. Nothing mentioned in the poem is known to have taken place after 4 April. So much, for the present, for the dating of the verse letter. What prompted Coleridge to write it that evening?

The poem itself suggests two somewhat conflicting answers to this question. As in the published versions of *Dejection*, so in the verse letter does Coleridge describe a scene and a state of mind and feeling which are radically out of joint with each other: this particular evening is one that forces upon him a poignant recognition of his present and maybe permanent incapacity to respond creatively to natural beauty. That recognition leads him and his reader temporarily away from the 'present' scene to a series of reminiscences and analyses which try to explain the origin of his 'Dejection' at the same time that they celebrate its opposite, creative 'Joy.' Sara Hutchinson's role in this part of the poem is important but confusing. Important, because she, in the Wordsworth–Hutchinson family context, epitomizes everything that is missing from his own domestic life:

Sister & Friend of my devoutest Choice!
Thou being innocent & full of love,
And nested with the Darlings of thy Love,
And feeling in thy Soul, Heart, Lips, & Arms
Even what the conjugal & mother Dove
That borrows genial Warmth from those, she warms,
Feels in her thrill'd wings, blessedly outspread—

The 'Edmund' or 'Lady' of the published versions has a similar though far less particularized role as the *Allegro* to Coleridge's *Penseroso*. In the verse letter, however, this role conflicts with what might be described as the private occasion of the verse letter, which emerges rather unexpectedly only after the poem is well-advanced:

Ah fair Remembrances, that so revive
The Heart, & fill it with a living Power,
Where were they, Sara?—or did I not strive
To win them to me?—on the fretting Hour
Then when I wrote thee that complaining Scroll
Which even to bodily Sickness bruis'd thy Soul!
And yet thou blam'st thyself alone! And yet
Forbidd'st me all Regret!

And must I not regret, that I distress'd
Thee, best belov'd! who lovest me the best?
My better mind had fled, I know not whither,
For O! was this an Absent Friend's Employ
To send from far both Pain & Sorrow thither

Where still his Blessings should have call'd down Joy!
I read thy guileless Letter o'er again—
I hear thee of thy blameless Self complain—
And only this I learn—& this, alas! I know—
That thou art weak & pale with Sickness, Grief & Pain—
And I—I made thee so!

Coleridge's writing here is commonplace by any public standards, but his meaning seems clear enough: the verse letter is his anxious and guilty answer to a recent letter from Sara blaming herself and telling him that she is unwell; he on the contrary is sure that a previous letter of his own, 'that complaining Scroll', is responsible for her illness. One wonders what she made of this reparation, if indeed she ever received it. For this 'Scroll' not merely frets and complains, it explains at length why his loss of Joy is permanent and withering while hers is but temporary. If his original diagnosis was correct, what more effective prescription for a relapse? Of course Coleridge was a deeply unhappy and confused man, and so it is scarcely surprising that he wrote an unhappy and confused poem. My point, however, is this: the verse letter does not give us a single or clear answer if we ask what was the occasion of its writing. Many scholars have felt, with de Selincourt, that the answer lies in Dorothy's Grasmere Journals.

On 5 March 1802, exactly one lunar month before the date given for the verse letter, Dorothy noticed a 'Beautiful new moon over Silver How' which she described just a few days later, on 8 March:

On friday evening the moon hung over the Northern side of the highest point of Silver How, like a gold ring snapped in two and shaven off at the ends it was so narrow. Within this Ring lay the circle of the round moon, as *distinctly* to be seen as ever the enlightened moon is. William had observed the same appearance at Keswick perhaps at the very same moment hanging over the Newlands fells. Sent of a letter to Mary H. also to Coleridge and Sara, and rewrote in the Evening the alterations of Ruth which we sent off at the same time.

At that moment, Coleridge was visiting with Sara Hutchinson, and it is possible that they too had observed what struck William and Dorothy many miles away. It is still more likely—the sight being unusual—that Dorothy described it in the letters she wrote to Coleridge on 6 and 8 March. But these are guesses, not known facts.

Later that month, after Coleridge's return to the chill hearth at Keswick, the Wordsworths paid a week-long visit there. This began on the day after Wordsworth drafted the opening strophes of the *Immortality* ode and ended the day after Coleridge is supposed to have drafted the verse letter to Sara Hutchinson. During that period Coleridge and Wordsworth took several excursions together, and the visit was concluded with the Coleridges on Sunday, 4 April:

> We drove in the gig to Water End. I walked down to Coleridge's. Mrs. C.[oleridge] came to Greta Bank to Tea. Wm walked down with Mrs. C. I repeated his verses to them. We sate pleasantly enough after supper.

Dorothy does not specify which of William's verses she repeated to the gathering, but it is possible that these included the unfinished ode. She does not mention a new moon, but neither does she mention many of the other things we should like to hear about. All that can be inferred with any certainty is that the Coleridges' marriage was functioning well enough for them to keep up appearances.

A few weeks later, on 21 April, we hear for the very first time of a poem which in all likelihood is a version of *Dejection*:

> William and I sauntered a little in the garden. Coleridge came to us and repeated the verses he wrote to Sara. I was affected with them and was on the whole, not being well, in miserable spirits. The sunshine—the green fields and the fair sky made me sadder; even the little happy sporting lambs seemed but sorrowful to me.

That she was so poignantly affected argues that the verses in question were not a poem like *Love* but were, rather, one of the several specially edited versions of *Dejection* which Coleridge prepared for his friends.

On the evening of 4 May, Dorothy again observed 'the crescent moon with the "auld moon in her arms"'. The association with the *Ballad of Sir Patrick Spens* is one that might have occurred to Dorothy Wordsworth without the prompting of the opening lines of *Dejection*, but in the circumstances we can reasonably infer that Coleridge was lending Dorothy a mythologizing eye.

Two and a half months later, Coleridge was including lengthy passages from the 'publishable' parts of the poem in letters to Sotheby and Southey, and he was naming Wordsworth as the addressee of the poem. On 4 October 1802, Wordsworth's wedding day and Coleridge's own seventh wedding anniversary, the poem was first published in the *Morning Post*—mutilated and incomplete, but called an ode now, and addressed to Wordsworth under the pseudonym of 'Edmund'. For the last time the poem was stated to have been 'Written April 4, 1802'. Coleridge made a few subsequent alterations and additions, but these need not concern us here.[4]

Such is the main evidence upon which scholars have based their speculations about the composition of *Dejection*, and I have tried to state it in a matter-of-fact and conservative way. It is of course much more extensive and detailed than such evidence usually is. Usually, however, we are not so tempted to look behind the published artefact in order to discover the relationship between the man who suffers and the mind that creates. After all, *Dejection* in all of its versions is a poem about precisely that relationship, and the verse letter gives a different, fuller, and arguably more honest account than does the *textus receptus*. My case is that we know too much not to push our inquiry further, but too little to reach any certain conclusions. Hence the many and conflicting readings of the evidence I have cited, by some of our greatest Coleridge and Wordsworth scholars: de Selincourt, Chambers, Meyer, Margoliouth, Moorman. When scholars of this calibre disagree and no definitive interpretation seems possible, it might seem wise to abandon the quest. I should do so if I did not believe that there is more evidence to be sifted more carefully than heretofore, and that, conjectural though all must be, some readings are more misleading than others as to the kind of poem *Dejection* is. I shall summarize some of these accounts and show how fictive, if intriguing, they can be.

John Livingston Lowes wrote about *Dejection* only in passing, and wrote about it before the verse letter was made public. But he knew Dorothy's journals and also knew, better perhaps than any other student of the subject, what went on between Coleridge and the Wordsworths. Lowes' guess, based on Dorothy's entries for 8 March and 4 April, was that her magnificent description of the new moon in March supplied Coleridge with the *donnée* for the opening passage of *Dejection*:[5]

On Monday evening, when she made her detailed note of the circumstances, she sent off a letter to Coleridge. And on the very day in the evening of which the poem was written, she had talked with him. Is it possible to believe that the rimmed circle of the moon . . . was in neither the letter nor the conversation?

According to Lowes, then, the poem was partly inspired by Dorothy's descriptions of the March new moon, but was not written until a month later when another new moon was in the sky. This seems plausible as far as it goes, and it might be taken much further. However, later scholars have followed de Selincourt in contending that it was William's rather than Dorothy's observation that fired Coleridge to write *Dejection*. Noting parallels of theme and imagery between *Dejection* and the recently begun *Immortality* ode, and verbal echoes of the latter in the verse letter, de Selincourt surmised that[6]

though those stanzas of the *Immortality* ode only state the problem, and the *Ode* was not to be completed till more than a year later, he must have recited what he had already written, and spoken to him of that mood of meditative ecstasy in which his poem was to close . . . Coleridge wrote *Dejection* while Wordsworth was still under his roof; and soon after Wordsworth had returned to Grasmere, his joyful mission to Mary accomplished, Coleridge came over and repeated to him and Dorothy 'the verses he wrote to Sara'.

In sum, during the week at Keswick, Wordsworth, who was about to make final arrangements for his marriage to Sara's sister Mary, not only recited the introductory strophes of the *Immortality* ode but also disclosed a projected happy ending to it: the parallels and the even more striking contrasts with his own losses and prospects led Coleridge to write the verse letter on the evening of 4 April. 'It was upon that night that Coleridge wrote, or more probably completed, *Dejection: An Ode*'.[7]

Now, de Selincourt did not explain why he supposed that Coleridge 'more probably completed' the poem that night, but possibly he found it hard to believe that even Coleridge could have drafted a poem so long and (in some of its passages) so finished as the 340-line verse letter. This difficulty has not disturbed some of his successors. Mary Moorman, apparently reading the verse letter as a straightforward autobiographical document, concluded that Coleridge wrote it 'between sunset and midnight'.[8] H. M. Margoliouth, on the other hand, decided that 4 April 'was the day on which it was begun. All its 340 lines can hardly have been written in one evening'.[9] The caution displayed by Mr. Margoliouth is the more striking when we contrast his thesis with that of G. W. Meyer, who began by asserting that Dorothy 'could not have forgotten *The Rainbow* and the opening stanzas of the *Intimations Ode*' when with the Coleridges, Mrs. Calvert, and William himself at tea on 4 April, she 'repeated his verses to them'.[10] 'That night, prompted no doubt by the pathetic contrast of his own comprehensive misery with Wordsworth's good health, philosophic cheerfulness, and happy personal prospects . . . Coleridge permitted his most intimate feelings to erupt in the misshapen first draft of *Dejection: An Ode*'.[11] Meyer's notion that the *Immortality* ode was first unveiled to Coleridge at the tea time gathering on 4 April, with volcanic consequences that night, has been accepted with few if any reservations in more recent studies by George Whalley and William Heath, and it is now enshrined in at least two undergraduate anthologies.[12]

Any one or none of these accounts might be right. My chief quarrel with their authors is not that I disagree with their interpretations (though I do) but that they tend to state as fact what is only conjecture, and that they usually fail to mention that there is any disagreement. This seems the less excusable because E. K. Chambers long ago provided a model of biographical tact and insight in his discussion of the making of *Dejection*. After accepting de Selincourt's contention that it 'must have owed much of its original inspiration to Wordsworth's stanzas of 27 March, which were doubtless shown to Coleridge at Keswick', Chambers goes on to explain why we should not build too much on those suppositions:[13]

There are parallels of phrase, which make clear the link between the two poems. The search for these has been pressed rather far, and some of those suggested are rather remote and may not be echoes at all. Moreover, echoes may have gone either way. We do not know the precise form in which Wordsworth's stanzas were when Coleridge first saw them. He was still working at them on 17 June, but laid them aside, and did not finish them until 1804. And the setting, as we have it, seems to be of May, rather than of March. But one passage is clear enough. When Coleridge wrote, 'I too will crown me with a Coronal', he must have had before him Wordsworth's 'my head hath its coronal'. Coleridge's line is not in the published version of *Dejection*. But whatever his first intention with regard to the poem, it had taken, if not already by 4 April, at latest by 21 April, a form in which it was addressed, not to Wordsworth . . . but to Sara Hutchinson.

This analysis is as pertinent today as it was in 1938. Though Chambers' approach makes for unexciting reading, and I am far from suggesting that we should not venture a bold hypothesis in order to make sense of such evidence as we actually possess, I believe we are bound to prefer his caution and uncertainty to the confident reconstructions of Professors Meyer and Whalley. With little to go on except Dorothy's bare statement that 'We sate pleasantly enough after supper' on 4 April, Whalley tells us that 'it was a sombre and uncomfortable visit'.[14] Perhaps it was, but the evidence can be construed to mean exactly the opposite. More seriously misleading is his statement that, after writing the verse letter the night before they left Keswick, Coleridge 'said nothing about it to the Wordsworths; but at tea time on 20 April, having written twice to Dorothy in the interval, Coleridge came to the door of Dove Cottage. The next morning he "repeated the verses he wrote to Sara".'[15] How does Professor Whalley know that Coleridge 'said nothing about it to the Wordsworths'? And what is the point of such an assertion? Certainly the impression conveyed by his account is that Coleridge kept his secret from his friends for some eighteen days, and then, with some of the macabre dramatic flair that Professor Meyer attributes to William and Dorothy on the occasion of the 4 April verse reading, suddenly dropped his bomb on the astonished Wordsworths while they were sunning themselves in their garden one fine morning. It is possible to imagine them staging their lives in this way, expostulating and replying to each other at intervals in a series of carefully timed readings of new poems. It is possible, and I concur with Professor Meyer's thesis that *Resolution and Independence* is an 'answer' to *Dejection*. But I cannot help suspecting that these distinguished scholars have been carried away by a literary gift of their own, and that, above all, they have failed to give due weight to what Lowes spoke of—'the influence of that fugitive thing, the spoken word, so often more deeply penetrating than the printed page. And we reckon ill, if, in our study of blending impressions of every provenance, we leave it out'.[16]

On one point all historians of *Dejection* agree, and that is on the importance of the date given by Coleridge: 4 April 1802. I shall have more to say about the authority and significance of that date, but it should be noted here that the dates Coleridge assigned to his poems are sometimes symbolic (or strategic) and sometimes indicative only of the beginning or ending of composition. For instance, when Coleridge first published *The Eolian Harp* in 1796 as 'Effusion XXXV', he assigned a date, 20 August 1795, which can have been no more than the date of its inception. As an 'effusion', it was ostensibly spontaneous, the improvisation of a particular moment; in point of fact, the poem was augmented and revised throughout Coleridge's lifetime. Another instance is his *Ode to the Departing Year*, which, though actually written many days previously, was stated in successive early editions to have been 'composed and . . . first published on the last day of . . . [1796]'. Clearly, this was an allowable fiction intended to perpetuate the convention that an occasional Pindaric ode was a wild and irregular outpouring rather than a work of study and refinement. *Dejection* is a much more complicated case, to be sure. But there is plenty of internal and external evidence that 4 April 1802 is scarcely more definitive, historically speaking, than 20 August 1795 or 31 December 1796. Much of this evidence has been gathered and analysed in recent searching studies by George Whalley and William Heath, who, nevertheless, adhered to the agreed date of composition. I reach different conclusions because I approach substantially the same evidence from a different perspective. To me, the verse letter does not look like a first draft of *Dejection: An Ode.*

2

Professor Heath says of the verse letter that 'Only Coleridge could have written a poem like this, and it is almost as clear that he could hardly have written it, or wanted to write it, at any other moment in his career'.[17] With the first part of this statement I can have no quarrel; only this particular man could have written this verse letter, with all of its highly personal, particular references and allusions, and with, as well, all of the passages of great and characteristic poetry which have survived in *Dejection: An Ode*. But on Professor Heath's own showing,[18] the central themes and theories, together with much of the actual phrasing of the verse letter, can be traced through Coleridge's correspondence and notebooks at least as far back as the winter of 1800–1801. And if we choose to be as impersonal and 'universal' as Coleridge did choose to be in *Dejection*, we can trace these much further back still. In the following chapter I shall show in considerable detail how Coleridge and his friends regularly cast him in the role of a composite Otway-Chatterton-Werther figure who was doomed to early literary extinction or actual death. For the moment I shall limit my discussion to statements and gestures which do not clearly belong to that fateful persona.

Writing to his brother the Rev. George Coleridge on 23 February 1794, young Silas Tomkyn Comberbache struck the pose, at once awkward and literary and sincere, which was to be used so often and at last earned and dignified by real suffering and real loss:[19]

My Brother would have heard from me long ere this, had I not been unwell—unwell indeed—I verily thought, that I was hastening to that quiet Bourne, Where grief is hush'd—And when my recovered Strength would have enabled me to have written to you, so utterly dejected were my Spirits, that my letter would have displayed such a hopelessness of all future Comfort, as would have approached to Ingratitude—

. . . . . .

Repentance may bestow that tranquillity, which will enable man to pursue a course of undeviating harmlessness, but it can not restore to the mind that inward sense of Dignity, which is the parent of every kindling Energy!—I am not, what I was:—*Disgust*—I *feel*, as if it had—jaundiced all my Faculties.

At twenty-one Coleridge not unnaturally identified adult 'Dignity' rather than childlike 'Joy,' as the 'parent of every kindling Energy'. But remote as these two concepts seem to be from each other, virtue or a clear conscience seems to have been at the root of both. The context in which 'Dignity' occurs certainly shows that he had something more in mind than what might be lost by his absurd caper with the King's Light Dragoons. For throughout this letter to his solemn brother, he makes his sins sound grotesquely un-dignified in their rudderless frenzy:[20]

My Agitations were delirium—I formed a Party, dashed to London at eleven o'clock at night, and for three days lived in all the tempest of Pleasure—resolved on my return—but I will not shock your religious feelings—I again returned to Cambridge—staid a week—such a week! Where Vice has not annihilated Sensibility, there is little need of a Hell! On Sunday night I packed up a few things,—went off in the mail—staid about a week in a strange way, still looking forwards with a kind of recklessness to the dernier resort of misery—An accident of a very singular kind prevented me—and led me to adopt my present situation—where what I have suffered—but enough—may he, who in mercy dis-penseth Anguish, be gracious to me!

This confession must have been more shocking (and gratifying) to Brother George and Sam himself than it can be to us, but I think it is not merely our different perspective that makes immature vice, in this immature self-portrait, appear foolish, hectic and helpless; the effect is deliberate. In the eyes of humiliated Sam and his Southey-like brother, virtue and dignity were doubtless closely allied if not absolutely confused with each other. And with virtue went not only dignity but power. It is a far cry from the cun-ning-contrite rhetoric of this letter to the sad lucidity of

Joy, virtuous Lady! Joy that ne'er was given,
Save to the pure, and in their purest hour,

but the springs of Coleridge's shallowest rhetoric and deepest convictions were alike Christian. Even the pious formulary check-and-prayer ('but enough—may he . . .') at the close of the letter is an habitual device which could be used honestly and with splendid dramatic effect in his poetry later on.

Perhaps I have made too much of an undergraduate letter, but when its message was repeated three years later, in early April 1797, Coleridge was a husband and father, and his poetry, sermons, and political writings had made him something more than a merely local celebrity. Indeed, it was on the eve of the *annus mirabilis* that Coleridge wrote to Joseph Cottle the following unprophetic sentences: [21]

> But when last in Bristol the day I meant to have devoted to you was such a day of sadness, that I could *do nothing*.—On the Saturday, the Sunday, and the ten days after my arrival at Stowey I felt a depression too dreadful to be described
>
> So much I felt my genial spirits droop!
> My hopes all flat, nature within me seem'd
> In all her functions weary of herself.
>
> Wordsworth's conversation, &c roused me somewhat; but even now I am not the man I have been—and I think never shall. A sort of calm hopelessness diffuses itself over my heart.—Indeed every mode of life which has promised me bread and cheese, has been, one after another torn away from me—but God remains.

I suppose that anything Coleridge wrote to Cottle has to be taken with a grain of salt. Here he is making his excuses for neglecting his helpful but scarcely acute publisher, and I believe it is not cynical to infer that he knows he has a ready audience for the posturings of blasted genius. Nonetheless, Coleridge had causes to be depressed, some of which are alluded to in this passage. One of his chief devices for securing bread and cheese was to act as paid companion and mentor to the unfortunate Charles Lloyd. But Lloyd, whom Coleridge then considered 'most certainly a young man of great Genius', [22] had just suffered a series of violent epileptic seizures which not only prostrated Lloyd and the Coleridges but enforced his departure in circumstances which left Coleridge harassed by economic fears for his own family and doubts that Lloyd would ever recover. It is possible that the 'day of sadness' to which Coleridge refers in his letter to Cottle was the day on which Lloyd left the care of the Coleridges to return to his parents' home in Birmingham. At all events, it is clear from the letters of this period that Lloyd's illness was a shattering experience for Coleridge, and I think it is by no means unlikely that his sympathies led him, as it were, temporarily to impersonate the broken figure of his friend. And at this time, as always, there were unfulfilled publishing commitments of various kinds to add to his sense of harassment and failure. [23]

B

The lines which Coleridge quotes from *Samson Agonistes*, and which are to be echoed resoundingly in *Dejection*, do irresistibly raise the question of his relations with Sara Coleridge before the advent of the Wordsworths. It is true that after a year and a half of marriage Mrs. Coleridge ceases to appear as the 'Beloved Woman' of her husband's poems, and there is reason to believe that they experienced rough times during their first year of marriage. But a couple of months before the letter to Cottle he declares that 'We are *very happy*',[24] and so they appear to have been until, and perhaps for some time after, the Wordsworths moved to Alfoxden. But if Mrs. Coleridge was not Dalila, Mr. Coleridge did cast himself, for a moment, in the role of Samson. As I shall explain later, the figure of Samson was almost certainly associated by Coleridge and Wordsworth with the more recent and cerebral figures of Chatterton and Burns, but the point to stress here is that Coleridge's preoccupation with Milton's Samson recurs during the very period when he is supposed to have written the verse letter to Sara Hutchinson—by which time, of course, Coleridge was more prone to blame his wife for the shearing of his creative power and glory.[25]

Milton, a Monody in the metres of Samson's Choruses—only with more rhymes/—poetical influences—political—moral— Dr Johnson/

This note, written sometime between 13 March and 16 April 1802, has no explicit autobiographical bearing. But there is a fascinating parallel between, on the one hand, the echo of *Samson* in *Dejection* accompanied by a notebook notation of 'Milton, a Monody', and, on the other, the quotation from *Samson* followed in the same letter to Cottle by an exhortation to

Observe the march of Milton—his severe application, his laborious polish, his deep metaphysical researches, his prayers to God before he began his great poem, all that could lift and swell his intellect, became his daily food.[26]

In both instances Coleridge echoes the words of Milton's hero at his volitionless nadir, and then, by a half-contradictory leap of association, invokes Milton himself, supreme example among English poets of willed achievement. In his letter to Cottle, Coleridge goes on:

I should not think of devoting less than 20 years to an Epic Poem. Ten to collect materials and warm my mind with universal science.

And so on. Before our eyes we see the foul rags of the Gaza slave cast off and the bardic robes of the heroic poet put on. Though unaccompanied by the 'Enough!' or 'That way no more!' which in other instances acts as the dramatic transition from abysmal confession to aspiring prayer, the impersonations and the reversal are characteristic of Coleridge as a writer and a man. One way of describing his tragedy after 1800 is to say that, while the heroic reversal becomes less and less convincing, the impersonation of the 'flat' Samson gradually usurps the reality of Coleridge's life. Though the reversal in *Dejection* has, I believe, a quite different meaning—for once Coleridge was able to relegate 'Milton' to a notebook entry—yet this letter to Cottle is a sort of sketch and audition combined for the great ode of 1802.

Whatever else they may be supposed to reveal to critical hindsight, these early letters prove that the loss of his 'shaping spirit of Imagination' was a fear that haunted Coleridge for years before he met Sara Hutchinson—or even Sara Fricker. I believe they also reveal characteristic patterns of thought and feeling which recur in the verse letter but are transcended or transformed in the moment of strength and self-knowledge which is *Dejection: An Ode*. They reveal more, in my opinion, than do many of the early poems which contain images or phrases that reappear in the verse letter and *Dejection*—such as *The Eolian Harp* (1795–6), *The Dungeon* (1797), *Lines Composed in a Concert-room* (1799), *The Mad Monk* (1800), and *The Triumph of Loyalty* (1800).[27] For the letters are, however crudely, *ur-Dejections*, while the poems are not. And yet this is not entirely true, since *Dejection* is a poem about Joy as well as Dejection, and several of the conversation poems of the *annus mirabilis*—*This Lime-Tree Bower My Prison*, *Frost at Midnight*, and *The Nightingale*—clearly anticipate the treatment of Joy in the ode. What is more, if we were to trace the way Joy was linked with creativity and perception, we should also have to examine the blank verse that Wordsworth wrote during this period, especially *Tintern Abbey* and the earliest books of *The Prelude*. But it should suffice here merely to affirm the importance of this 'background' to the praise of Joy in *Dejection*. The poems in question are known to every student of English poetry, and the subject is complicated and important enough to warrant a chapter to itself.

The period that commenced shortly before the Wordsworths' arrival at Alfoxden in the summer of 1797 and which concluded when the Coleridges arrived at Greta Hall some three years later, was scarcely a period of unadulterated Joy. The estrangement from Southey, complicated as it was by marital connexions, shadowed a large part of it; the child Berkeley died while Coleridge was sojourning in Gottingen; the Wordsworths once found were then desperately missed; and but a few days before his first meeting with Sara Hutchinson there appeared clear portents of marital dissatisfaction: 'for the Wife of a man of Genius who sympathizes effectively with her Husband in his habits & feelings is a rara avis with me; tho' a vast majority of her own sex & too many of ours will scout her for a rara piscis'.[28] Nonetheless, the entire period was one of comparative happiness and achievement, and I can find only an occasional hint that Coleridge then reckoned himself fated to poetic impotence and an early grave. But from midsummer 1800 onwards the premonitions of *Dejection* crowd in so thick and fast that, in an essay of this kind, I can offer only a drastic summary and selection of the evidence.

He inaugurated his residence at Keswick with a fortnight of illness which left him with these reflections, communicated to his patron Josiah Wedgwood:[29]

That Tom receives such pleasure from natural scenery strikes me as it does you—the total incapability, which I have found in myself to associate any but the most languid feelings with the godlike objects which have surrounded me lately, & the nauseous efforts to *impress* my admiration into the service of nature, has given me a sympathy with his former state of health which I never before could have had.—I wish from the bottom of my soul that he may be enjoying similar pleasures with those which I am now enjoying with all that newness of sensation; that voluptuous correspondence of the blood & flesh about me with breeze & sun-heat; which make convalescence more than repay one for disease.

He was able to speak later, as he had previously, of the 'nutritive' value of natural scenery.[30] but his discovery that the 'godlike objects' of Nature had no 'correspondence' with or healing effect on an unwell man was one which would surely not be forgotten—

especially during the long winter evenings of 1801–2 when he and Tom Wedgwood engaged in abstruse research together. And a year before then he was to suffer the winter-long illness which broke him, and from which there never was a full convalescence.

During the late summer and autumn of 1800 he was able to will himself to complete Part II of *Christabel* and important revisions of *The Ancient Mariner*, just as earlier in the year he had been able to complete his superb translation of *The Piccolomini* and *The Death of Wallenstein*—in spite of his disgust with these tasks. These were not major productions of the Secondary Imagination, it is true, but they represented victories of a particularly significant kind for Coleridge. It is therefore the sadder to find him returning on 17 September 1800 to the theme of his letter to Cottle: [31]

Every line [of *Christabel*, Pt. II] has been produced by me with labor-pangs. I abandon Poetry altogether—I leave the higher & deeper Kinds to Wordsworth, the delightful, popular & simply dignified to Southey; & reserve for myself the honorable attempt to make others feel and understand their writings, as they deserve to be felt & understood.

Here it is Coleridge who abandons Poetry, rather than Poetry that abandons Coleridge; but a little later he gives a different account: [32]

the deep unutterable Disgust, which I had suffered in the translation of that accursed Wallenstein, seemed to have stricken me with barrenness—for I tried & tried, & nothing would come of it. I desisted with a deeper dejection than I am willing to remember. The wind from Skiddaw & Borrowdale was often as loud as wind need be—& many a walk in the clouds on the mountains did I take; but all would not do—till one day. . . .

Once again Coleridge's correspondent is Josiah Wedgwood, to whom he regularly sent descriptions of lengthy paralysis (to excuse non-performance) and recent bouncing recovery (to justify the Wedgwoods' investment). There was nothing hypocritical in this. As we have seen, the manic-depressive swing from Samson to Milton was the way he frequently felt about his own destiny. Moreover, as the *Dejection* ode itself brilliantly manifests, Coleridge *was* able to make astonishing recoveries. And yet he clearly did love to dramatize his ups and downs, even to the point of self-caricature. There is even a delightful whimsy in the picture he paints of himself as the songless Bard seeking Elevation by taking 'many a walk in the clouds on the mountains' and seeking an Aeolian Visitation from the wind that 'was often as loud as wind need be'. It is startling to realize that this whimsical *Tale of the Tub* imagery was to become the central image-metaphor of *Dejection*: startling, and yet the prefiguring itself now seems inevitable, both because the metaphor itself was virtually inevitable and because *Dejection* was much the most elaborately rehearsed of all his performances. As the winter and with it his illness wear on, he continues to play with variations on the basic wind-as-inspiration metaphor: [33]

yet still [m]y animal spirits bear me up—tho' I am so weak, that even from sitting up to write this note to you I seem to sink in upon myself in a ruin, like a Column of Sand informed and animated only by a Whirl-blast of the Desart.

The Poet is dead in me — my imagination (or rather the Somewhat that had been imaginative) lies, like a Cold Snuff on the circular Rim of a Brass Candle-stick, without even a stink of Tallow to remind you that it was once cloathed & mitred with Flame. That is past by!—I was once a Volume of Gold Leaf, rising & riding on every breath of Fancy—but I have beaten myself back into weight & density, & now I sink in quicksilver, yea, remain squat and square on the earth amid the hurricane, that makes Oaks and Straws join in one Dance, fifty yards high in the Element.

These variants on the wind figure are more novel, more striking than the one Coleridge used in the letter-ode, where, though his confession of poetic failure had to be ironic in so far as the poem itself had to be an actual poetic success, he could not risk a witty irony or brilliant exotic imagery.

By April 1801 he was again prophesying not merely the death of the poet but the death of the man as well in a series of letters to his friends. [34] Whatever the nature of his illnesses that winter, it is virtually certain that he did suffer a great deal of physical pain and that he became addicted to opium at that time as a result of his efforts to escape from the pain. This was also the period during which he first took refuge from physical pain by engaging in 'abstruse research'. What this meant is not entirely clear to me, but it did involve philosophical speculation supported by empirical research in which he used himself as a guinea pig: [35]

I have not only completely extricated the notions of Time, and Space; but have overthrown the doctrine of Association, as taught by Hartley, and with it all the irreligious metaphysics of modern Infidels—especially, the doctrine of Necessity. . . . At Wordsworth's advice or rather fervent intreaty I have intermitted the pursuit—the intensity of thought, & the multitude of minute experiments with Light & Figure, have made me so nervous & feverish, that I cannot sleep . . . it seemed to me a Suicide of my very soul to divert my attention from Truths so important, which came to me almost as a Revelation/

This was written to Poole; writing to Godwin a few days later, he is less boastful and more aware of the dangers of his research:[36]

In my long Illness I had compelled into hours of Delight many a sleepless, painful hour of Darkness by chasing down metaphysical Game. . . . You would not know me—! all sounds of similitude keep at such a distance from each other in my mind, that I have *forgotten* how to make a rhyme—I look at the Mountains (that visible God Almighty that looks in at all my windows) I look at the Mountains only for the Curves of their outlines; the Stars, as I behold them, form themselves into Triangles. . . . The Poet is dead in me—

which is followed by the passage describing the loss of an imagination that was once like a 'Volume of Gold Leaf, rising & riding. . . .' What seemed a 'Suicide' of his soul *not* to pursue has been found suicidal indeed:[37]

I am not dissembling when I express my exceeding scepticism respecting the sanity of my own Feelings & Tone of Intellect, relatively to a work of Sentiment & Imagination.—I have been compelled, (wakeful thro' the night, & seldom able, for my eyes, to read in the Day) to seek resources in austerest reasonings—& have thereby so denaturalized my mind, that I can scarcely convey to you the disgust with which I look over any of my own compositions—

Still other passages from Coleridge's letters might be cited to show how he explained the causes and effects of his 'abstruse research,'[38] but enough has been quoted to show that it was pursued for its own sake as well as for the sake of distraction from physical pain—and that it was pursued in spite of Wordsworth's 'fervent intreaty'.

How far it was also a refuge from psychological pain is impossible to say. In the letters to Poole and Godwin 'abstruse research' was invariably associated with physical illness, and this was the case as late as 31 October 1801 when in a letter to Poole he exclaimed, 'O how I *watched* myself while the Lancet was at my Leg!—*Vivat Metaphysic!*'[39] But although the surviving evidence points to physical suffering as the first and chief cause of his recourse to 'abstruse research', it is hard to believe that mental suffering was not an important factor from the start. From the moment the Coleridges settled in Greta Hall there were financial problems, there was the unwelcome presence of Charles Lloyd nearby, and there was Wordsworth's unnervingly equivocal attitude towards both *The Ancient Mariner* and *Christabel*.[40] And even if there had not been such comparatively plausible grounds for sieges of depression, Coleridge was not the man to rest secure and easy in any Paradise. In a passage of self-analysis which anticipates *Dejection*, he quotes from *Tintern Abbey* in a way which may help us to understand how Wordsworth's precepts and example both sustained and intimidated his friend:[41]

> & this greatly alarms me.—So much for the doleful! Amid all these changes & humiliations & fears, the sense of the Eternal abides in me, and preserves unsubdued
>
> > My chearful Faith that all which I endure
> > Is full of Blessings!
>
> At times indeed I would fain be somewhat of a more tangible utility than I am, but so, I suppose, it is with all of us—one while cheerful, stirring, feeling in resistance nothing but a joy & a stimulus; another while drowsy, self-distrusting, prone to rest, loathing our own Self-promises, withering our own Hopes, our Hopes, the vitality & cohesion of our Being!—

The tone of this is relatively cheerful, but it acquires a certain pathos from our knowledge that his Wordsworthian 'Faith' would not survive the winter of 1801–2 and that this letter was written to Humphry Davy, then on the threshold of his brilliant success in London and described in this letter as one of the 'few who combine the "Are" & the "will be"'. In his concern for Davy's welfare as a scientist (and even poet) of great promise, he enquires anxiously whether Davy might 'have not exposed yourself to unwholesome influences in your chemical pursuits'. There is perhaps no connexion between this enquiry and Coleridge's description of his own periods of despair, of 'loathing our own Self-promises, withering our own Hopes. . . .' But it soon turns out that Davy had damaged himself in the course of his researches—but not, apparently, of his laboratory experiments: Davy, Coleridge tells Southey, 'complained in a deep tone of the ill effect which perpetual analysis had on his mind'.[42] Again, there may be no connexion between this statement and Coleridge's earlier enquiry. But these apparently unconnected remarks to or about Davy do at least show Coleridge groping towards a theory of causal relationships between mental depression, 'abstruse research', and creativity—the theory which is expressed with something less than perfect connectedness in *Dejection*.

Thus far I have said little about the mental distress occasioned by Mrs. Coleridge's 'dyspathy' and Coleridge's hopeless love for 'the other Sara'. I have reserved this discussion for two reasons. First, very little is known about the early stages of his love for the one and his break-up with the other; it becomes a documentable part of the story only as we draw nearer the date when the verse letter is said to have been written. Second, I have wished to establish that, so far as main themes and images and theories are concerned, the ode—as distinct from the verse-letter—*could* have been written at least a year before the 4 April 1802 date which Coleridge carefully assigned to all versions of the poem whenever he mentioned or quoted from one of them during 1802. Now I do not suppose it *was* written so early as that, and I do suppose that his troubles with the two Saras began some time before they came to the surface in his (surviving) letters and notebook entries for the late summer and autumn of 1801. But on my reading of the evidence these troubles were perhaps no more than subordinate factors in Coleridge's collapse during the winter of 1800–1801, and they may well have been as much effects as causes of that collapse. This is partly to say that Coleridge emerged from that terrible winter with a greater need than ever for unqualified sympathy and reassurance—which Sara Fricker had been unable to provide in the best of times. It is also to say that he emerged with a need to explain and perhaps even excuse a collapse which—in actuality and in the account given in the ode—had something mysterious and self-engendered about it. However this may be, the verse letter survives as proof that, in the changed circumstances of the early spring of 1802, he was telling Sara Hutchinson and himself that his ill-starred marriage was at the bottom of it all: of his loss of Joy, of his 'abstruse research' and therefore

41

of his loss of the shaping spirit of Imagination. This can only be described as a radical reshaping of the views recorded in his correspondence with Godwin, Poole, and Davy the year before. Was the verse letter also a reshaping of lines already written—and written in a spirit nearer that of the correspondence of 1800–1801 and of the *textus receptus* of 1817? As I have shown, the external evidence proves that this was possible, and the internal evidence in the verse letter does, to my mind, argue strongly in favour of such a conclusion.

Before turning to the text of the verse letter, however, I must give a brief summary of Coleridge's relations with the two Saras from the time he first met the Hutchinson family until *Dejection's* first mutilated appearance in print on 4 October 1802. As I have already stated, very little is known for certain about the matter. We can perhaps assume that Coleridge would never have fallen in love with Sara Hutchinson had he not grown indifferent or hostile to his wife, and, aside from the homesick letters from Germany, there certainly is a noticeable decline in the number of affectionate references to her in poems and letters after the summer of 1797, when Wordsworth and his 'exquisite Sister' became their neighbours. But before that time and in spite of the inauspicious beginnings of their courtship, there had been an extended period of mutual warmth and affection which must have strengthened the good marital intentions of both parties even after Sara came to know that sister Edith had, in Southey, the kind of husband every Fricker girl needed and deserved, and after Coleridge came to understand fully what a woman like Dorothy Wordsworth might mean to a man like himself. At any rate, Coleridge had known Dorothy over four years and Sara Hutchinson nearly two years before the first definite evidence of discord at home made its appearance in a letter to Godwin dated 22 September 1801 where Coleridge refers to recent 'additional sources of Disquietude' which are unmistakably domestic.[43] By this time there could be no doubt, in his mind or Mrs. Coleridge's, that he was in love with Sara Hutchinson and determined to continue what he considered an innocent relationship. However, convinced as he was that his marriage was indissoluble, he also determined to effect a reconciliation with his wife if he could.[44] By 19 February 1802, and after three months of separation, Coleridge found it possible to write to her in these terms:[45]

I attribute my amendment to the more tranquil State of my mind —& to the chearfulness inspired by the thought of speedily returning to you in love & peace—I am sure, I drive away from me every thought but those of Hope & the tenderest yearnings after you—And it is my frequent prayer, & my almost perpetual aspiration, that we may meet to part no more—& live together as affectionate Husband & Wife ought to do.

That this may have happened for a short time at least is indicated by the fact that a child was conceived shortly after his return to Keswick in mid-March 1802.[46] But if the directly personal sections of the verse letter were composed on 4 April 1802, the reconciliation must have been very short-lived.[47] And if his letters to Southey and Tom Wedgwood are to be believed,[48] his relations with Mrs. Coleridge must have deteriorated yet farther after the verse letter was written. For they describe a state of marital warfare and desperation that is not easily reconciled with Dorothy's narrative of the Wordsworths' visit to Keswick in early April. Then, whatever tensions Dorothy may have sensed, Mrs. Coleridge joined her husband and the Wordsworths in a variety of activities, though perhaps only for the sake of maintaining appearances. At any rate, the appalling battle of wills ended with the spring, and throughout the summer and autumn the Coleridges enjoyed a time of 'more Love & Concord in my House, than I have known for years before.'[49] What is more, in the same letter of 29 July to Southey, Coleridge appears to have been having second thoughts about what had driven him to 'abstruse research':

As to myself, all my poetic Genius, if ever I really possessed any *Genius*, & it was not rather a mere general *aptitude* of Talent, & quickness in Imitation/is gone—and I have been fool enough to suffer deeply in my mind, regretting the loss—which I attribute to my long & exceedingly severe Metaphysical Investigations—& these partly to ill-health, and partly to private afflictions which rendered any subject, immediately connected with Feeling, a source of pain & disquiet to me/

As we have seen, this explanation squares with the historical record as it is preserved in Coleridge's correspondence over a period of several years.[50] And it was in this more honest and perhaps forgiving spirit that he undertook the editorial labours which issued in the publication of *Dejection: An Ode* in the *Morning Post* for 4 October 1802.

We are left with the problem of Sara Hutchinson's relationship to the events I have been recounting. When, in the first place, did it begin? Coleridge may have become consciously in love with her as early as their first meeting in the late autumn of 1799 (as George Whalley seems to believe) or as late as Coleridge's long visit with the Hutchinsons during the summer of 1801 (as E. K. Chambers concluded) or (as E. L. Griggs argues) during the winter of 1800–1 when she visited the Wordsworths for several months.[51] Frankly, the evidence is so sparse and inconclusive that a biographer has a right to choose the date that suits his own convenience as an interpreter of other events in Coleridge's life. My own guess is that Griggs is right when he speculates that an attachment 'ripened into love during Sara's protracted stay with the Wordsworths in the winter of 1800–1' and that Coleridge's 'month-long visit with the Hutchinsons in the summer of 1801 precipitated a crisis' at Greta Hall. My reasons for guessing that there was no love at first sight in 1799 are, first, that Coleridge seems to have made no effort to see her until after she visited him at Keswick a full year later; second, that with the doubtful exception of *Love* (1799) Coleridge wrote no love poems to Sara which can be dated certainly before 1801; and third, that Coleridge assured Southey on 12 February 1800 that, in spite of basic temperamental conflicts with his wife, he was content—indeed, happier than he had been during his early married life when he was sometimes made almost miserable by their differences.[52] If I am right about this, the love for Sara Hutchinson developed about the time that physical suffering was driving him into opium addiction and 'abstruse research'. Or, if Chambers is right, these addictions had taken hold of him before he found himself in love with Sara. In either case, his initial recourse to 'abstruse research' cannot well be blamed solely on frustrated love for Sara. At all events, by the end of the summer of 1801 he was most definitely in love with her and out of love with his wife; his finest 'Asra' poem, the sonnet to her, was perhaps written about then; and then ensued the first of Coleridge's deliberate separations from his wife. Unhappy and in miserable health during the autumn and winter of 1801, Coleridge burdened Sara and the Wordsworths with complaints, as Dorothy's *Journals* make painfully clear. And although his health and attitude to his wife greatly improved in January and February, he found it necessary on his way home to stop with Sara for eleven days and therefore to arrive for his joyful reconciliation with Mrs. Coleridge a week later than promised. As William Heath and Geoffrey Yarlott have observed,[53] the notes Coleridge made during this visit with Sara show considerable strain. One of the notes,[54]

Friday, March 12th/"& wept aloud."—you made me feel uncomfortable/

suggests that there may have been some sort of crisis between them, and clearly, at this juncture, their Platonic affair cannot have been making either of them happy. Possibly they agreed not to see each other for a time? In any case, with the exception of a conceivably accidental meeting in passing in November, he did not see Sara again until Christmas 1802 when she was staying with the Wordsworths once more. The letters to Sara which have survived from this period do, however, belong to that Indian Summer of health and conjugal rapport which seems to have commenced in June or July; and they are loving, cheerful letters which must have made Sara not dread the thought of seeing him again.[55]

There is no way of knowing what she thought, or what Coleridge may have explained to her, about the ode entitled *Dejection* which was published in the *Morning Post* on the day of Wordsworth's wedding and his own seventh wedding anniversary. Some of the 'Asra' poems, notably the fine sonnet *To Asra*, did not see print during their lifetimes. But this one passed easily enough as a poem to Wordsworth. To whom was the poem really meant to be addressed? Many of the 340 lines of the verse letter can have been addressed only to Sara; the *Morning Post* version of 139 lines certainly reads like a poem to Wordsworth; and we know that between 3 April and 4 October 1802 Coleridge felt able to tell his dear friend Thomas Poole that 'on 4th of April last I wrote you a letter in verse; but I thought it dull & doleful—& did not send it—'.[56] There was only one other friend comparably intimate and important to Coleridge the poet, and that of course was Dorothy. The claims of Sara and William seem obvious enough, and it is easy to believe that the verse letter is simply an amalgamation of lines written at different times with one or the other in mind as the person addressed. Poole's claims are also strong, and there are lines in the ode that are strikingly anticipated by this passage in a letter to him, dated 1 February 1801:[57]

O my dear dear Friend! that you were with me by the fireside of my Study here, that I might talk it over with you to the Tune of this Night Wind that pipes it's thin doleful climbing sinking Notes like a child that has lost it's way and is crying aloud, half in grief and half in the hope to be heard by it's Mother.

The rhythm, syntax, and imagery of this passage are untypical of Coleridge's epistolary prose, and I suspect he is quoting from something already composed, recalled in this context because of nostalgic associations with Poole's 'great windy Parlour'.[58] But important as Poole's friendship was to him, Coleridge it was whose 'animal Spirits corrected his [Poole's] inclinations to melancholy.'[59] I therefore doubt that the poem could have been intended for him in anything like the ode or verse-letter versions, where the person addressed does—in spite of some temporary sickness—possess the pristine Joy to which the poet has lost access. As for Dorothy, about the only reason I can think of for supposing that the poem was not addressed to her is that, to my knowledge, Coleridge never said it was. As we have seen, she may have supplied him with the crucial donnée for the poem; and her role at this time as chief comforter and support to both hypochondriacal bards certainly merited the address of any number of their poems. Substitute 'Rotha' (Coleridge's affectionate nickname for her) for 'Sara', 'William', 'Edmund' or 'Lady', and the poem in any of its versions would require very few adjustments to make perfect biographical sense.

However, I suppose the poem belonged to each and all of them, and to others besides who were less intimate and deserving. Earlier in this essay I suggested that letters Coleridge wrote to his brother George in 1794 and to Joseph Cottle in 1797 might be regarded as ur-Dejections, and the same can surely be said of various letters which he sent to Davy, Godwin, the Wedgwoods, and Southey between 1800 and 1802. In one letter he not infrequently repeated ideas, rhetorical devices, and actual phrases that he used in another letter the same day or a week before. That was his way. He gave the best that he had (whether 'his own' or not) to each of his correspondents, and yet he never forgot their individual interests and concerns. (When writing to Godwin, for instance, he repeats ideas that appear in letters to Poole or Davy, but he does not fail to mention Godwin's little Fanny and Mary.) Possibly the final change of address from 'Edmund' to 'Lady' in the 1817 text of the poem implies that, in the end, Coleridge perceived that it was his letter to all who might care to understand. Possibly, too, it was a way of restoring to Sara what, like his heart, once belonged to her more than it did to anybody else, though it was something he gave to many people. We shall never know. By the time of *Sibylline Leaves* Coleridge could no longer describe Wordsworth as perfectly 'pure of heart'; and even Sara, Dorothy, and good Tom Poole were either estranged or practically lost to him as close friends. The same self-destructive habits and demands described or alluded to in *Dejection* as costing him his shaping spirit of Imagination had also cost him friendships as true and dear as man ever had.

3

The pioneer studies of Richard Harter Fogle and Humphry House have shown in some detail how Coleridge excised and rearranged passages from the verse letter when he prepared the *Morning Post* and *Sibylline Leaves* versions of the poem for publication.[60] House has made out as good a case as possible, I think, for the moral and aesthetic integrity of the letter. I have tried to show that, as a matter of historical record, the verse letter misrepresents by oversimplifying the relationship between, on the one hand, his loss of Joy and the shaping spirit, and on the other, his domestic miseries and practice of 'abstruse research'. And though I agree with House that there is one marvellous passage in the letter, re-grettably though necessarily expurgated from the ode,

> Thou being innocent & full of love,
> And nested with the Darlings of thy Love,
> And feeling in thy Soul, Heart, Lips, & Arms
> Even what the conjugal & mother Dove
> That borrows genial Warmth from those, she warms,
> Feels in her thrill'd wings, blessedly outspread—

I am bound to agree with Fogle and most other critics that the ode is incomparably the better poem. But if our critical conclusions are, broadly speaking, the same, our historical premises are so different after all that I find House and Fogle in one camp and myself in another. For I believe that the essential components of *Dejection: An Ode* existed as actual stanzas of poetry *before* the verse letter to Sara Hutchinson was drafted.

One indication that a fragmentary ode preceded the verse letter is so obvious that I hesitate to mention it: the stanzaic pattern of the poem in all its known versions is that of an irregular 'Pindaric' ode. It is true that during the eighteenth century this form was often associated with hasty improvisation, so that, for example, Cowper could write to a correspondent, 'I am very Pindaric, and am obliged to be so by the hurry of the hour'.[61] Therefore Coleridge *might* have chosen to employ the irregular Pindaric stanza in a verse epistle—and especially in a high-spirited burlesque epistle. But as I shall show in my fifth chapter, the odds are more strongly in favour of his having chosen this form in the first place because his main themes—Joy and Dejection, Inspiration and its loss—were themes that belonged traditionally to the ode. Thereafter, because of its other (though less essential) associations with impromptu writing, the same stanzaic pattern could have been used without shocking incongruity to expand the unfinished ode into a long private verse letter. Such arguments from generic usage can never be conclusive, but I believe that, especially in the fuller context of Chapter Five, they are very persuasive.

However this may be, it must be true that at some stage the making of *Dejection* involved a transformation of raw private experience into relatively finished public utterance. The question is whether the chief labour to objectify and universalize took place before or after the composition of the verse letter. If we assume that it took place afterwards, we have to explain how it was that during the evening of 4 April 1802 Coleridge was, for fifty lines here and sixty lines there, one of the greatest and most polished poets in the language, and, for stretches of a hundred or seventy lines at a time, no better than a clumsy off-the-top-of-the-head versifier. It may have been simply that the gusts of inspiration blew intermittently that evening, but if that was the case they left the bard drifting in a dead calm whenever he tried to allude to William's latest poems or to express his love and concern for Sara. The two distinct echoes of the *Immortality* ode are these:

When thou, & with thee those, whom thou lov'st best,
Shall dwell together in one happy Home,
One House, the dear *abiding* Home of All,
I too will crown me with a Coronal—
Nor shall this Heart in idle Wishes roam
Morbidly soft!

No! let me trust, that I shall wear away
In no inglorious Toils the manly Day,   (133–141)
And only now & then, & not too oft,

But oft I seem to feel, & evermore I fear,
They are not to me now the Things, which once they were.
    (294–295)

Certainly these lines bear all the marks of impromptu writing: the padded lines with their mechanical jog-trot rhythm; the unscanable line of misremembered quotation; the couplet (beginning 'No! let me trust. . . .') which might have been pirated from *Peri Bathous*; and the strange ambiguity of lines 133–135 where it isn't clear whether he is wishing the Wordsworths and Hutchinsons all dead and in Heaven or all living together in one house in Grasmere. The allusion to *Peter Bell* is more adroit:

Yon crescent Moon, as fix'd as if it grew
In it's own cloudless, starless Lake of Blue—
A boat becalm'd! dear William's Sky Canoe!
    —I see them all, so excellently fair!
I see, not feel, how beautiful they are.   (39–43)

Though there is an extraordinary sequence of four successive rhymes on '—ower' in Stanza V, there are no triplets in the *textus receptus*. What this means, so far as the allusion to *Peter Bell* is concerned, can only be appreciated by a careful study of the rhythmic structure of the whole of Stanza II of the ode in its final state. For the rhythmic structure of that stanza *is* a whole. In its closing phases it is articulated through a series of three noun clauses each of which exhausts itself syntactically within a couplet before the series, and indeed the entire stanza, achieves a resolution in the closing couplet. The charming local surprise of 'A boat becalm'd! dear William's Sky Canoe!' wrecks the beautiful, painstakingly developed cadence as it also shatters the intimate yet immeasurably sad and dignified tone of the stanza.

Of course the line had to be retained in the *Morning Post* version of the ode, but Coleridge did manage to eliminate a number of lines (italicized) which clog the movement at the beginning of Stanza II:

A Grief without a pang, void, dark, & drear,
A stifling, drowsy, unimpassion'd Grief
That finds no natural Outlet, no Relief
    In word, or sigh, or tear—

This, Sara! well thou know'st,
Is that sore Evil, which I dread the most,
And oft'nest suffer! In this heartless Mood
To other thoughts by yonder Throstle woo'd,
That pipes within the Larch tree, not unseen,
(The Larch, which pushes out in tassels green
It's bundled Leaflits) woo'd to mild Delights
By all the tender Sounds & gentle Sights
Of this sweet Primrose-month—& vainly woo'd
O dearest Sara! in this heartless Mood
All this long Eve, so balmy & serene,   (17–31)

The awkwardness, the padding of the 'know'st/most' couplet, perhaps require no critical comment, but some of the lines which
follow are not, in themselves, poetically worthless by any means.
Yet Coleridge was absolutely right to cancel them. For in the first
place it is essential that the throstle *not* succeed in drawing the
poet's eyes to itself and the Larch tree with its interesting tassels,
etc. This is partly a question of logical consistency, but much more
a question of tone and movement. As Coleridge himself stresses,
this is no place for 'mild Delights' and 'gentle Sights'; anything
more specific than 'other thoughts' is an intrusion. The cancelled
passage also blurs the powerful contrast between the claustro-
phobic grief of the opening lines and the vast open spatial images
of the remainder of the stanza. No less important, the busy run-
over rhythms of the Larch tree/Throstle passage form a grotesque
and disruptive contrast with what precede and follow them: the
magnificently heavy and exhausted rhythms of the opening lines,
and the slow yet graceful end-stopped lines mid-stanza. For all
these reasons Coleridge's excisions made the difference between the
poetic wholeness of Stanza II and mere scattered brilliance. What
is more, the ungainly partial repetition of the 'heartless mood/
woo'd' couplets makes what falls between them look suspiciously
like a hastily improvised interpolation. Yet the author of *Dejection*
was too great a poet not to perceive that such an interpolation
was ruinous. What can have possessed him to do it—if indeed he
did? The answer I think can be found in Coleridge's notebooks
for early March 1802, when he was visiting Sara at Gallow Hill:[62]

The Larches in spring push out their separate bundles of Leaves
first into green Brushes or Pencils, which soon then are only small
tassels. . . .

There is no knowing whether this entry records one of Sara's observations, one of Coleridge's, or, for that matter, one that has no direct connexion with the visit to Gallow Hill. But that it was almost certainly written during that visit and then included, rather ineptly, in the verse letter to her strongly suggests that it was meant especially for her in the hope that she would recall—what? A walk together on a fine March morning? A happy moment of shared perception? Alas, this touching lover's gesture, like the amiable allusion to *Peter Bell* later in the stanza, is an aesthetic disaster.

But to say so is to take the verse letter altogether too seriously as an aesthetic object which surely it was never meant to be. There is therefore no point in further demonstration that the distinctly private passages are, with the single exception already noticed, distinctly ill-written as well. What is to the point is to try to determine what part the composition of the verse letter may have played in the gestation of a work which *is* an aesthetic object—namely, *Dejection: An Ode*. Here I must ask my reader to bear with me while I venture some hypotheses which, though unverifiable in the present state of our knowledge, seem to me to make better sense of what we do know.

I have tried to show that lines 17–43 of the verse letter, which emerge finally as Stanza II of *Dejection*, bear the marks of interpolations which appear there for the sake of purely private gestures of affection or recognition. That prodigies of revision were later performed on later sections of the letter I do not doubt, but, bearing in mind what I have said about the nature of the suspected interpolations and their lack of relation to the surrounding lines, I cannot persuade myself that the glorious wholeness of Stanza II was achieved by scissoring away parts of an original text which were written during a momentary fit of nostalgia or lulls of inspiration. The same can be said of lines 1–51 (corresponding to Stanzas I–III of the ode) altogether. Whatever questions may be raised about the history and unity of *Dejection* in its entirety, these opening lines (minus the private incrustations) clearly do form a continuous and unified body of poetry, incomplete but superb as far as it goes. Since the interpolated passages (and the subsequent passages which allude to the *Immortality* ode) can be dated with some confidence as belonging to a period in March/ early April, or at any rate not earlier than that period, it might

51

seem that the lines now comprising Stanzas I–III were composed well before 4 April 1802, as far back, perhaps, as the preceding spring or even the summer of 1800! This is possible, but in the absence of any definite evidence to the contrary it is probably best to assume that the lines in question were written not long before 4 April 1802, inspired maybe by Dorothy's description of the new moon which she and William saw on 5 March and which, very likely, Sara and Coleridge saw the same evening at Gallow Hill. I suppose we can also accept 4 April as the date of the verse letter, that is, the date when Coleridge assembled a letter to Sara out of some lines that already existed and some that were improvised for the occasion. (I confess to a radical scepticism about that date, which I suspect Coleridge insisted on partly because it camouflaged the conglomerate nature of the letter, it being the date of the new moon in April 1802; but it is as good a date as any for the poem which must have been put together about that time.)

Having argued that the opening lines, in something very close to their final form, existed before, I find it tempting to make the same claim for nearly all the lines that have survived into the final version of the ode. But I am afraid that the process of writing and rewriting cannot have been so simple as that. In the first place, if the ode had existed as much more than a great fragment, it would surely have been circulated among his friends before 4 April as it was in letters afterwards. Second, the version sent to Sotheby on 19 July 1802 shows that, even at this stage, Coleridge did not perceive the dramatic function of the Wind-as-Actor-and-Poet (Stanza VII), for he says that he will 'annex' this passage as a 'fragment'.[63] Apparently it was some time between late July and late September that Coleridge first perceived that this passage was the emotional as well as meteorological fulfilment of the lines,

> O! Sara! that the Gust ev'n now were swelling,
> And the slant Night-shower driving loud & fast!   (15–16)

which in the *Morning Post* version he proceeded to strengthen by adding these, the *only*, wholly new lines:

> Those sounds which oft have rais'd me, whilst they aw'd,
> And sent my soul abroad,
> Might now perhaps their wonted impulse give,
> Might startle this dull pain, and make it move and live!

Accustomed as we are to experiencing Stanza VII as a necessary climax and purgative, we find it difficult to imagine that there ever was a time when Coleridge failed to perceive its true function in the poem. This is partly because *we* fail to perceive the full novelty of this dramatic lyric, which in its use of symbolist techniques anticipates the radical innovations of *When Lilacs Last in the Dooryard Bloom'd* and *The Waste Land*. Moreover, I am not even sure that this passage and its immediate sequel ''Tis Midnight! . . .' (Stanzas VII and VIII) were originally intended to be parts of the poem which commenced with 'Well! if the Bard was weatherwise. . . .' (Stanzas I–III), though their relative finish and impersonality would seem to argue that they too existed before the verse letter was drafted. For there is a conflict between the prayer in the opening passage,

> O! Sara! that the Gust ev'n now were swelling,
> And the slant Night-shower driving loud & fast!   (15–16)

presumably for the sake of the ailing poet, and the prayer that occurs after the Wind passage,

> Cover her, gentle Sleep! with wings of Healing.
> And be this Tempest but a Mountain Birth!
> May all the Stars hang bright above her Dwelling,
> Silent, as tho' they *watch'd* the sleeping Earth!   (219–222)

Fortunately, the conflict does not affect the functioning of Stanza VII; and since it seems as natural to wish for calm at this stage as it did to wish for storm earlier, the reader may be prepared to overlook the fact that only now, having achieved a measure of release with the wished-for tempest, is the selfish poet prepared to wish it away for the sake of his friend. This fault persists in the ode, because, I should imagine, Coleridge was rightly anxious to conclude the poem with a firm turning away from the self and a refusal to indulge in facile expectations of quick recovery for himself. We cannot be certain whether it occurred in the first place because of an expedient marriage of two slightly incompatible fragments of extant poetry, or because the prayer passage at the end actually was improvised for the verse letter. But the sudden interruption of the prayer in the verse letter

> Healthful & light, my Darling! may'st thou rise
> With clear & chearful Eyes—

And of the same good Tidings to me send!

For, oh! beloved Friend!

I am not the buoyant Thing, I was of yore—   (223–227)

looks remarkably like another interpolation of urgent personal matter into an already achieved passage of poetry. In this case the interruption lasts for rather more than one-hundred lines, some of them exquisitely beautiful and retained elsewhere in the ode, before the prayer starts up again.

I have carried conjectural analysis of the verse letter as far as I feel is reasonable, or necessary, to support my contention that it is, in effect, an intermediate and in many ways deviant draft of *Dejection: An Ode*. Of all Coleridge's poems *Dejection* was probably the least an extempore performance. Of all his great poems, it was at once the most dearly earned and richly inherited. I believe that Wordsworth and Coleridge's other intelligent literary contemporaries would have understood that *Dejection* was a culmination of something in Coleridge's career and of an important tradition as well.

NOTES

1. Ernest de Selincourt, 'Coleridge's Dejection: an Ode', *Essays and Studies*, XXII (1937), 7–25. Reprinted in *Wordsworthian and Other Studies* (Oxford, 1947), 57–76, which is the text I have consulted. *Journals of Dorothy Wordsworth* (London, 1941), 2 vols. As noted above, my citations are from more recent transcriptions.

2. The most forceful apologist for the superior honesty and clarity of the verse letter is Humphry House in his Clark Lectures, published as *Coleridge* (London, 1953), 133–41. A fuller case is made out by David Pirie in 'A Letter to [Asra]', *Bicentenary Wordsworth Studies*, ed. Jonathan Wordsworth (Ithaca & London, 1970), 294–339. Most critics clearly prefer the ode and maintain that, in revising the verse letter, Coleridge did create a new—though perhaps imperfect—whole. Among the important cases made out for the essential wholeness of the ode are R. H. Fogle, 'The Dejection of Coleridge's Ode', *ELH*, XVII (1950), 71–77. Donald Davie, *Purity of Diction in English Verse* (London, 1952), 122–31. Harold Bloom, *The Visionary Company* (New York, 1961), 216–23.

3. Important literary biographical studies are G. W. Meyer, 'Resolution and Independence: Wordsworth's Answer to Coleridge's *Dejection: An Ode*', *Tulane Studies in English*, II (1950), 49–74. George Whalley, *Coleridge and Sara Hutchinson and the Asra Poems* (Toronto, 1955). Marshall Suther, *The Dark Night of Samuel Taylor Coleridge* (New

54

York, 1960). William Heath, *Wordsworth and Coleridge: A Study of Their Literary Relations in 1801–1802* (Oxford, 1970). For a balanced appraisal of biographical and critical studies of the poem, see the commentary by T. M. Raysor and Max F. Schultz in *The English Romantic Poets: A Review of Research and Criticism*, ed. Frank Jordan (3rd edn., New York, 1972), 199–203.

4. The *Morning Post* version of the poem has as part of its title 'Written April 4, 1802'. The *Sibylline Leaves* version, thrice reprinted during Coleridge's lifetime, was not dated. In letters to Thomas Poole (7 May 1802) and William Sotheby (19 July 1802) Coleridge mentions 4 April as the date of the poem: *Letters*, II, 801 and 815.

5. *The Road to Xanadu* (Boston & New York, 1927), 175.

6. *Wordsworthian and Other Studies*, 66.

7. *Ibid*, 64.

8. *William Wordsworth: The Early Years* (Oxford, 1957), 528.

9. *Wordsworth and Coleridge 1795–1834* (Archon Books edn., 1966; first published London, 1953), 105.

10. Meyer, *TSE*, 54.

11. *Ibid*, 54.

12. *English Romantic Poetry and Prose*, ed. Russell Noyes (Oxford U.P.: New York, 1956), 417–19. *Coleridge: Selected Poems*, ed. John Colmer (Oxford U.P.: London, 1965), 40, 214–15.

13. *Samuel Taylor Coleridge: A Biographical Study* (Oxford, 1938), 151, 152.

14. *Coleridge and Sara Hutchinson*, 44.

15. *Ibid*.

16. *The Road to Xanadu*, 173.

17. Heath, *Wordsworth and Coleridge*, 94.

18. *Ibid*, 69–92.

19. *Letters*, I, 66–67.

20. *Letters*, I, 68.

21. *Letters*, I, 319–20.

22. *Letters*, I, 243. This letter is dated 1 November 1796, and it may be that Coleridge's admiration for Lloyd's genius had somewhat moderated by the following Spring. But he was not ashamed to appear with Lloyd and Charles Lamb in the second edition of his *Poems* (1797).

23. These unfulfilled commitments are detailed in a letter of 16 March 1797, *Letters*, I, 316.

24. *Letters*, I, 308. This was written to Thelwall on 6 February 1797 and projects a half-humorous Pantisocratic fantasy of life at Nether Stowey. But the happiness seems real enough.

25. *Notebooks*, I, n. 1155.

26. *Letters*, I, 320.

27. *The Dungeon* excepted, these and other Coleridge poems connected in one way or another with *Dejection* are discussed by George Whalley in *Coleridge and Sara Hutchinson*.

28. *Letters*, I, 540, dated 15 October 1799, to Robert Southey.

29. *Letters*, I, 609.

30. *Letters,* I, 620, dated 8 September 1800, to William Godwin.
31. *Letters,* I, 623.
32. *Letters,* I, 643, dated 1 November 1800.
33. *Letters,* II, 663, dated 11 January, to Humphry Davy; *Letters,* II, 714, dated 25 March 1801, to William Godwin. Professor Griggs notes that the image of the column of sand is taken from Coleridge's own dramatic fragment *The Triumph of Loyalty,* drafted a couple of months previously, which uses the phrase 'shaping spirit'.
34. *Letters,* II, 719, 721, 724, 726, to Greenough, Poole, Thelwall, and Davy.
35. *Letters,* II, 706–7, dated 16 March 1801, to Poole.
36. *Letters,* II, 713–14, dated 25 March 1801.
37. *Letters,* II, 725, dated 28 April 1801, to Godwin.
38. E.g. *Letters,* II, 731, 751.
39. *Letters,* II, 772.
40. The Coleridges appear to have based their standard of living on the assumption that he would earn a modest sum by his writings to supplement the Wedgwood legacy, but his illness did of course prevent that. The quarrel with Lloyd is discussed in the next chapter. A good short discussion of Wordsworth's attitude towards Coleridge's *annus mirabilis* masterpieces is in Professor Griggs' notes in *Letters,* I, 592, 602, 631.
41. *Letters,* I, 649, dated 2 December 1800.
42. *Letters,* II, 751, dated 12 August 1801.
43. *Letters,* II, 761–62.
44. *Letters,* II, 767, dated 21 October 1801, to Southey.
45. *Letters,* II, 785–86.
46. Sara Coleridge was born on 24 December 1802. Cf. Chambers, *Samuel Taylor Coleridge,* 150.
47. That it was short-lived or may never have happened seems to be confirmed by his letter of 20 October 1802 in which he says simply that his domestic misery began again 'after my return to Keswick' (*Letters,* II, 875–76, to Tom Wedgwood). But the same letter telescopes what must have been three or four months of domestic concord into two. As in his letters to Josiah, Coleridge seems here to be adjusting personal history to suit the expectations of his patrons; but I suppose that what he says is 'broadly true.
48. *Letters,* II, 832, 875–76, dated 29 July and 20 October 1802.
49. *Letters,* II, 832.
50. The same explanation is given in a letter to William Sotheby dated 19 July 1802 (*Letters,* II, 814): 'Sickness & some other & worse afflictions, first forced me into *downright metaphysics'.*
51. Whalley, *Coleridge and Sara Hutchinson,* 35–39; Chambers, *Samuel Taylor Coleridge,* 142–43; *Letters,* II, 762.
52. *Letters,* I, 571.
53. Heath, *Wordsworth and Coleridge,* 91–92; Yarlott, *Coleridge and the Abyssinian Maid* (London, 1967), 246–47.
54. *Notebooks,* I, 1151.

55. *Letters*, II, 825–28, 834–45, and 852–55, dated 27 July, 1–6 August, and 25 August 1802. Contrary to Patricia Adair, *The Waking Dream* (London, 1967), 201, Sara most certainly was not with the Wordsworths during their visit to Keswick in April 1802.

56. *Letters*, II, 801, dated 7 May 1802. Surely the least probable recipient of the poem in any version was Sara Fricker Coleridge, but she has been identified as the addressee of the *Morning Post* version by Allen Grant in *A Preface to Coleridge* (London, 1972), 140.

57. *Letters*, II, 669.

58. *Letters*, I, 643.

59. *Letters*, I, 643. That Poole was something of a melancholiac is confirmed by Mrs. Henry Sandford, *Thomas Poole and His Friends* (London, 1888), I, 118.

60. Fogle, *ELH*, XVII (1950), 71–77; House, *Coleridge*, 133–41.

61. Quoted by George N. Shuster, *The English Ode from Milton to Keats* (New York, 1940), 238.

62. *Notebooks*, I, 1142.

63. *Letters*, II, 818.

2

Blue Coat Boys

What most elates them sinks the Soul as low;
When Spring Tide Joy pours in with copious flood,
The higher still the exulting Billows flow,
The farther back again they flagging go,
And leave us groveling on the dreary Shore:
Taught by this Son of Joy, we found it so.

—Thomson, *The Castle of Indolence*

As I have not been blessed with the talents of Burns or Chatterton. I have been happily exempted from the influence of their violent passions, exasperated by the struggle of feelings which rose up against the unjust decrees of fortune.

—Scott, *Memoir* dated 26 April 1808

1

When we recall the important male friendships of Coleridge's early manhood, we are apt to think especially of those with Robert Southey of Bristol, Thomas Poole of Nether Stowey, William Wordsworth of Cumberland and Charles Lamb of London. Not merely these men but their places have to figure prominently in any serious biography of this period of his life. To say so is not to deny the vast scope of his life with books and ideas, outside the confines of any particular time, place or friendship. It is rather to insist on the vulnerable side of what came to be symbolized by his felt orphanage from the Coleridges of Ottery St. Mary. Whatever the origins of this feeling, it seems to have driven him to seek one foster home after another. And while no place, no people could give him what he needed during these years, a very great deal was given both by his friends, notably Poole and Wordsworth, and by Coleridge himself in return. These friends had extraordinary opportunities to see Coleridge through his and their own eyes, and their testimony therefore has extraordinary value both because of what they saw truly and what they saw with a distortion shared with or provoked by him. In this chapter I shall be concerned with only a small part of what they knew or thought about the Friend, the Orphan, the life-long Guest. I believe it is a significant part of the personal and intellectual history of English Romanticism. Other friends and enemies and legendary figures belong in the story as well, and they will appear in due course.

Of these friendships, the last formed but much the most important for Coleridge and English literature was that with Wordsworth. The quality of their communication with and concern for each other can be gauged at least in part from the journals of Dorothy, the third person of that Trinity. For all Dorothy's ingenuousness, William's reticence and Coleridge's submissive evasiveness, I believe they left as little unsaid between them as any other three men and women of their time, and even if much was left unstated (as had to be the case, considering the strangeness of their experience) they also carried on a private discourse through symbolic places and gestures, which further extended an astonishing range of expressive means. In these circumstances it must always be a bit risky to assert that *Dejection* was an 'answer' to the *Immortality* ode or that *Resolution and Independence* was an 'answer' to *Dejection*. For very often the poems must have seemed (from one point of view) mere public crystallizations of what had been discussed more candidly and at greater length in private. However, it is also true that Coleridge and Wordsworth were not just friends communicating with each other, but professional writers for whom (from another point of view) the 'mere' public crystallizations were all-important. This was the more true in 1801–1802 when each was experiencing a crisis of confidence in his power to go on writing poetry, and at the same time was watching the other anxiously and sympathetically. We may suppose that in these circumstances each poem did become the next speech, the next event in a drama of poetic survival. In this sense we may accept George Meyer's thesis that *Resolution and Independence* is an 'answer' to *Dejection*. We may accept this thesis even while we note that the longer poems Wordsworth wrote during this phase of his emergence as a fully professional poet—the *Immortality* ode, *Resolution and Independence*, the *Castle of In-*

dolence stanzas—no longer pretend to answer or converse with anybody except himself or an anonymous Common Reader.

Who can doubt that, in the two following stanzas, Coleridge heard an apt admonishment directed personally to himself?[1]

> My whole life I have liv'd in pleasant thought
> As if life's business were a summer mood,
> And they who liv'd in genial faith found nought
> That grew more willingly than genial good
> But how can he expect that others should
> Build for him, sow for him, and at his call
> Love him who for himself will take no heed at all.

> I thought of Chatterton, the Marvellous Boy,
> The sleepless soul who perish'd in his pride:
> Of him who walk'd in glory and in joy
> Behind his plough upon the mountain side;
> By our own spirits are we deified:
> We Poets in our youth begin in gladness;
> But thereof comes in the end despondency & madness.

Now neither Wordsworth nor Coleridge lived so heedlessly as the first of these stanzas claims: the truth—if truth it be rather than moralistic caricature—is that of a fictional portrait resembling both poets as they had once been, in the happier days of Pantisocracy or the French Revolution. True, there were moments when guilt-ridden Coleridge and his exasperated friends and benefactors uttered something very like the three last lines of this stanza. For the moment I should like to pass by the reference to Burns, noting only that Wordsworth surely had himself as well as Coleridge in mind when he alluded to the Scottish poet's fate. But I have found no evidence that he felt any specially strong kinship with Chatterton: that was Coleridge's problem.

Wordsworth's famous epithet for Chatterton certainly appears to have been a calculated allusion to Coleridge's early poem *On Observing a Blossom on the First of February 1796:*

> Flower that must perish! shall I liken thee
> To some sweet girl of too, too rapid growth
> Nipp'd by Consumption mid untimely charms?
> Or to Bristowa's Bard, the wond'rous boy!
> An Amaranth, which Earth scarce seem'd to own,
> Blooming mid poverty's drear wintry waste,

Till Disappointment came, and pelting Wrong
Beat it to earth?

Of course Wordsworth's distich is incomparably finer than these lines of thickly clichéd diction and metaphor—metaphor which, by transforming the 'wond'rous boy' into an amaranth beaten to earth by 'pelting Wrong', relieves him of any responsibility for his own death. The lines *On Observing a Blossom* conclude with a passage which also faintly anticipates the poetic situation in *Dejection*—the distant sick female friend, the image of the Aeolian Harp, in this case so merged with that of the poet's faculties as to be nearly invisible:

Farewell, sweet blossom! better fate be thine
And mock my boding! Dim similitudes
Weaving in moral strains, I've stolen one hour
From black anxiety that gnaws my heart
For her who droops far off on a sick bed:
And the warm wooings of this sunny day
Tremble along my frame, and harmonize
Th' attemper'd brain, that ev'n the saddest thoughts
Mix with some sweet sensations, like harsh tunes
Play'd deftly on a soft-ton'd instrument.

It is something of a shock to realize that 'her who droops far off on a sick bed' is Sara Coleridge. It is impossible to know whether Wordsworth's glancing allusion to this early poem led either poet to notice the faint ironic parallels between it and *Dejection*. Coleridge at least did not revise it for the 1803 edition of his poems, though he did remove the reference to Mrs. Coleridge when he prepared *Sibylline Leaves* for the press many years later.

His chief literary connexion with Chatterton, however, was through his *Monody on the Death of Chatterton*, a poem which has a very special place in the Coleridge canon. Apparently first drafted in 1790 at Christ's Hospital as a Pindaric ode, but incorporating lines that go back to his thirteenth year, an expanded version of the *Monody* was first published in an edition of Chatterton's poems that appeared in 1794. For several years thereafter Coleridge was often identified as 'the author of the *Monody on the Death of Chatterton*', and although it was a title of which he quickly grew tired, the poem was his first public literary success. What attracted the brilliant schoolboy to this subject in the first place can be readily conjectured. Chatterton lived out in sordid but easily romanticised actuality the dream of many a moody adolescent: he was astonishingly gifted, he was neglected and exploited by the adult world, and he did take fate in his own hands and end it all. What is more, he too was a charity boy at a blue coat school which belonged to the same foundation of Christ's Hospital.[2] There may have been other early associations between the two which I have failed to notice; it is certain that the associations grew stronger after Coleridge went up to Cambridge. There, harassed by financial problems and occasional bouts of ill health, he appears to have contemplated suicide as a way out—and this at about the time he was revising the *Monody* for publication in the Cambridge edition of Chatterton's poems.[3] Shortly thereafter, his connexion with Southey and, through him, with Sara Fricker, propelled Coleridge not only into a marriage at Chatterton's native city of Bristol but into a residence in Chatterton's (and the Frickers') parish church, St. Mary Redcliff. Coleridge was not one to overlook such an omen:[4]

On Sunday Morning I was *married*—at St Mary's, Red Cliff—poor Chatterton's Church—/The thought gave me a tinge of melancholy to the solemn Joy, which I felt—united to the woman, whom I love best of all created Beings.

This was to Tom Poole. A year later, after the collapse of Pantisocracy and *The Watchman*, he wrote to Poole about some of the consequences of being united to the woman whom he loved best of all created beings:[5]

Surely, surely, you do not advise me to lean with the whole weight of my Necessities on the Press?—Ghosts indeed! I should be haunted with Ghosts enough—the Ghosts of Otway & Chatterton, & the phantasms of a Wife broken-hearted, & a hunger-bitten Baby! O Thomas Poole! Thomas Poole! if you did but know what a Father & Husband must feel, who toils with his brain for uncertain bread! I dare not think of it—The evil Face of Frenzy looks at me!

As we shall soon see, Poole must have regarded this letter as a suicide threat. Confronted with moral blackmail, he arranged what turned out to be the happiest and most productive living situation that Coleridge ever enjoyed. At Nether Stowey, I think, Coleridge simply outgrew the identification with Chatterton: the *Monody* became a literary embarrassment,[6] and as a husband and father in his middle twenties he could no longer picture himself as a 'wond'rous boy'.

Before the Nether Stowey years, however, Coleridge was not alone in perceiving some possibly sinister resemblance between himself and Chatterton. Charles Lamb, who was Coleridge's wisest critic, wrote a slight but revealing imitation of the *Monody* at a time when he was planning to visit its author in Bristol:[7]

Or, with mine eye intent on Redcliffe towers,
To drop a tear for that Mysterious youth,
Cruelly slighted, who to London Walls,
In evil hour, shap'd his disastrous course.

Complaints, begone; begone, ill-omen'd thoughts—
For yet again, and lo! from Avon banks
Another 'Minstrel' cometh! Youth beloved,
God and good angels guide thee on thy way,
And gentler fortunes wait the friends I love.

Lamb's prayer for the transplanted 'Minstrel' might not mean that he really felt any serious apprehensions; a complimentary verse letter such as this is at once too literary and too casual to mean anything very precisely. But the identification of Chatterton with his monodist is made once again by a very shrewd judge of Coleridge's strengths and weaknesses, and the form of Lamb's imitation of the *Monody* is striking in as much as it reproduces the important new structural device which Coleridge had added to the 1796 version of the poem:

Poor Chatterton! farewell! of darkest hues
This chaplet cast I on thy unshaped tomb;
But dare no longer on the sad theme muse,
Lest kindred woes persuade a kindred doom:
For oh! big gall-drops, shook from Folly's wing,
Have blacken'd the fair promise of my spring;
And the stern Fate transpierc'd with viewless dart
The last pale Hope that shiver'd at my heart!

Hence, gloomy thoughts! no more my soul shall dwell
On joys that were! no more endure to weigh
The shame and anguish of the evil day,
Wisely forgetful!

As Coleridge was soon to realize, this is the most turgid adolescent melodrama. And yet the poetic idea is a good one—the monodist himself sliding into a suicidal identification with his subject, and then abruptly pulling himself back from the precipice. As A. Alvarez has but recently pointed out,[8] what happens here in the *Monody* is remarkably like what happens at the end of Stanza VI and the beginning of Stanza VII of the final (1817) version of *Dejection*. I agree with him that this is very unlikely to be a coincidence, and I shall return to the matter in my final chapter. At the moment, I am concerned to establish why, with *Dejection* before him, Wordsworth 'thought of Chatterton' in particular rather than of a dozen other poets who came to a bad end. The answer is that Coleridge and his friends had been 'thinking' of Chatterton in this connexion long before Wordsworth and Dorothy appeared on the scene to put those thoughts temporarily to rest.

One of these friends was Tom Poole. As a practical and largely self-educated man, he had small measure of literary sophistication; his critical opinions were mostly derived from his brilliant young friends Southey, Coleridge, and Wordsworth. But he had qualities of mind and heart that were sufficiently rare. I think those qualities emerge movingly from the following letter, written shortly after one of Mary Wollstonecraft's suicide attempts. The passage is a long one, but it is important for what it tells us about Poole himself, Coleridge, and the constellation of melancholy geniuses who were associated with Chatterton at the end of the eighteenth century:[9]

I have heard with pain from my sister Mrs. Wollstonecraft's story . . . it is a bulbin [*sic?*] though melancholy instance of the justice of Providence, that we seldom see great talents, particularly that class which we peculiarly denominate genius, enjoying an even tenour of human happiness. A continuation of the rapturous intellectual delights which beings of this description often experience would be inconsistent with that looking forward, which is certainly a duty, to a state of superior existence. Their souls seem, at times, to start from the flesh, and to mingle with their native skies. But on their return, as if wearied by the exertion, they feel more bitterly the sad weight which surrounds them, and seem sunk even below the common standard of human nature. Doubtless he who can, with calmness, and most frequently, abstract himself from the body, and come home again with becoming dignity, is of human beings the most perfect. But it behooves him who possesses this faculty, so nearly allied to superior spirits, to keep a strong guard over his feelings, to consider that he is at present connected with a mortal part that is earthly, low, has passions and appetites which must be, in a certain degree, indulged. The neglect of this consideration seems to me the great rock against which men of genius are wrecked. In their moments of mind, if I may be allowed the expression, they form plans which would be practicable only if those moments were of continued duration; but in their career they feel like other mortals the sad burdens of mortality, and these being overlooked in their schemes of life, in the form of various passions they enter the fenceless field, making unbounded havoc.

What a striking instance of this is Mrs. Wollstonecraft! What a striking instance is my beloved friend Coleridge! Spenser, Milton, Dryden, Otway, and last of all, the "sweet Harper of time-shrouded minstrelsy," Chatterton, were the same... Is genius a misfortune? No. But people of genius ought imperiously to command themselves to think *without* genius of the common concerns of life. If this be impossible—happy is the genius who has a friend ever near of *good sense*, a quality distinct from genius, to fill up by his advice the vacuity of his character.

And happy was Coleridge to have a friend like Tom Poole. In his first paragraph Poole appears to be describing both the genius he had been able to observe at first hand and the 'Genius' as that figure had taken literary shape by the end of the eighteenth century. In Poole's eyes Coleridge was genius incarnate, the mighty innocent with whom he, the wifeless tanner of Nether Stowey, had been entrusted by Providence. His second paragraph, with its direct and indirect echoes of the *Monody*, demonstrates that he feared his friend might share the fate of the 'sweet Harper' or, if not that, then one of the dark fates reserved for other members of the gallery of English poetic genius:

Is this the land of song-ennobled line?
Is this the land, where Genius ne'er in vain
   Pour'd forth his lofty strain?
Ah me! yet Spenser, gentlest bard divine,
Beneath chill Disappointment's shade,
His weary limbs in lonely anguish lay'd
   And o'er her darling dead
   Pity hopeless hung her head,

While 'mid the pelting of that merciless storm,'
Sunk to the cold earth Otway's famish'd form!

Coleridge here alludes to Collins' allusion to Otway in the *Ode to Pity*, and Collins himself might be added to Coleridge's and Poole's roll-call of tragic genius. These names and others will recur in this and the following chapter, not because I am ambitious to rewrite *The Gloomy Egoist*,[10] but because they were part of the common intellectual currency of Coleridge's circle around the turn of the century. No theme could yield better evidence of the validity of eighteenth-century associationist psychology: of the way a virtually predictable association of names and personal legends came to tyrannize over the thoughts and actions of some of the most gifted people of that or any other age.

A last word on the subject of Coleridge's identification with Chatterton may be left to a not-so-very-gifted friend of the Bristol and Nether Stowey days, Joseph Cottle, before whom, as we have already seen, the burnt-out young bard liked to posture in the guise of Samson Agonistes:[11]

In certain features of their character, there was a strong resemblance between Chatterton and S. T. Coleridge, with a reverse in some points, for Chatterton was loved and cherished by his family, but neglected by the world. In the agony of mind which Mr. C. sometimes manifested on this subject, [resemblance to Chatterton? neglect by his family?] I have wished to forget those four tender lines in his Monody on Chatterton.

'Poor Chatterton! farewell! of darkest hues,
This chaplet cast I on thy unshaped tomb:
But dare no longer on the sad theme muse,
Lest kindred woes persuade a kindred doom!'"

2

By the time Wordsworth wrote *Resolution and Independence*, his reference to Chatterton was pointed but out of date so far as Coleridge was concerned. The career of Burns, on the other hand, offered a lesson that Wordsworth as well as his friend could apply immediately to his own life. So different from Burns in most essentials, Wordsworth cannot have failed to notice a few striking parallels between his own current experience and that of the

Ayrshire peasant. He suffered from the same mysterious chest and headaches that presaged Burns' early dissolution; he too had an illegitimate child whose mother he had been long prevented from marrying by untoward circumstances; and he also was a man with 'Jacobin' sympathies to live down. Though he knew and learned from Burns' poems at an early period and even grew up not very far from where the Scottish poet lived, it was not until 1803 that Wordsworth made a pilgrimage to Dumfries. In the fullness of time, that visit to Burns' home yielded three indifferent poems. The best of them, *At the Grave of Burns*, has a few memorable lines:

> I mourned with thousands, but as one
> More deeply grieved, for He was gone,
> Whose light I hailed when first it shone,
>   And showed my youth
> How Verse may build a princely throne
>   On humble truth.

But the lines to which I wish to direct attention are these:

> And have I then thy bones so near,
> And thou forbidden to appear?
> As if it were thyself that's here
>   I shrink with pain;
> And both my wishes and my fear
>   Alike are vain.

> Off weight—nor press on weight!—away
> Dark thoughts!—they came, but not to stay. . . .

This looks very like another gauche imitation of Coleridge's *Monody*, though the imitation may not have been conscious. In any case, its author lacked Lamb's excuse of tossing off an affectionate compliment. Though the passage invites citation, I cannot pretend to explain what Wordsworth's conscious or unconscious motives were when he wrote it; I do venture to suggest this might be an instance of slack associational 'inspiration'—the grave of Burns invoking *Resolution and Independence* and the grave of Chatterton, and Coleridge's *Monody and Dejection*, and . . . What is more important and revealing, finally, is the soul-shrinking conclusion to his poem addressed in 1807 *To the Sons of Burns*:

> Let no mean hope your souls enslave;
>   Be independent, generous, brave;

Your Father such example gave,
And such revere;
But be admonished by his grave,
And think, and fear!

There can be little doubt that, well before he visited that grave, the example of Burns' early and appalling disintegration led Wordsworth to 'think and fear'. That thought and fear are to be felt in *Resolution and Independence* and also, I think, in the *Immortality* ode. We know that he was deeply moved, as well he should have been, by Burns' *Despondency, an Ode*, a poem which anticipates both his own and Coleridge's odes of 1802:[12]

Oh! enviable, early days,
When dancing thoughtless pleasure's maze,
    To care, to guilt unknown!
How ill exchang'd for riper times,
To feel the follies, or the crimes,
    Of others, or my own!
Ye tiny elves that guiltless sport,
Like linnets in the bush,
Ye little know the ills ye court,
    When manhood is your wish!
The losses, the crosses,
    That *active man* engage!
The fears all, the tears all,
    Of dim-declining *age*!

As in Hardy's poems of loss a century later, this is the more effective for the song lilt that enters at the end of the stanza, without a hint of irony but with full commitment to the artifice of popular pathos. How different is the artifice, how different and yet like is the pathos of the *Immortality* ode.

Relevant as the example of Burns may have been to Wordsworth in 1802, it was still more relevant to the author of *Dejection*. Surely Coleridge recalled that, six years previously, *he* had written a poem of admonishment to Charles Lamb on the subject of Burns' death. This was when Lamb, shattered by Mary's murder of their mother, had destroyed his manuscripts and forsworn poetry. *To a Friend Who Had Declared His Intention of Writing No More Poetry* does not tell us why the friend made such a declaration, nor does it hint at any temperamental affinity between Lamb and Burns. Rather (at its best) does it swell up to a splendid rage against those who neglected the bard:

> And shall he die unwept, and sink to earth
> 'Without the meed of one melodious tear'?
> Thy Burns, and Nature's own beloved bard,
> Who to the 'Illustrious of his native Land
> So properly did look for patronage.'
> Ghost of Maecenas! hide thy blushing face!
> They snatch'd him from the sickle and the plough—
> To gauge ale-firkins.

> Oh! for shame return!

> On a bleak rock, midway the Aonian mount,
> There stands a lone and melancholy tree,
> Whose agéd branches to the midnight blast
> Make solemn music: pluck its darkest bough,
> Ere yet the unwholesome night-dew be exhaled,
> And weeping wreath it round thy Poet's tomb.
> Then in the outskirts, where pollutions grow,
> Pick the rank henbane and the dusky flowers
> Of night-shade, or its red and tempting fruit,
> These with stopped nostril and glove-guarded hand
> Knit in nice intertexture, so to twine,
> The illustrious brow of Scotch Nobility!

Other writings of this period (1796) suggest that the intended therapeutic function of this poem was to rouse the person addressed from a preoccupation with private misery by enlisting him in an act of public protest. One such writing is the sonnet *Addressed to a Young Man of Fortune* (Charles Lloyd), which begins,

> Hence that fantastic wantonness of woe,
> O Youth to partial Fortune vainly dear!
> To plunder'd Want's half-shelter'd hovel go....

In Lamb's case, Coleridge could not speak honestly or discreetly of any 'fantastic wantonness of woe'. But that something might startle Lamb's dull grief and make it move and live was evidenced by his own powerful sonnet of 1794, a poem which Coleridge considered 'divine':[13]

> O! I could laugh to hear the midnight wind,
> That, rushing on its way with careless sweep,
> Scatters the ocean waves. And I could weep
> Like to a child. For now to my raised mind

On wings of winds comes wild-eyed Phantasy,
And her rude visions give severe delight.
O winged bark! how swift along the night
Pass'd thy proud keel! nor shall I let go by
Lightly of that drear hour the memory,
When wet and chilly on thy deck I stood,
Unbonnetted, and gazed upon the flood,
Even till it seemed a pleasant thing to die,—
To be resolv'd into th'elemental wave,
Or take my portion with the winds that rave.

The midnight wind that both inspires and relieves is a common-place of eighteenth-century poetry; but in spite of the hackneyed and contorted language which blights the middle of the poem, this sonnet sets forth with unforgettable gusto and continues to develop to the end. It has affinities of mood, theme, and imagery not only with *To a Friend* and *Dejection*, but with such poems of Burns as *Despondency* and *Winter, a Dirge*:[14]

"The sweeping blast, the sky o'ercast,"
The joyless winter-day,
Let others fear, to me more dear
Than all the pride of May:
The tempest's howl, it sooths my soul,
My griefs it seems to join,
The leafless trees my fancy please,
Their fate resembles mine!

It is not certain that Wordsworth had any such complex web of associations definitely in mind when he referred to Burns in *Resolution and Independence*, but none of the poems I have cited were strangers to him, and it may be that a half-conscious recollection of some of them confirmed his sense of the aptness of that particular admonishment.

What I am pretty sure he did have clearly in mind when he spoke of Burns' fall from glory and joy was James Currie's analysis of that phenomenon in his *Life of Robert Burns*. Wordsworth probably learned about Currie's edition and *Life* of Burns in the first place from Coleridge, who met Currie during a visit to Liverpool in July 1800. Coleridge was enthusiastic about his discovery:[15]

Currie is a genuine philosopher; a man of mild and rather solemn manners. . . . I would have you by all means order the late

Edition in four Volumes of Burns's Works—the Life is written by Currie, and a masterly specimen of philosophical Biography it is.

Currie's *Life* is not quite that good, but it is a humane and thoughtful book which testifies to the high state of civilization in British provincial cities at the turn of the century. One of its sections is so pertinent to what began to happen to Coleridge shortly after he read it that it seems more like an inspired prognosis of his disaster than like a *post mortem* on Burns. Nothing but extensive quotation can show just how pertinent Currie's analysis must have seemed to Coleridge and Wordsworth in 1802:[18]

He knew his own failings; he predicted their consequence; the melancholy foreboding was never long absent from his mind; yet his passions carried him down the stream of error, and swept him over the precipice he saw directly in his course. The fatal defect in his character lay in the comparative weakness of his volition, the superior faculty of the mind, which governing the conduct according to the dictates of the understanding, alone entitles it to be denominated rational; which is the parent of fortitude, patience, and self-denial; which, by regulating and combining human exertions, may be said to have effected all that is great in the works of man, in literature, in science, or on the face of nature. The occupations of a poet are not calculated to strengthen the governing powers of the mind, or to weaken that sensibility which requires perpetual control, since it gives birth to the vehemence of passion as well as to the higher powers of imagination. Unfortunately, the favourite occupations of genius are calculated to increase all its peculiarities; to nourish that lofty pride which disdains the littleness of prudence, and the restrictions of order; and by indulgence, to increase that sensibility, which in the present form of our existence is scarcely compatible with peace or happiness, even when accompanied with the choicest gifts of fortune!

But though men of genius are generally prone to indolence, with them indolence and unhappiness are in a more especial manner allied. The unbidden splendours of imagination may indeed at times irradiate the gloom which inactivity produces; but such visions, though bright, are transient, and serve to cast the realities of life into deeper shade. In bestowing great talents, nature seems very generally to have imposed on the possessor the necessity of exertion, if he would escape wretchedness. Better for him than sloth, toils the most painful, or adventures the most hazardous.

It is more necessary that men of genius should be aware of the importance of self-command, and of exertion, because their indolence is peculiarly exposed, not merely to unhappiness, but to diseases of mind, and to errors of conduct, which are generally fatal. . . . Relief is sometimes sought from the melancholy of indolence in practices, which for a time sooth and gratify the sensations, but which in the end involve the sufferer in darker gloom. To command the external circumstances by which happiness is affected, is not in human power; but there are various substances in nature which operate on the system of the nerves, so as to give a fictitious gaiety to the ideas of imagination, and to alter the effect of the external impressions which we receive.

Opium is chiefly employed for this purpose by the disciples of Mahomet and the inhabitants of Asia; but alkohol, the principle of intoxication in vinous and spirituous liquors, is preferred in Europe, and is universally used in the Christian world. Under the various wounds to which indolent sensibility is exposed, and under the gloomy apprehensions respecting futurity to which it is so often a prey, how strong is the temptation to have recourse to an antidote by which the pain of these wounds is suspended, by which the heart is exhilarated, visions of happiness are excited in the mind, and the forms of external nature clothed with new beauty!

It is the more necessary for men of genius to be on their guard against the habitual use of wine, because it is apt to steal on them insensibly. . . .

It is the more necessary for them to guard against excess in the use of wine, because on them, its effects are, physically and morally, in an especial manner injurious. In proportion to its stimulating influence on the system (on which the pleasurable sensations depend) is the debility that ensues; a debility that destroys digestion, and terminates in habitual fever, dropsy, jaundice, paralysis, or insanity. As the strength of the body decays, the volition fails; in proportion as the sensations are soothed and gratified, the sensibility increases; and morbid sensibility is the parent of indolence, because, while it impairs the regulating power of the mind, it exaggerates all the obstacles to exertion. Activity, perseverance, and self-command, become more and more difficult, and the great purposes of utility, patriotism, or of honorable ambition, which had occupied the imagination, die away in fruitless resolutions or in feeble efforts.

These extracts from Currie's *Life of Robert Burns* speak for themselves. That they fit Coleridge's case just as well as they fit Burns' is only partially coincidental. As Coleridge said, Currie's book is a 'masterly specimen of philosophical Biography', which is a way of saying that Currie is a good deal more interested in the species than in the individual—even when that individual is Robert Burns! His method is to narrate the particulars of Burns' life by quoting a number of eye-witness accounts, and to devote his own efforts to philosophic meditations on the species Poet or the species Scottish Peasant. The 'character' of Burns that results is consequently even more generalized than those in Dr. Johnson's *Lives*, in spite of the scope Currie has to build up a more novelistic portrait. The weakness of such a method—where for pages at a time he might as well be describing the problems of one who was anything but an Ayrshire ploughboy—that weakness is immediately obvious. But the strength is nearly as great. Currie wrote as a highly respectable English professional man for a principally English middle-class audience. Genius or not, Burns was a drunkard, ribald writer, fornicator, peasant, and a Scot. Currie could not, and did not wish to, explain away all of these embarrassments. What he could do was show that a Scottish peasant was rather better educated, more self-sufficient and clean-lived than his English counterpart; and that a poetic genius, regardless of background, was too commonly subject to those weaknesses of temperament and character which destroyed Burns. Thus was he able to turn the edge of prejudice against his subject. Writing at the end of a century which had witnessed the early destruction of so many fine poetic talents through the fatality of Sensibility, Currie cannot have suspected himself of combating one prejudice by reinforcing another. He mentions Gray and Shenstone as examples of melancholy indolence, but he might have cited many more and more striking cases in illustration of this thesis about the character of Burns. Any poetaster of the period could have supplied two dozen tragic names, some of them still famous like Chatterton, some of them all but forgotten like Michael Bruce and John Bampfylde. Coleridge and his circle had a strong, almost obsessive, interest in all of the early dead and mad among them, and it is easy to see why. That circle *was* the next generation of English poetic genius, knew it, and believed that English poetic geniuses were marked men.

I have shown that the references to Burns and Chatterton in *Resolution and Independence* were very pregnant ones for Wordsworth and Coleridge, but we may still wish to inquire why Wordsworth cited two poets of such humble birth and education when he might have named (for instance) Otway or Collins or some other University-trained poet. One answer is that Wordsworth named the poets who fitted his poem rather than the poets who were most like himself and Coleridge. 'Otway' will do in a poem which also has an Aeolian lute in it and the phrase 'poor loveless ever-anxious crowd', but a bookish reference to a bookish poet would be out of place with the old leech-gatherer and the lonely moor. To say so, however, is to remind ourselves that Wordsworth was the man to exploit such an indecorum if he had wished to blame 'books' for the mercurial sensibility of poets. Clearly he did not wish to do so; the theory of genial creation developed in the Preface to the *Lyrical Ballads* was supposed to apply to all poets, and it had, as its unacknowledged tragic corollary, self-destructive despondency. When the corollary was acknowledged, in *Resolution and Independence*, Wordsworth found *exempla* which had both a very particular private significance for himself and his friend and a general public significance which suited the character of the poem. The character of this poem is to be severely reductive in more ways than one, and especially in its bold generalizations about poets:

> By our own spirits are we deified:
> We poets in our youth begin in gladness;
> But thereof comes in the end despondency & madness.

The encounter with the old leech-gatherer is supposed to show a way out of the fatalistic inclusiveness of these generalizations, but the poem nowhere denies their force and accuracy for the bardic tribe as a whole. On the contrary, the citation of two relatively untutored bards of genius goes to confirm the view that the history summed up in the 'gladness'/'madness' couplet is the 'natural' one for a poet. It is not false education but his own nature that the poet must transcend by experiencing a

> peculiar grace,
> A leading from above, a something given. . . .

The explicitly Christian terms of reference here and elsewhere in the poem not only lend dignity to 'the problem of Sensibility', but they invite us to carry the process of generalization farther and regard the poet as Man writ large.

3

Considered in this light, the figure of the Poet in *Resolution and Independence* is, not less than in *Dejection*, a Samson of the mind. In Coleridge's poem it is not merely the line 'My genial spirits fail' that echoes *Samson Agonistes*, but also his description of 'unimpassioned grief', which finds no natural outlet, no relief'.[17] Wordsworth, who echoes the same line from *Samson* in his *Tintern Abbey* (l. 113), cannot have missed the allusion to Milton's poem nor have failed to perceive that, unlike the speaker of *Tintern Abbey*, Coleridge really had donned the persona of Samson in earnest. In *Resolution and Independence*, I believe Wordsworth sought to match that earnestness by a fuller exploration of the implications of the persona. Though I could wish for more certain evidence that Wordsworth did have *Samson* in mind when he wrote some of the stanzas of his 'reply' to *Dejection*, the reader who is not convinced will perhaps bear with me for the sake of the insights to which a hypothetical parallel may lead.

Though we first encounter Milton's hero at the absolute nadir of his fortunes and spirits and are not permitted to witness his final triumph, we are constantly reminded of his former glory—frequently by means of the starkest antitheses that Milton's rhetoric can create:[18]

My race of glory run, and race of shame. . . .

As signal now in low dejected state
As erst in high'st, behold him where he lies.

These violent contrasts are essential to Milton's conception of a tragic hero who is great not because of social but because of natural endowments of a high order:

The rarer thy example stands.
By how much from the top of wondrous glory,
Strongest of mortal men,
To lowest pitch of abject fortune thou art fall'n.

For him I reckon not in high estate
Whom long descent of birth
Or the sphere of fortune raises;
But thee whose strength, while virtue was her mate,
Might have subdued the earth,
Universally crown'd with highest praises.

In so far as Milton himself is known to have shared some of his hero's traits, he encouraged the easy translation of terms, of physical into mental strength, which we find in *Dejection* and *Resolution and Independence*. Wordsworth in turn, in his metaphors for poetic genius and its operations, employs vehicles of great physical force and activity:

And mighty Poets in their misery dead. . . .

But, as it sometimes chanceth from the might
Of joy in minds that can no farther go,
As high as we have mounted in delight
In our dejection do we sink as low. . . .

After a century which saw the rise of the cult of Genius and Milton's elevation alongside Shakespeare as the supreme example of poetic genius in modern literature, it was inevitable that the Poet should assume the rank of tragic hero which Milton claimed for Samson. Not indeed that the poet's career had to be tragic; but nobody had greater natural potential for tragedy, as was demonstrated by the lives of the plebeian Burns and Chatterton.[19]

The view of the Poet in *Resolution and Independence* is very like the view of Man in the Christian tradition generally and in such moralizing poems as *Night Thoughts* and the *Essay on Man* particularly. In those poems, quite as much as in Milton's, Man is depicted in terms of sublime contrasts of exaltation and debasement, ecstasy and despair. But without denying the grandeur that Pope and Young are able to achieve at times, I would argue that Milton's fable lends his rhetoric much additional leverage and, partly by virtue of its association with Milton himself, becomes a great paradigm account of the might and misery of creative genius. All three poets have a view of Man which is very like Wordsworth's view of the Poet, but Milton's statement of that view is most powerful just as his influence on Coleridge's *Dejection* is most naked and direct. And therefore, given as well Wordsworth's general openness to Milton's influence, I am persuaded that *Samson* helped Wordsworth to shape his 'answer' to *Dejection*. And most appropriately, too. For by the contagious power of his lyric genius he doubtless also fostered many a hectic eighteenth-century poetic Sensibility. *L'Allegro* and *Il Penseroso* both defined some of the dominant moods of the literature of Sensibility and supplied the conventions to express them. As paired opposites the two poems linked these moods (and their more extreme variants) in a stylized pattern which came to seem as inevitable and firmly articulated in life as in art.

I have to turn now to a particularly flamboyant strain in that literature: to that English Wertherism which was quick to seize upon parallels between Chatterton and Goethe's protagonist, which flourished for a time in the Coleridge circle, and which may have guided Coleridge to some of his finest insights into his own condition.

4

Mrs. Mary Robinson made her debut at Drury Lane as a protégée of David Garrick; Herbert Croft made an early reputation as author of the *Life* of Young under the protection of Dr. Johnson. From such auspicious beginnings, Mrs. Robinson went on to become—as 'Perdita', the Lost One—mistress of the Prince of Wales ('Florizel') for a season, literary inamorata of Robert Merry ('Della Crusca'), and finally, with most of her great beauty gone, and almost destitute and a cripple, dead at the age of forty. Herbert Croft went on to become Sir Herbert, the Rev. Sir Herbert, and one of the great rogue men of letters of his age. So far as I am aware, they never met each other and presumably would not have wished to; they must have known each other's writings, however, since these achieved considerable notoriety and popularity during the last quarter of the eighteenth century. Had they been born a half century earlier, they might have been immortalized in the *Dunciad*; as it was, they got off with fugitive pilloryings in print during their lifetimes, and with comparatively merciful if infrequent attentions since.[20] I introduce them here partly because their careers impinged on that of Coleridge, but mainly because they had a gift for crude synthesis of the literary fashions with which Coleridge grew up. They began publishing a few years after Coleridge was born, when 'Rowley' and 'Werther' were the crazes of

77

England and Europe; they did much to advance and fuse those crazes.

Croft's special qualification for writing the *Life of Young* was that, as the intimate friend of the poet's son, he was much better placed than Dr. Johnson to draft an informed biography. What Dr. Johnson doubtless did not know was that the son had many irrational grievances against his dead father, and that the price of privileged information was a distorted interpretation of it. Although Dr. Johnson redrafted the most offensive passages, the Croft-Johnson *Life* poisoned the reading public against Edward Young for well over a century.[21] However, it is not with the ostensibly scholarly *Life* of Young that I am concerned here, but with a book which was frankly sensational in its appeal to sordid appetites for sex, scandal, and suicide. This was *Love and Madness*, a book first published in 1780 which purported to be a collection of love letters written by James Hackman, a dashing young soldier and clergyman, and by the woman he murdered, Miss Martha Reay, mistress of the Earl of Sandwich.[22] The letters between Hackman and Martha Reay are largely Croft's own fabrications; but imbedded in this tawdry, unimaginative fiction are a number of genuine letters of Thomas Chatterton which Croft had obtained by trickery from Chatterton's mother and sister. The interest of 'Hackman' in Chatterton is accounted for by the real James Hackman's attempt to kill himself after slaying Martha Reay; Croft's 'Hackman' is accordingly supplied with an obsessive interest in suicides of all descriptions, ranging from the lugubrious lovers' double-suicide of Faldoni and Teresa Meunier to the magniloquent conclusion of *Othello*. These are so many premonitions *à la Werther* of Hackman's own suicide attempt, and Werther is of course the special favourite and model of the hero of this amateurish epistolary novel. Early in the book 'Hackman' begs his mistress to send him a copy of the recent French translation of Goethe's novel, assuring her that Werther's example will not influence him; but he quickly identifies with the German youth and even writes a poem entitled *Lines Found after Werther's Death, upon the Ground by the Pistol.*

Clearly, Croft's opportunism was of the crudest variety, but he showed some ingenuity in yoking together three sorts of sensational appeal: the gutter press attractions of the Hackman–Reay affair; the more elevated and dangerous fascination of the Werther story; and the odd ink-tallow-and-arsenic lure of the Rowley controversy. In *Love and Madness* there was something for everybody and judging from the number of editions it went through everybody did read it.[23] One reader, certainly, was the man who Englished *The Sorrows of Young Werther* in 1786; he linked the 'love and madness' of Hackman with that of Werther and he saw a particularly close affinity between Werther and Chatterton.[24]

Nature had infused too strong a proportion of passion in his composition: his feelings, like those of our CHATTERTON, were too fine to support the load of accumulated distress; and like him, his diapason closed in death.

The parallel once established, Goethe's translator was quick to see further resemblances, e.g. the reluctance of both heroes to accept practical counsels of compromise—a reluctance which doubtless led to their destruction but which was perhaps the preservative of their genius for so long as they survived.[25] Such resemblances between Werther and Chatterton must have occurred to many readers without the prompting of Croft or the anonymous translator of *The Sorrows of Young Werther*. But given that prompting, just about every literate Englishman of the 1780s and 1790s must have reflected a moment on the kinship between the boy-poet from Bristol and the German youth self-slain in his famous blue frock coat.

Coleridge probably knew *Love and Madness* during his Christ's Hospital days when he wrote the first version of the *Monody on the Death of Chatterton*. He certainly knew it by 1797 when he agreed to assist Southey in preparing an edition of Chatterton's poems for the benefit of Chatterton's sister.[26] In the event, the work fell on Southey, Cottle and George Dyer, but Coleridge did follow the slow progress of the edition with a good deal of sympathy and attention. One of Southey's first objects was to retrieve the holographs of the letters which Croft had purloined from Chatterton's relatives and then reproduced in *Love and Madness*. This task was made almost impossible because Croft, after serving a term in prison for debt, had fled to Denmark to escape further prosecution. Powerless to do anything else, Southey denounced Croft in the *Monthly Magazine* in November 1799; badly caught out as a cheat, and a very shabby one at that, Croft was powerless to do much more than counter-attack Southey in the *Gentleman's*

Magazine in early 1800 as an atheistical incendiary. Coleridge was moved to threaten, 'If that Reverend *Sir* continues his Insolence, I will give him a scourging that shall flea him. . . .'[27] However, the public controversy was dropped and we hear no more of Croft in Coleridge's letters. The edition was at last published in 1803, a work which said much for the moral qualities of Southey and his associates but rather little for their editing abilities. Needless to say, the holographs in Croft's possession were not put at the disposal of Chatterton's editors.

It would be a great mistake to suppose that Croft's vulgar compilation could not have deeply interested and affected Coleridge. In common with his own and the immediately previous generation of English poets, Coleridge was fascinated by suicide cases. He assumed his readers would be too. In *The Watchman* in 1796, he recounted with loving (and partially invented) detail the attempted joint suicide of the French poet Louis de Boissy and his wife, prefacing the story with this question: 'Who has not sighed over the fates of Otway, Collins and Chatterton, and forgotten their imprudence in the contemplation of their miseries?'[28] If we are to judge from the double suicide story he related to Tom Poole from Germany, the more florid and melodramatic such cases were the better he liked them. This one concerned an unhappily married German officer who arranged a pleasure party culminating in the joint suicide of himself and his mistress, who spent her last moments writing a *leibestod* in 'wild irregular verse'. This suicide tale, Coleridge assured Poole, was but one of eleven ('and many of them curious enough') which he had heard since his arrival in Germany; 'I have a number of affecting Stories of this kind to tell you, of winter Evenings'.[29] The note of connoisseurship is not misleading. Among the flotsam of his year in Germany were two anthologies of suicide stories, which his notebooks show he consulted or recollected at least a couple of times during the period when *Dejection* was in gestation. The tale of *selfmordor* to which his notebook entries recur was that of the unfortunate Englishman, Lord Pisport, unhappily married, unhappily in love with another woman.[30] That such stories were all too pertinent to Coleridge's own situation is obvious: we must be grateful for the ultimate strength and orthodoxy of his Christian convictions, and also, I suppose, for the lively down-to-earthness of Miss Sara Hutchinson, who was scarcely a likely partner in anybody's suicide pact.

If *Love and Madness* and Coleridge's two German anthologies belonged to the popular sub-literature of suicide, there was likewise a vast late eighteenth-century European literature of suicide which ranged in seriousness and intelligence from Goethe's great novella down to Della Crusca's *Elegy for Werther*.[31]

Sure he was right, for if th'Almighty hand,
    That gave his pulse to throb, his sense to glow,
Gave him not strength his passions to withstand,
    Ah! who shall blame him? he was forc'd to go.

In England, according to Professor Atkins, there were more 'Werther poems', written than in any other country, including Germany.[32] There must have been nearly as many 'Chatterton poems'.[33] The common theme of such poems (as of Dr. Currie's *Life* of Burns) is stated with uncommon clarity in Thomas Warton's *The Suicide*, an ode which Coleridge considered 'exquisite':[34]

"'Is this, mistaken Scorn will cry,
"'Is this the youth whose genius high
      "Could build the genuine rime?
"Whose bosom mild the favouring Muse
"Had stor'd with all her ample views,
"Parents of fairest deeds, and purposes sublime."

Ah! from the Muse that bosom mild
By treacherous magic was beguil'd
    To strike the deathful blow:
She fill'd his soft ingenuous mind
With many a feeling too refin'd
And rous'd to livelier pangs his wakeful sense of woe.

Though doom'd hard penury to prove,
And the sharp stings of hopeless love;
    To griefs congenial prone,
More wounds than nature gave he knew,
While misery's form his fancy drew
In dark ideal hues, and horrors not its own.

According to Warton's editor, this poem was written without a knowledge of Chatterton's doom and before the publication of *The Sorrows of Young Werther*. This was very possibly the case. The notion that the heightened sensitivity and imagination of the lyric poet made him especially vulnerable to suicide was given

81

archetypal expression, not originated, by Chatterton or Goethe. Warton's poem is no such masterpiece; its diction and rhythm are utterly commonplace; it is 'exquisite', if at all, only in its paraphrasable analysis of the suicidal psychology. However, his treatment of the subject is neither shrill nor lachrymose; unlike many later treatments, his is an analysis rather than an exhibition of Sensibility.

One very 'sensible' poet, but with a great courage for life, was the notorious Perdita, whose once radiant beauty, as captured by Reynolds and Gainsborough, still shines forth in the Wallace Collection. Coleridge appears to have known her either through Godwin or as a result of their mutual connexion with Daniel Stuart's *Morning Post* where both regularly published poems for a number of years. I know of no evidence that they spent many hours in each other's company, and, pathetically crippled and dropsical as she was during the last decade of her life, Perdita cannot have been an object of romance when Coleridge knew her. Nonetheless, they felt the warmest admiration for each other and left several poems as a testament of their friendship. His opinions of her and her work are recorded with unusual fullness in his correspondence, but only the following passage, from a letter to Southey, need be quoted at length here:[35]

I have enclosed a Poem which Mrs Robinson gave me for your Anthology—She is a woman of undoubted Genius. There was a poem of her's in this Morning's paper which both in metre and matter pleased me much—She overloads every thing; but I never knew a human Being with so *full* a mind—bad, good, & indifferent, I grant you, but full, & overflowing. This poem I *asked* for you, because I thought the metre stimulating—& some of the Stanzas really *good*—The first line of the 12th would of itself redeem a worse Poem.—I think, you will agree with me; but should you not, yet still put it *in*, my dear fellow! for my sake, & out of respect to a Woman-poet's feelings.

The redeeming line, as Professor Griggs notes, is 'Pale Moon! thou Spectre of the Sky!' from the mediocre poem *Jasper*. The same line, directly quoted in a poem (*A Stranger Minstrel*) which Coleridge addressed to her, may well have suggested the 'phantom light' of the moon in *Dejection*.

Coleridge also admired the moonlight imagery of her *The Haunted Beach*, in which the moon appears as part of a Gothick scene that recurs obsessionally in her poetry. This is of a cliff over-looking the sea at night, from which a bereaved or betrayed girl plunges to her death. With slight variations this scene also appears in *The Progress of Melancholy, Ode to Hope, Poor Marguerite, The Weeping Willow,* and *Stanzas to Him Who Asked, 'What is Love?'* None of these is a good poem, though the range of styles they exhibit is somewhat interesting—from the Pindaric rant of *Ode to Hope:*[86]

> *Hence, dark Despondency!* away!
>   Parent of *Frenzy* and *Despair!*

to the neo-Elizabethan ballad of the same period:

> "Then, *fare thee well,* false rover!
>   'Tis now too *late* to save!
> My grief will soon be over!"
>   She plung'd amidst the wave!

And yet, as Coleridge maintained, her poems have sometimes their redeeming moments, as in these lines from the poem just quoted, *The Weeping Willow:*

> *"My love,"* said she, "lies dreaming,
>   Beneath yon foamy deep;
> Where lonely SEA-BIRDS screaming,
>   With restless pinions sweep!
> Ah! where is now the laurel,
>   That bound his golden hair,
> He wears a crown of *Coral,*
>   Of PEARLS and JEWELS rare."

Only for a moment, in the third and fourth lines, do the imagery and diction seem really fresh; but the other lines, with their echoes of *The Tempest,* are at least a passable imitation of a great model. More often, however, Perdita's poems are 'literary,' through and through. Her own rich experience of life and considerable courage give way before hollow allegorical abstractions which rush frantically to the Cliff that o'erlooks the Gulf of Despair. It was therefore inevitable that she should have tried her hand at poems on the two most famous literary suicides of her age. They lie there cheek by jowl in her *Poetical Works*: a long-winded *Monody to the Memory of Chatterton* and a briefer but (if pos-sible) emptier *Elegy to the Memory of Werter.*[88] As they do not

83

lend themselves very well to quotation, the following couplet from *Ainsi Va Le Monde* will serve to illustrate the predictability of form and content in Perdita's poetry on this theme:[39]

> Her [the Muse's] eye beheld a CHATTERTON oppress'd,
> A famish'd OTWAY—ravish'd from her breast;

'Oppress'd' calls up 'breast' just as surely as 'CHATTERTON' calls up 'OTWAY'. One feels that she should have been able to do better. She was a Bristol girl herself who had known poverty and even debtor's prison in her youth; she experienced a good deal of physical and mental suffering later in life. But when she wrote on the theme of desperate genius, she was little better than a ventriloquist's dummy perched on the all-accommodating knee of the *Zeitgeist*.

I do not wish to suggest that Perdita's various poems on the subject of suicide influenced *Dejection* in any direct or important way. They were themselves mere concentrates of 'Influence'. Nonetheless, Coleridge was so much a child of his age that he could describe their author as 'a woman of undoubted Genius'. And in so far as the final version of *Dejection* invoked Otway and bade 'viper thoughts' go 'Hence', it participated in the poetic movement to which Perdita Robinson's, Anna Seward's, Samuel Marsh Oram's, Robert Merry's, and Henry Hedley's poems also belonged.[40] If Coleridge seems out of place in this company, it is only fair to Perdita to say that she too rose above it at the very end of her life. In a letter to her daughter written after Perdita's death, Coleridge speaks of her Christian aspirations and of 'One of her poems written in sickness which breathes them so well & so affectingly, that I never read it without a strange mixture of anguish & consolation.'[41] I cannot identify this poem positively, but it is probably *To Spring, Written after a Winter of Ill Health in the Year 1800*.[42] This is an unambiguous example of the spring elegy, which William Heath argues is the genre to which both *Dejection* and the *Immortality* ode belong. It is also a poem which at moments seems faintly to recall Coleridge's *The Nightingale* and, even more faintly, to anticipate *Dejection*:

> On the thorn
> Which arms the hedge-row, the young birds invite
> With merry minstrelsy, shrilly and maz'd
> With winding cadences; now quick, now sunk

84

BLUE COAT BOYS

In the low twitter'd song, The ev'ning sky
Reddens the distant main, catching the sail
Which slowly lessens, and with crimson hue
Varying the sea-green wave; while the young Moon,
Scarce visible amid the warmer tints
Of western splendours, slowly lifts her brow
Modest and icy-lustred! O'er the plain
The light dews rise, sprinkling the thistle's head,
And hanging in clear drops on the wild waste
Of broomy fragrance. Season of delight!
Thou soul-expanding pow'r, whose wond'rous glow
Can bid all *Nature* smile!—Ah! why to me
Come unregarded, undelighting still
This ever-mourning bosom? So I've seen
The sweetest flow'rets bind the icy urn,
The brightest sun-beams glitter on the grave
And the soft zephyr kiss the troublous main
With whisper'd murmurs.

The good writing in this passage, which is to say all but the last
half dozen lines, appears to be modelled on her young admirer's
conversation poems. The rhythms are less sure, the images less
subtly shaded, but here is something to substantiate Coleridge's
claims for her. It is striking nonetheless that the writing falls to
pieces exactly at the point where she attempts to go beyond, to
qualify, the rapturous affirmation of the conversation poems. Had
she lived to read *Dejection*, she might have learned how to do that,
too.

Croft and Mrs. Robinson impinged on the Coleridge circle in ways
that necessarily enforced its awareness of the resemblance between Werther and Chatterton and the prevalence of ill fortune and
suicide among men of genius generally. But the men who were
close to Coleridge doubtless required no such intermediaries: they
felt the 'relevance' of Werther with tingling—if transient—Sensibility, and made their own contributions to Wertheriana. Lloyd's
ambition to rival Goethe as an epistolary novelist led him in the
almost unforgivable *Edmund Oliver* (1798) to portray Coleridge
himself as a sort of grotesque Werther figure drenched but still
afloat in the destructive element. Southey, who had had a very
feverish case of Sensibility at Westminster and Balliol, produced

his own much more distinguished imitation-cum-rejection of Werther during the same year. Before the breach occasioned by *Edmund Oliver*, Coleridge and his friends must have spent more than a few minutes discussing the German novella which was both a literary triumph and shrewd diagnosis of what was ailing the lot of them more or less acutely.

The diseased life and writings of Charles Lloyd are a tragi-comic chapter in the story of Coleridge's struggle with the Werther or Chatterton or Otway or Collins he saw within himself and his friends. I have already mentioned the seizures Lloyd suffered while he was living as a student-companion in the Coleridges' home at Nether Stowey; these were the prelude to lengthy periods of madness which later obliged his family to keep him in asylums most of the time. Though he deserved the pity and forgiveness of his friends, it has to be said that he was fortunate to receive abundant love and practical assistance necessary to his condition but out of proportion to his personal worth. Through his friendship with Coleridge and his sister's marriage to Wordsworth's brother, Christopher, he became acquainted with the entire Wordsworth–Coleridge circle. In time, they all learned that he was not to be trusted, but not before he hurt Coleridge a good deal and disrupted his friendships with Southey and Lamb. The full irony and cruelty of the book that did the damage cannot be appreciated unless we recall Coleridge's sonnet to Lloyd, entitled *Addressed to a Young Man of Fortune, Who Abandoned Himself to an Indolent and Causeless Melancholy:*

Hence that fantastic wantonness of woe,
O Youth to partial Fortune vainly dear!
To plunder'd Want's half-shelter'd hovel go,
Go, and some hunger-bitten infant hear
Moan haply in a dying mother's ear:

Coleridge's admonitory poem was doubtless occasioned by Lloyd's behaviour; but it might have been an answer to a poem like The *Melancholy Man,* a work in which echoes of Gray's *Elegy* and Collins' *Ode to Evening* consort harmoniously enough with Wertherian Sensibility. A stanza will show how badly Lloyd had been bitten:[43]

Why flutters thy tumultuous heart,
Thy looks unspoken feelings tell,

If chance beneath thy devious feet
Thou see'st the lover's last retreat,
The cold and unblest grave of pale despair?
Why dost thou drop a feeling tear
Upon the flowret lurking near
And bid it ever droop, a meek memento there?

Subject as Lloyd was to a mysterious disease, such verses could not be dismissed as mere literary vapourings; the melancholy might be 'fantastic' but it might also be dangerous.

What is more, since Genius was prone to such suicidal melancholy, perhaps Lloyd was the great genius Coleridge and Southey believed him to be. I can find no other evidence to support their belief. Apparently on the strength of *Edmund Oliver*, Southey was able to write as follows about Lloyd's promise as a novelist: [44]

Lloyd has begun another novel, also in Letters. He tells me that one only character is introduced in it, and that it will more resemble Werter than any other book. In that stile of writing, in anatomising the feelings, I believe Lloyd will exceed any writer that this country has ever produced, and perhaps—almost equal Goethe and Rousseau.

This judgment would astonish more if Southey were not so erratic as a critic. For *Edmund Oliver* is essentially an unimaginative and morally vicious *roman à clef* worked up out of Lloyd's recollection of the conversations of Coleridge and Coleridge's friends. The story concerns one Edmund Oliver's hopeless love for Lady Gertrude Sinclair, a brilliant woman of advanced ideas who is, alas, infatuated with the scoundrel D'Oyley. D'Oyley abandons Lady Gertrude who, after bearing an illegitimate child, kills herself and leaves the bereft Edmund totally prostrate. Edmund's sage friend Charles Maurice (apparently a compound of Southey and Lloyd himself) delivers this consolatory reflection on the hero's sufferings: [45]

experience is necessary for all minds, but for those of wild and luxuriant growth like his, no discipline that does not utterly blast, and annihilate, can be too severe;—it converts the passions, to energies of patience, and fortitude; and raises selfish sensibilities . . . to general benevolence.

Thus are the tables turned on Lloyd's erstwhile mentor and friend. It must have seemed a good joke to judge Coleridge's personal history by his own teachings and preachings; but how painful to have exposed for public consumption his adventure with the King's Light Dragoons, his use of opium, and even passages of private conversation which have a very authentically Coleridgean ring to them, as this one from the mouth of Edmund:[46]

taking for granted that whosoever puts away his wife is guilty of adultery, let us picture a man of extraordinary intellect, of the acutest sensibilities, linked to a woman of the foulest disposition, and of a temper that is the torment of his life;—further conceive him as strongly tempted to separate himself from her: —he alleges that in his present situation his talents are frittered away by vexations, all his moral usefulness lost. . . . to part from that woman would be highly criminal: it would not only be feeling a weakness, but acting in consequence of that feeling; such conduct would pamper the subtleties of self-adulation;—

Who can doubt that Coleridge supposed something very like this in Lloyd's hearing, and that Lloyd, as a member of the Coleridge household, saw through the supposition quickly enough? *Edmund Oliver* is a mine for the biographer if he knows how to use it, and so I suppose we ought to be grateful that it exists. But what spiteful and sanctimonious feelings led Lloyd to write it, Lamb and Southey to sponsor it, and Cottle to publish it!

The nastiest aspect of *Edmund Oliver* does not concern Coleridge directly. Gertrude Sinclair is closely modelled on Mary Wollstonecraft, whose tragic death as a result of childbirth in 1797 should surely have prevented *Edmund Oliver* from ever going to press. After being abandoned by Gilbert Imlay (D'Oyley in Lloyd's novel), Mary attempted suicide several times before she succeeded in pulling herself together and found most loving and secure marriage with William Godwin. What is peculiarly unfeeling about Lloyd's portrait of Gertrude Sinclair, therefore, is that Godwin's philosophy (though it is not named) is held responsible for her fate:[47]

I have endeavoured to portray a woman of warm affections, strong passions, and energetic intellect, yielding herself to these loose and declamatory principles, yet at the same time uncorrupted in her intentions, unfortunate from error, and not from deliberate vice.

You evidently see, in this case, the horrible effect of playing with human passions, and throwing down wantonly the barriers which religion and morality have erected—and of adopting a method of cold and generalising calculation in conduct, which stands aloof from nature and human sympathies.

It will be remembered that Lamb, to whom *Edmund Oliver* was dedicated, was an intimate of the Godwin household, and that Southey and Coleridge had been frequent guests of Godwin. Southey, in particular, had admired Mary Wollstonecraft so greatly that he dedicated his *The Triumph of Woman* to her in 1795, and, hearing of her death in 1797, wrote these clumsy but doubtless sincere lines:[48]

Who among women left no equal mind
When from the world she passed; and I could weep
To think that *She* is to the grave gone down!

How could this fugitive triumvirate face Godwin, let alone Coleridge, after this crude libel? The answer, apparently, was that they didn't expect Coleridge or Godwin to suffer more than a brief and salutary shock of recognition, and that they believed in all seriousness that *Edmund Oliver* was a masterpiece in the tradition of *Clarissa* and *Werther*.

Sensibility was generally known to be dangerous and unprofitable like an indulgence in Courtly Love. That clearly was a large part of its appeal. And like that of Courtly Love, the literature of Sensibility was littered with the palinodia of men who either lost their nerve, or retaining their courage and idealism, sought to redirect the aspirations of a secular cult towards equally impractical but higher objects. It is tempting to say that Coleridge is an example of the latter, Southey of the former.

Tempting, but not quite fair to Southey. So far as Wertherism is concerned, Southey's career somewhat resembles that of Lloyd; but it is much more interesting simply because Southey himself was much more interesting and important, both in his own right and as an influence on Coleridge. Southey was very frank in later life about his adolescent enthusiasm for *Werther* and Rousseau's *Confessions* and *Nouvelle Héloise*; his surviving early letters show just how responsive he was:[49]

Take care Horace, the crimes of St. Preux were of a less dreadful nature than that of Werter.

I need not tell you with what pleasure my frequent perusals of *Werter* have been attended. For six months I was never without it in my pocket—the character is natural—at least it appeared so when tried by the touch-stone of my own heart.

This was written but a few months before Southey first met Coleridge in 1794. It would be easy to dismiss it as adolescent posturing, especially when we reflect on the well-drilled conservatism of Southey the Laureate. But I am convinced that Southey's radicalism up until shortly after he met Coleridge was quite genuine, and a good deal more extreme than Coleridge's ever was. Whatever occasioned Southey's change of heart—and it is difficult to believe that Coleridge's negative example was not a contributing factor—it had made considerable progress by the time he and Coleridge were reconciled in 1799. It was about this time that Southey described to William Taylor of Norwich the 'cure' he had undergone.[50]

Once, indeed, I had a mimosa-sensibility, but it has long been rooted out: five years ago I counteracted Rousseau by dieting upon Godwin and Epictetus; they did me some good, but time has done more. I have a dislike to all strong emotion, and avoid whatever could excite it; a book like 'Werter' gives me now unmingled pain. In my own writings you may observe that I rather dwell upon what affects than what agitates.

Now nobody who knows what it is can wish a life of Sensibility on anybody; as Wordsworth truly said, 'thereof comes in the end despondency & madness'. Yet there is something disturbing about the way Southey retreated from the radical commitments of his youth. I am not talking now about the 'apostasy' with which he and his generation were charged by the Radicals of the 1820s, but about a much more sudden and immediately personal revolution of principle and outlook that began with his abandonment of Pantisocracy in 1795, and (after considering the Church) his decision to study Law. It is true, of course, that young men who leave University and take a wife tend to become very practical all of a sudden; and so we have to admit that Coleridge was being rather ingenuous when he charged Southey with a great betrayal.[51] Nonetheless, what happened to Southey was exceptional: a most passionate rejection of passion and impractical schemes. But we need only examine the metaphors in his letter to Taylor ('rooted out', 'unmingled pain') to see that the strong emotion he so disliked was not as thoroughly eradicated as he claimed. One does not have to be a follower of Freud or Lawrence to conclude that Southey inflicted a form of emotional castration on himself in order to become a good husband, a good citizen, and a good man of letters; or, to put it less positively, to escape what must have seemed the likely fate of Coleridge. How revealing, after all, that admirable act of charity—his edition of Chatterton's poems.

Southey, like Wordsworth and Coleridge, inherited and in some measure accepted an eighteenth-century theory of poetic genius which at its crudest left them with a wreched dilemma: to save the poet (for a while) or to save the man. If Southey anticipated the advice Wordsworth gave Burns' sons—to 'be admonished by his grave, / And think, and fear!'—we have no moral right to condemn him or Wordsworth for taking the prudent course. It might be that their decisions to risk as little as possible, in both cases connected with decisions to marry, had something to do with poetic failure. It might be but we can never know. The problem of Wordsworth's decline is too complex to be analysed here or to be satisfactorily resolved anywhere. There is no 'problem' in Southey's case, because at no time was he a major poet and, even at his best, never wrote better than good minor poetry. It is pointless to conjecture whether he might have earned the golden opinions of his poetry which Coleridge recorded in Chapter Three of the *Biographia* if only he had retained a little more of Coleridge's superabundant Sensibility. What is sure is that he and Wordsworth thoroughly understood the psychology of Sensibility, and beheld in Coleridge especially but also in such other friends as Lloyd and the Lambs, a present portent of dissolution, of despondency and madness.

Out of that understanding and fear, Wordsworth made one of his greatest poems, *Resolution and Independence*, and Southey wrote in 1798 what I think is his finest short poem, *Autumn*. Geoffrey Carnall believes that this poem was partly inspired by a passage in *Werther*, and I am sure he is right.[52] The passage from Goethe is this one:[53]

What saps my heart is that destroying, hidden power, which exists in every thing. Nature has formed nothing which does not consume itself, and every thing that is near it; so that, surrounded by earth and air, and by all the active powers, I wander with an aching heart; and the universe to me is as a fearful monster, which devours and regorges its food.

91

This passage occurs in the context of a famous letter in which Werther's former creative relationship with nature, perceived as itself creative, through God the creator, is very sharply contrasted with the state of mind depicted here. *Werther* is built on such bold contrasts: spring and winter, Homer and Ossian, Nature the creator and Nature the destroyer—these and a host of lesser paired opposites are the projections and correlatives of the hero's sensibility as the course of his love for Lotte proceeds from ecstasy to despair. Southey's poem *Autumn*, originally entitled *The Contrast*, is a much more modest exploitation of a similar relationship between literary structure and subjective vision. In this case the speaker of what can be read either as a conversation poem or Wertherian verse letter, is rebutting (and at the same time expressing) a deeply pessimistic view of the relationship between man and nature. The optimistic view gets the last word and is clearly meant to be taken as Southey's view, but, with a bit of help from Goethe's masterpiece, the contrary view is stated with considerable force. Since this fine poem is not available in any twentieth-century edition, I quote it in its entirety:[54]

Nay, William, nay, not so! the changeful year
In all its due successions to my sight
Presents but varied beauties, transient all,
All in their season good. These fading leaves,
That with their rich variety of hues
Make yonder forest in the slanting sun
So beautiful, in you awake the thought
Of winter, ... cold, drear winter, when these trees
Each like a fleshless skeleton shall stretch
Its bare brown boughs; when not a flower shall spread
Its colours to the day, and not a bird
Carol its joyaunce, ... but all nature wear
One sullen aspect, bleak and desolate,
To eye, ear, feeling, comfortless alike.
To me their many-colour'd beauties speak
Of times of merriment and festival,
The year's best holiday: I call to mind
The school-boy days, when in the falling leaves
I saw with eager hope the pleasant sign
Of coming Christmas; when at morn I took
My wooden kalendar, and counting up
Once more its often-told account, smooth'd off

92

BLUE COAT BOYS

Each day with more delight the daily notch.
To you the beauties of the autumnal year
Make mournful emblems, and you think of man
Doom'd to the grave's long winter, spirit-broken,
Bending beneath the burthen of his years,
Sense-dull'd and fretful, "full of aches and pains,"
Yet clinging still to life. To me they shew
The calm decay of nature, when the mind
Retains its strength, and in the languid eye
Religion's holy hopes kindle a joy
That makes old age look lovely. All to you
Is dark and cheerless; you in this fair world
See some destroying principle abroad,
Air, earth, and water full of living things,
Each on the other preying; and the ways
Of man, a strange perplexing labyrinth,
Where crimes and miseries, each producing each,
Render life loathsome, and destroy the hope
That should in death bring comfort. Oh, my friend,
That thy faith were as mine! that thou could'st see
Death still producing life, and evil still
Working its own destruction; could'st behold
The strifes and troubles of this troubled world
With the strong eye that sees the promised day
Dawn through this night of tempest! All things then
Would minister to joy; then should thine heart
Be heal'd and harmonized, and thou would'st feel
God, always, every where, and all in all.

This is the final text of the poem. The conclusion of the version Southey published in the *Morning Post* on 8th September 1798 is yet more strikingly like those of the conversation poems and *Dejection:*

        All things then
Would minister to joy, and in thine heart
So harmonis'd, these lovely scenes would wake
The deep delight that feels the present God.

Southey in 1798 was of course more conventional than either Wordsworth or Coleridge in his piety as well as in his diction and imagery; he was also more complacent. Yet *Autumn* is not a merely conventional or complacent poem. What rescues it, by creating rather more intellectual and emotional tension than he may have intended,—what rescues it is precisely that not entirely eradicated 'mimosa-sensibility' which finds effective expression in, for instance, the rhythmic and syntactical guttering-out of

> but all nature wear
>
> One sullen aspect, bleak and desolate,
> To eye, ear, feeling, comfortless alike.

On the other hand, where it should be, the rhythm in *Autumn* is firm and confident, and the syntax relatively compact for a poem in the descriptive-meditative mode. The writing in this poem is not great, but it is distinguished in the same way that some passages in *Roderick* are. We do not feel that *Autumn* is a triumph, human and artistic and in spite of great difficulties, in the way that *Dejection* and *Resolution and Independence* are. But this is partly to say that Southey has nearly succeeded in following his own formula for minor poetry: 'I have a dislike to all strong emotion. . . . In my own writings you may observe that I rather dwell upon what affects than what agitates'.

Southey and Coleridge were not on speaking terms when *Autumn* was published in the *Morning Post*, a few days before Coleridge sailed for Germany. Probably he read the poem when it first appeared, but it is impossible to say what impression it made on him. If he connected it with a specific passage in *Werther*—and this is supposing a good deal—he might also have noticed what immediately precedes it in the same letter:

That which constitutes the happiness of man, must it then change and become the source of his misery? that ardent sentiment which animated my heart with the love of nature, which poured in upon me a torrent of pleasure, which brought all heaven before me, is now changed to an insupportable torment. . . . Ragged rocks, untrodden wilds . . . are animated by the breath of *life*, and every atom to which he has given animation, exults and finds favour in his sight. Ah me! how often at that time has the flight of a sea bird . . . inspired my soul with the desire . . . to partake . . . of the sublime beatitude of the creator, *in whom we live, and move, and have our being!*

Once again we encounter the idea that man's greatest joy and greatest dejection are intimately, even inevitably, linked. We also encounter in the controlling 'breath of life' metaphor, in the

94

associated Psalm-like personifications, and in the direct citation of Acts 17:28 at the end of the passage, scriptural figures and doctrines which are at the heart of *Dejection* and much else that Coleridge and Wordsworth wrote during their greatest years. And of course these very figures and doctrines, as reinterpreted in the eighteenth century, must therefore be the subject of much that I shall write in the following chapters. For the moment, I note only that there is a marked pattern of associations which connect *Dejection* and its author with *Werther* and Wertherism.

That there are close affinities between *Dejection* and parts of *Werther* should not surprise us or, on the other hand, lead us to assume any direct influence. Both works had a common ancestry in the Protestant mystical tradition and in the writings of Young, Richardson, Percy, and 'Ossian'. Moreover, the central ideas and images of *Werther* were rapidly diffused and vulgarized by, among many others, the English writers I have just discussed. One need go only slightly further afield and read *Réné* to see how a more gifted literary opportunist than Croft or Lloyd could exploit Goethe's achievement and keep it current in a degraded form. *Dejection* may well be, like *Werther* itself, an entirely fresh sublimation of some of the grosser elements of the life and literature of Sensibility. Nevertheless, the resemblances between the two works are so striking that we must pause to consider whether *Dejection* is not perhaps the most distinguished English contribution to Wertheriana.

Quite early in his career, Coleridge perceived that Sensibility, though no friend to Established Interests, was also no ally of humanitarian reform. I have already quoted poems which Coleridge addressed to Lamb and Lloyd in 1796 admonishing them to forget their private troubles and throw themselves into benevolent public causes; during the same year he made what I believe was his first reference to Goethe's novel:[55]

She sips a beverage sweetened with human blood, even while she is weeping over the refined sorrows of Werter or Clementina. Sensibility is not Benevolence. Nay, by making us tremblingly alive to trifling misfortunes, it frequently prevents it, and induces effeminate and cowardly selfishness.

To say so, however, was not to deny the brilliance and accuracy of Goethe's portrayal of suicidal youth, and years later (when he was less concerned with the slave trade) Coleridge admitted the excellence of *Werther*: [56]

He [Coleridge] spoke with more than usual candour of Goethe, and said if he spoke in seeming depreciation of him, it was only because he compared him with the very greatest poets. He said that Goethe appeared to him from some sort of caprice to have underrated the kind of talent he had in his youth so eminently displayed, viz. the power of exhibiting man in a state of exalted sensibility as in *Werther*.

Possibly he thought the same in 1802. All that can be said with certainty is that there are letters in *Werther*, the following one and the one quoted earlier in connexion with Southey's *Autumn*, which afford uncanny anticipatory glimpses of the imagery, creative theory, and phrasing of Coleridge's ode. These qualities come through even in the clumsy contemporary translation already cited in relation to Chatterton and *Love and Madness*: [57]

In the morning I arise, behold the bright orb of day, and am un-happy. Oh! that I were hipped! that I could impute my sadness to a clouded atmosphere, or an unsuccessful undertaking—my sufferings would grow somewhat tolerable; but, alas! I feel too sensibly that the source of my grief is in myself. This bosom, formerly the seat of delight, is now the seat of misery—am I not the same man, who formerly knew nothing but exquisite sensa-tions, who, at every step, saw paradise before him, whose expanded heart was full of benevolence to all the world. But this heart is now torped—quite dead to all sentiment—my eyes are dry, and my senses no longer moistened by the tears of sensibility, daily wither, and exhaust my brain. My afflictions are many—I am de-prived of my only consolation—that inspiring power which created worlds around me is now no more! I contemplate the distant mountain from my window, and behold the rising sun, immerging from the clouds, illuminate the gladdened plains with his rays! . . . But all the magnificent beauties of nature cannot elevate my dejected soul, nor raise one lively sensation in my breast—I am totally inanimate. On my knees I have implored heaven for tears, as the countryman prays for rain to moisten his parched corn. But 'tis in vain; the Almighty does not grant rain or sun-shine to importunities—Why were those times so happy, the memory of which so torments me? When I waited the blessings of the

Great Creator of all things with patience, and accepted them with a heart filled with gratitude.

Here are the grief which 'finds no natural outlet, no relief, / In word, or sigh, or tear'; the suspension of the 'shaping spirit of Imagination'; the failure 'from outward forms to win / The passion and the life, whose fountains are within'. With regard to the crucial question of the suspended Imagination, it is important to point out that the original ('denn ich habe verloren, was meines Lebens eizige Wonne war, die heilige belebende Kraft . . .'[58]) is closer to *Dejection* in its stress on the joyous, sacred and active nature of the power with which Werther formerly created worlds around him; and some eighteenth-century translations of these phrases are closer to the German than the one I have quoted. By 1802, of course, Coleridge could have read the German text, but his first reading must have been of a translation. All that need be noted here is that all of the eighteenth-century English translations I have checked are faithful enough to the original passage to have afforded Coleridge a synopsis of some of the leading ideas of *Dejection*.

There is simply no way of knowing whether *Werther* played any direct role in the making of *Dejection*. Coleridge's references to *Werther* before 1802 are so infrequent and vague that we have to conclude, I think, that no direct influence was involved. And even if we suspect that *Werther* was under Coleridge's pillow during the winter of 1801–2, we have to allow that *Dejection* is a fresh artistic synthesis of ideas and experiences that Goethe in his turn had synthesized in a very different literary form and with very different implications. Each is a masterpiece of the literature of Sensibility, intimately related to the other and yet unique and irreplaceable.

NOTES

1. *Letters*, II, 967. This letter to Sir George and Lady Beaumont, dated 13 August 1803, includes early versions of both *Resolution and Independence* and *Dejection*, and it is possible that their being copied together in the same letter is significant. Unless noted otherwise, my quotations from *Resolution and Independence* are taken from this text. The subsequent quotations from 'On Observing a Blossom', are taken from *The Watchman*, ed. Lewis Patton (London, 1970), 202–3.

D

2. A point duly noted by Linda Kelly in *The Marvellous Boy* (London, 1971), 85.

3. See the letter to George Coleridge dated 23 February 1794, *Letters*, I, 68.

4. *Letters*, I, 160, dated 7 October 1795. The coincidence of the marriage in Chatterton's church is also noted by Miss Kelly, *The Marvellous Boy*, 90.

5. *Letters*, I, 275, dated 13 December 1796.

6. For Coleridge's own shrewd criticism of the *Monody*, see his letter to Southey, dated 17 July 1797, *Letters*, I, 333.

7. *The Letters of Charles and Mary Lamb*, ed. E. V. Lucas (London, 1935), I, 34–35, dated 5 July 1796. This verse letter was subsequently revised for publication, but the revisions have no biographical significance.

8. A. Alvarez, *The Savage God* (London, 1971).

9. Mrs Henry Sandford, *Thomas Poole*, I, 132–34, letter to Henrietta Warwick, dated 6 February 1796.

10. E. M. Sickles, *The Gloomy Egoist* (New York, 1932).

11. Cottle, *Reminiscences of Samuel Taylor Coleridge and Robert Southey* (London, 1847), 72.

12. *The Letters of William and Dorothy Wordsworth*, ed. de Selincourt and Shaver (2nd edn, Oxford, 1967), I, 256: dated 27 February 1799, to Coleridge: 'His Ode to Despondency I can never read without agitation'. *The Works of Robert Burns*, ed. James Currie (Liverpool, 1800), III, 170.

13. *Letters*, I, 136, dated 11 December 1794, to Southey. Lamb's poem was first published in Coleridge's *Poems* (Bristol, 1796), 57, with the suicidal concluding lines omitted. The version quoted here, the 1818 text given in E. V. Lucas' *The Works of Charles and Mary Lamb* (London, 1903), V, 4, does not differ significantly from earlier drafts.

14. *The Works of Robert Burns*, III, 172.

15. *Letters*, I, 607, dated 24 July 1800, to Thomas Poole.

16. *The Works of Robert Burns*, I, 236–37, 246–47, 248–50, 251–52, 252.

17. Lines 21–24 of *Dejection* employ some of the same words and metaphors as *The Dungeon*, which is a poem Coleridge made by simply lifting a speech without alteration from his tragedy *Osorio*, Act V. *Osorio* was written during a period when Milton was much on his mind, when in fact he quoted lines 594–96 of *Samson* in his letter of early April 1797 to Joseph Cottle. The lines in *The Dungeon* are very like lines 617–22 of *Samson*.

18. *Samson Agonistes*, lines 597, 338–39, 166–75. Anderson, V, 132, 130, 128–29.

19. It must be obvious that the shift from physical to mental might is accompanied by shifts in the meaning of 'genial'. In the fourth chapter I try to amplify somewhat the account given in the *Oxford English Dictionary*, the learned editors of which long ago traced the curious history of Milton's phrase.

20. Perdita wrote her own memoirs, several times reprinted during the

nineteenth century, and has been fortunate in her most recent biographer, Marguerite Steen, whose *The Lost One* (London, 1937) is a sensible if sometimes 'novelistic' treatment.

21. Henry C. Shelley, *The Life and Letters of Edward Young* (London, 1914), pp. v, and 256–58.

22. I have consulted both the first edition of *Love and Madness* (London, 1780) and the 'new' London edition of 1786; they are substantially the same. But I should note that my final readings are based on the 1786 edition.

23. See S. P. Atkins, *The Testament of Werther in Poetry and Drama* (Cambridge, Mass., 1949), for further information about the popularity of *Love and Madness* and other Wertheriana in England during the last quarter of the eighteenth century.

24. *Werter and Charlotte, a German Story* (London, 1786), 169, 164, iii.

25. *Werter and Charlotte*, 20.

26. *Letters*, I, 332–33, dated 17 July 1797, to Southey; I, 340, dated August 1797, to Joseph Cottle.

27. *Letters*, I, 585, dated 10 April 1800, to Southey.

28. *The Watchman* (London, 1970); first published 5 May 1796), 313–15.

29. *Letters*, I, 491–93, dated 6 May 1799.

30. *Notebooks*, I, 874 and 1045, dated respectively December 1800 and November 1801–January 1802.

31. Robert Merry, 'Elegy, written after having read the Sorrows of Werter', *The British Album* (London, 2nd edn., 1790), I, 14.

32. Atkins, *The Testament of Werther*, 16–17.

33. Some of these are mentioned in Linda Kelly, *The Marvellous Boy* (London, 1971).

34. *Letters*, I, 381–82, dated January 1798, to the Editor of *The Monthly Magazine. Poetical Works of the Late Thomas Warton* (Oxford, 1802), I, 146.

35. *Letters*, I, 562–63, dated 25 January 1800.

36. *Poems by Mrs M. Robinson* (London, 1793), II, 118.

37. *Poems by Mrs M. Robinson*, II, 109–11.

38. *The Poetical Works of the Late Mrs. Mary Robinson* (London, 1806), I, 246–50, 251–53. These poems appear paired in her *Poems of 1793* as well.

39. *Poetical Works*, I, 16.

40. This list of minor late eighteenth-century poets who shed tears over Chatterton or Werther might be extended considerably, but it will do for sampling purposes.

41. *Letters*, II, 904, dated 27 December 1802.

42. *Poetical Works*, II, 368–70.

43. *Poems* by S. T. Coleridge, (2nd edn., Bristol & London, 1797), 155.

44. *New Letters of Robert Southey*, ed. Kenneth Curry (New York & London, 1965), I, 161, dated 7 March 1798.

45. Charles Lloyd, *Edmund Oliver* (Bristol, 1798), II, 190–91.

46. *Edmund Oliver*, II, 145.

47. *Edmund Oliver*, I, ix–x; II, 86–87.

48. Lines from Southey's metrical introduction to Joseph Cottle's *Icelandic Poetry*, dated 1 November 1797. Cited by W. Clark Durant, Preface to the *Memoirs of Mary Wollstonecraft* (New York, 1927), xxxi.

49. *New Letters of Robert Southey*, I, dated 24 January 1794.

50. A *Memoir of the Life and Writings of the Late William Taylor of Norwich*, ed. J. W. Robberds (London, 1843), I, 262, letter dated 12 March 1799.

51. *Letters*, I, 163–73, dated 13 November 1795, to Robert Southey.

52. Geoffrey Carnall, *Robert Southey and His Age* (Oxford, 1960), 64–65.

53. *The Sorrows of Werter: A German Story* (New edn., London, 1794), I, 155–56. Carnall quotes a mid-nineteenth-century translation, but I have chosen the Graves translation, which is slightly closer to Southey's poem and might well have been the one he read, since it seems to have been the most commonly available English translation during the eighteenth century. My second quotation from Goethe's novella is from the translation quoted previously, i.e. the translation of 1786 by a different hand than Graves' (*Werter and Charlotte*, 70–73). I cite the latter whenever I am making a point about Coleridge's possible indebtedness to *Werther*, though of course it is impossible to know which translation he used or whether he used one at all after 1798.

54. *The Minor Poems of Robert Southey* (London, 1815), I, 237–39.

55. *The Watchman*, 25 March 1796, 139.

56. *Henry Crabb Robinson on Books and Their Writers*, ed. Edith J. Morley (London, 1938), I, 122. Coleridge's remarks are dated 2 March 1813.

57. *Werter and Charlotte*, 117–18.

58. Goethe, *Die Leiden des jungen Werthers* (Mainz, 1938): 1774 edn., p. 80; 1787 edn., p. 194.

3

Nature's Music

On one of those dark days which sadden the end of the year . . . listen, while reading Ossian, to the fantastic harmony of an Aeolian harp hung at the top of a leafless tree; and I defy you not to experience a feeling deep and sad, of surrender, of a vague and infinite longing for another existence . . . in a word, a strong attack of spleen joined with a temptation to suicide.

—Berlioz, *Voyage Musical*

David Hartley is well, saving that he is sometimes inspired by the God Eolus, & like Isaiah, his 'bowells sound like an Harp'!

—Coleridge, letter dated 5 November 1796

1

The Harp of Aeolus has long since disappeared from the window casements, the hills and gardens of Europe. But when Coleridge wrote *Dejection*, the vogue of the wind harp was at its height. During the same decade of 1800–10, London musical comedy impresario Charles Dibden published the lyrics of this High Class song:[1]

> But most, the senses to ensnare,
>   Give me the soft celestial strain
> That gently floats upon the air,
>   That all can feel but none explain;
> In sounds the ear so smoothly greet
> From the seraphic, self-play'd, sweet
>   Aeolian harp.

Recalling the lost friends of his youth in the Dedication to *Faust*, Part I, Goethe was seized[2]

by long forgotten yearning
For that kingdom of spirits, still and grave,
To flowing song I see my feelings turning,
As from aeolian harps, wave upon wave....

While in the year of *Faust* (1808), the Farmer-Boy poet Robert Bloomfield brought out a pamphlet, *Nature's Music*, which not only anthologized previous writings on the Aeolian harp but also advertised the poet's own manufacture of that wonderful instrument.[3] Coleridge himself had contributed to the vogue by describing or alluding to the wind harp in a number of early poems, most notably *The Eolian Harp* (1795). In doing so, he was perpetuating a tradition that began with James Thomson in *The Castle of Indolence* (1748) and included Collins, Akenside, Smollet, Smart, Bowles, and Wordsworth. He was also contributing to a related but much older tradition of literary reference to stringed instruments which, though not designed for Aeolian performance, were played upon by the wind when the poet's hand was stilled by death or sleep. Coleridge and his literary friends and peers knew these traditions well: for them, if not for us, the dull sobbing draft that moaned upon the Aeolian lute in the opening stanza of *Dejection* must have invoked a host of meanings beyond its immediate and primary meaning.

The Aeolian harp sounds twice but very briefly in *Dejection.* In the opening sentence:

Well! If the Bard was weather-wise, who made
    The grand old ballad of Sir Patrick Spence,
This night, so tranquil now, will not go hence
Unroused by winds, that ply a busier trade
Than those which mould yon cloud in lazy flakes,
Or the dull sobbing draft, that moans and rakes
    Upon the strings of this Æolian lute,
        Which better far were mute.

And at the beginning of Stanza VII:

Hence, viper thoughts, that coil round my mind,
    Reality's dark dream!
I turn from you, and listen to the wind,
    Which long has raved unnoticed. What a scream
Of agony by torture lengthened out
That lute sent forth!

102

About six of the total one hundred and thirty-nine lines of the poem refer directly to the playing of the wind harp. (Coleridge calls the instrument a harp or lute without distinction, apparently according to the local exigencies of the sound pattern.⁴) But the importance of this image is much greater than my arithmetic implies. First, integrated as it is with the setting of evening sky, rising wind and storm, we are obviously meant to imagine the lute playing on all the while the poet is speaking. Second, though the lute is described as an actual instrument actually present and playing, we quickly perceive that it is also a metaphor for the poet himself and that the dull sobbing draft of Stanza I is the figurative counterpart of the

> stifled, drowsy, unimpassioned grief,
> Which finds no natural outlet, no relief,
> In word, or sigh, or tear—

of Stanza II. At this level, then, the utterance of the lute is the poem itself. Later on, references to 'My shaping spirit of Imagination' and to the wind as 'Thou mighty Poet' reveal what is only latent in the opening stanza, the traditional idea of Pythian inspiration. That it is only latent at first has to be insisted on: for working as he does in this poem with symbolic images which bear many and even contradictory associations, much of Coleridge's art consists in keeping unwanted associations in the shadows of the mind, until they are wanted. The lute's first appearance in the poem is in a metaphorical role which is essentially a variation on familiar eighteenth-century usage—the Aeolian harp as a figure for the highly responsive, helplessly passive sensibility of genius. This primary meaning is easily comprehended by the careful reader of English literary tradition may bring it into sharper focus.

2

The Aeolian harp made its first literary appearance in the Spenserian stanzas of Thomson's *Castle of Indolence* (1748). Though the Castle is not quite the Bowre of Bliss and its inhabitants not quite Lotus-eaters held in thrall, Thomson's False Paradise, like those of Spenser and Keats and Tennyson, is the bone-yard of them whose senses have triumphed over their creative will. Beauti-

ful as the Aeolian strains are conceded to be, they are the siren
music of a wicked Prospero:[5]

Each sound too here, to languishment inclin'd,
Lull'd the weak bosom, and induced ease.
Aerial music in the warbling wind,
At distance rising oft by small degrees,
Nearer and nearer came, till o'er the trees
It hung, and breath'd such soul-dissolving airs,
As did, alas! with soft perdition please:
Entangled deep in its enchanting snares,
The listening heart forgot all duties and all cares.

A certain music, never known before,
Here lull'd the pensive melancholy mind;
Full easily obtain'd. Behoves no more,
But sidelong to the gently-waving wind,
To lay the well-tun'd instrument reclined;
From which, with airy flying fingers light,
Beyond each mortal touch the most refin'd,
The god of winds drew sounds of deep delight;
Whence, with just cause, The harp of Aeolus it hight.

Ah me! what hand can touch the string so fine?
Who up the lofty diapasan roll
Such sweet, such sad, such solemn airs divine,
Then let them down again into the soul?
Now rising love they fann'd; now pleasing dole
They breath'd, in tender musings, through the heart;
And now a graver sacred strain they stole,
As when seraphic hands an hymn impart:
Wild warbling nature all, above the reach of art!

Thomson included himself among the inmates of the Castle of
Indolence (1, lxviii), and rightly, too. For in his enthusiasm for
the wind harp he soon forgets to be a Spenserian moralist. Indeed,
that role is undermined from the beginning by his allusions. These
deserve careful attention. Besides the obvious one to *The Tempest*,
there are less obtrusive ones to *Il Penseroso*, *L'Allegro* and the
Essay on Criticism:[6]

As may with sweetness, through mine ear,
Dissolve me into extacies,
And bring all Heav'n before mine eyes.

NATURE'S MUSIC

Or sweetest Shakespear, Fancy's child,
Warble his native wood-notes wild.

Music resembles Poetry; in each
Are nameless graces which no methods teach,
And which a master-hand alone can reach.

. . . . .

From vulgar bounds with brave disorder part,
And snatch a grace beyond the reach of art. . . .

Lines which implicitly compare the Aeolian harp with Shakes-peare and which recall Shakespeare's and Milton's celebration of the power of music are not well-calculated to score a Puritanical point. Without perhaps fully intending to, Thomson reaffirms Shakespeare's recognition that there is something frightening about the power of music but something sadly lacking in us if we do not succumb:[7]

Therefore, the poet

Did feign that Orpheus drew trees, stones, and floods;
Since nought so stockish, hard, and full of rage,
But music for the time doth change his nature:
The man that hath no music in himself,
Nor is not mov'd with concord of sweet sounds,
Is fit for treasons, stratagems, and spoils;
The motions of his spirit are dull as night,
And his affections dark as Erebus. . . .

In the passage immediately following his praise of Shakespeare's 'wood-notes wild', Milton describes the power of music in images which, slightly adjusted, might well describe a Bowre of Bliss. His eye precociously fixed on the problems of temptation and fall, he yields with more wariness than Thomson does when describing a supposedly sinister engine of enthrallment!—[8]

And ever, against eating cares,
Lap me in soft Lydian airs,
Married to immortal Verse,
Such as the meeting soul may pierce
In notes with many a winding bout
Of linked sweetness long drawn out
With wanton heed, and giddy cunning,
The melting voice through mazes running,

105

Untwisting all the chains, that tie
The hidden soul of harmony';
That Orpheus self may heave his head
From golden slumber on a bed
Of heapt Elysian flow'rs, and hear
Such strains as would have won the ear
Of Pluto, to have quite set free
His half-regain'd Eurydice.

As the passage develops, invoking Orpheus in magnificent hyperbole, the power of music is shown to be a potentially liberating as well as anaesthetizing force when experienced by 'the meeting soul'. Perhaps the idea of liberation (from a man's own 'stockish, hard', enraged nature) is also present in the speech Shakespeare gives to Lorenzo. At any rate, both Shakespeare and Milton affirm that there is a music within and a music without, and that the affective power of the one is proportionate to the active response ('motions of his spirit') of the other. Thomson makes no such affirmation, and of course it is no part of his scheme to do so. On the contrary. The inhabitants of his Castle are essentially passive, victims of necromantic artifice. To the principle of passivity he adhered—perhaps less as a disciple of Spenser than as a disciple of Locke—even while he betrayed his scheme by celebrating the 'Nature' of the Aeolian harp and hinting at connexions with the music of Shakespeare and Milton.

An instrument with such ravishing influence over the sensibility might be put to more philanthropic uses. Though James Beattie wrote of a friend who 'has been once and again wrought into a feverish fit by the tones of an Eolian harp', many eighteenth-century observers believed that the harp might have important therapeutic value for the mentally disturbed.[9] Other forms of music, from the remotest periods, had been invested with supposed powers of enchantment, seduction or healing; and so it is scarcely surprising that this novel engine of musical entertainment should have been invested with them, too. Yet there was something special about the Aeolian harp. As Christopher Smart makes especially clear, it was the instrument through which, not man, but the very forces of Nature expressed themselves:[10]

O rich of genuine nature, free from art!
Such the wild warblings of the sylvan throng,
So simply sweet the untaught virgin's song.

Add to this that the performer, Aeolus, acted invisibly and therefore (while the novelty lasted) mysteriously, and it becomes easy to understand why his music was imagined by some to be endowed with extra virtue and potency.

Yet the instrument which produced this highly active music might itself be considered the very type of trembling feminine passivity. Although its utterances were neither more nor less voluntary than those of any other instrument, the Aeolian harp could be much more readily anthropomorphized and projected full of human powers to will and initiate action: [11]

Hail heav'nly harp, where Memnon's skill is shown,
That charm'st the ear with music all thine own!
Which though untouch'd, can'st rapturous strains impart.....

Alas for Smart's claims, the harp and its owner had in practice to wait patiently for Aeolus to act upon it. What was patently and merely an instrument could arouse no painful sense of its beautiful helplessness, but the Aeolian harp was something both more and less than an object to be taken up and played upon by man. As the century wore on and man himself came more and more to seem a determined being, man and harp tended to trade places: the Aeolian harp became a major metaphor for the human sensibility, especially the mercurial and delicately responsive sensibility of genius.

A few examples with which Coleridge was certainly familiar will illustrate my point. One very susceptible genius, as Wordsworth reminded the world, was Robert Burns, who never knew 'why the tones of her voice made my heart-strings thrill like an Æolian harp'.[12] Another was Mary Wollstonecraft: 'what misery, as well as rapture, is produced by a quick perception of the beautiful and sublime, when it is exercised in observing animated nature, when every beauteous feeling and emotion excites responsive sympathy, and the harmonized soul sinks into melancholy, or rises to extasy, just as the chords are touched, like the aeolian harp agitated by the changing wind'.[13] Even the Rev. W. L. Bowles found the Aeolian harp an indispensable metaphor:[14]

Though the long night is dark and damp around,
And no still star hangs out its friendly flame;
And the winds sweep the sash with sullen sound,
And freezing palsy creeps o'er all my frame;

I catch consoling phantasies that spring
　　From the thick gloom, and as the night-airs beat,
They touch my heart, like the wild wires that ring
　　In mournful modulations, strange and sweet.

As early as March 1795, Coleridge himself used the closely related image of the statue of Memnon to describe a delicate sensibility: 'The finely-fibred Heart, that like the statue of Memnon, trembles into melody on the sun-beam touch of Benevolence, is most easily jarred into the dissonance of Misanthropy'.[15] In a poem that belongs to the same year as the passages quoted from Bowles and Mary Wollstonecraft, *On Observing a Blossom on the First of February 1796*, Coleridge has forebodings of the 'keen North-East' that must drive out an unseasonable Zephyr, and a gloomy train of associations that includes Blossom, consumptive girl, and the 'wondrous boy' Chatterton. Of course the poem is implicitly about his fears for himself, but in the manner of Bowles he makes the best of a pleasurably painful situation:

And the warm wooings of this sunny day
Tremble along my frame, and harmonize
Th' attemper'd brain, that ev'n saddest thoughts
Mix with some sweet sensations, like harsh tunes
Play'd deftly on a soft-ton'd instrument.

A sensibility as delicate as that had better be kept indoors. Though self-indulgent and facile, the poem neatly exemplifies the sudden modulations of mood which made the wind harp such a favourite metaphor of the Age of Sensibility.

That is one part of the background of the opening lines of *Dejection*. The great difference is that the note of self-indulgence, the pleasure in the pain, which is present not only in early Coleridge but in Bowles and Mary Wollstonecraft too, has been purged away. The Aeolian lute has lost all of its glamour; what is no more than an instrument, with an instrument's helpless sensitive responsiveness, 'better far were mute'. And that is all. In the course of the poem Coleridge goes on to develop the related metaphors of music and wind in ways that expose the inadequacy of the wind harp as a metaphor for the human sensibility in a state of health. In doing so, he harks back to a conception of aesthetic psychology which antedates Hobbes and Locke; which is, as we have seen, the conception of Shakespeare and Milton:

And from the soul itself must there be sent
 A sweet and potent voice, of its own birth,
Of all sweet sounds the life and element!

O pure of heart! thou need'st not ask of me
What this strong music in the soul may be!

To say that the Aeolian harp is an inadequate metaphor is not to say that it fails to serve its purpose in the opening section of *Dejection*. On the contrary, it introduces precisely the right associations and attitudes for future affirmation or rejection.

3

Dejection is a poem about Death-in-Life; more specifically, it is a 'greater ode' about the death of a poet. It is therefore appropriate that a form of the lyre or harp, ancient bardic instrument and emblem, should sound mournfully in the opening lines of the poem. It seems even more appropriate if we recall (as Southey, Wordsworth and many another contemporary reader must have done) the long line of elegiac poems in which an ordinary harp, played on by the sympathizing winds, laments its dead master. Coleridge experimented with this idea on two occasions before *Dejection*,[16] commented on lines in which Southey did the same, and certainly knew its classic embodiment in the poetry of Ovid, Spenser, and Collins. Probably he meant us to perceive these connexions with earlier literature—the more so because they oblige us to think further about the relationship between Nature and the poetic imagination.

Both Lucian and Ovid describe how, after Orpheus is torn to pieces by the Thracian women, his head is placed upon his lyre and sent floating down the river Hebrus: the dissevered head sings and the marvellous lyre is played by river breezes in mournful yet triumphant accompaniment.[17] Virgil tells the same story but does not mention the Aeolian accompaniment of the lyre.[18] Lucian adds that Orpheus' lyre was eventually hung up in the temple of Apollo, within reach of the winds. All three accounts stress the perfect sympathy that existed between Orpheus and nature. In these versions the myth was transmitted to Milton, Spenser, Coleridge and the many other English schoolboys who were obliged to read portions of the *Metamorphoses and Georgics*.

Spenser's treatment of the wind-played harp in *The Ruins of Time* was duly noted by eighteenth-century commentators on the Aeolian harp and gracefully echoed in Thomson's line, 'Aerial music in the warbling wind'.[19] This was as it should have been. For of all English poets Spenser was the one peculiarly gifted to exploit the possibilities of this image in a poetry of pastoral elegy, richly allusive and emblematic:[20]

Whilest thus I looked, loe adowne the *Lee*,
I sawe an Harpe strong all with siluer twyne,
And made of golde and costlie yourie,
Swimming, that whilome seemed to have been
The harpe, on which *Dan Orpheus* was seene
Wylde beasts and forrests after him to lead,
But was th' Harpe of *Philisides* now dead.

At length out of the Riuer it was reard
And borne aboue the cloudes to be deuin'd,
Whilst all the way most heauenly noyse was heard
Of the strings, stirred with the warbling wind,
That wrought both ioy and sorrow in my mind:
So now in heauen a signe it doth appeare,
The Harpe well knowne beside the Northern Beare.

In this tribute to Sidney the old image of the wind-played Orphic harp is given its most daring and memorable restatement in English. So much so that direct imitation must have seemed a very risky venture. One might hope to refine on some aspect of Spenser's soaring figures, but where, for many years to come, would one find such a legend of untimely poetic death as Sidney's to justify, and be perpetuated by, such figures? Milton is very much to the point here, since he developed the pastoral elegy in the tradition of *The Ruins of Time* and since he certainly felt the full archetypal force of the Orpheus myth. He identified Orpheus with himself in the great opening passage of *Paradise Lost*, Book VII, and with his friend Edward King in *Lycidas* 58–63:[21]

What could the Muse herself that Orpheus bore,
The Muse herself for her enchanting son,
Whom universal Nature did lament,
When by the rout that made the hideous roar,
His goary visage down the stream was sent,
Down the swift Hebrus to the Lesbian shore?

Milton chose the generalized personification, 'Whom universal Nature did lament', rather than the symbolic particular of the wind playing the dead poet's harp. Whatever his reasons, he quietly dropped the vehicle but not the tenor, and pointed up the relevance of the myth for English nature poetry. It was all the more appropriate, therefore, that Collins should have alluded to that myth while restoring the 'airy Harp' in his elegiac *Ode on the Death of Mr. Thomson:*[22]

> In yon deep bed of whisp'ring reeds
>   His airy harp shall now be laid,
> That he, whose heart in sorrow bleeds,
>   May love thro' life the soothing shade.
>
> Then maids and youths shall linger here,
>   And, while its sounds at distance swell,
> Shall sadly seem in pity's ear
>   To hear the woodland pilgrim's knell.

Professor McKillop rightly comments that Collins 'identifies the harp with Thomson's poetic genius and adapts the passage to the uses of pastoral elegy'.[23]

Elegy in *Ossian* is not classical in origin or feeling, and when the winds play Ossian's harp they do not do so for a dead poet. None-theless, it is necessary to mention Macpherson's remarkable prose poem in passing, because elegy after *Ossian* could never be quite the same again and because the mournful wind-played harp was one of his favourite atmospheric props. Along with all other moans, whistles and shrieks of the wind in the trees, valleys and peaks, the wind in the harp occurs at least four times in *Ossian*.[24] Per-haps its most memorable occurrence is in *Dar-thula*, where Ossian recalls:

> The wind was abroad, in the oaks; the spirit of the mountain shrieked. The blast came rustling through the hall, and gently touched my harp. The sound was mournful and low, like the song of the tomb . . . 'I hear the sound of death on the harp of my son. Ossian, touch the sounding string; bid the sorrow rise; that their spirits may fly with joy to Morven's woody hills'.

In a footnote Macpherson explains that 'By the spirit of the moun-tain is meant that deep and melancholy sound which precedes a storm; well known to those who live in a high country'. For him nature was neither the treasury of moral emblems that it was for Spenser nor the book of moral wisdom that it was for so many of his eighteenth-century contemporaries. It was, rather, a vast theatre of the pathetic fallacy into which a shaft of sunlight sometimes fell, not to irradiate the gloom, but to make it more intense. Romantic writers, like the author of *Werther*, had to come to terms with *Ossian*'s world, appropriating its powerful expressive means without succumbing (as Schiller said Goethe's hero did) to its fatal formlessness.[25] *Dejection* is another, later fruit of such discipline: which is not to argue for any direct or conscious influence, but only to remind the reader that *Ossian* was in the bones and bloodstream of the early Romantics.[26]

The live poet in *Dejection* has an Orpheus-like power to animate nature, and, in his 'purest hour', enjoys a sacramental relationship with her. But once that power is gone, through death or the loss of 'Joy', so too must that relationship go: the things of nature are mere 'outward forms'. Therefore,

> Upon the strings of this Æolian lute,
>
> the dull sobbing draft, that moans and rakes

must not be confused with the winds which express the grief of 'universal nature', when Orpheus, Sidney or Thomson die, by playing upon the dead poets' harps. Indeed, in this as in other respects *Dejection* can be read as a sad repudiation of some of the most cherished portions of Coleridge's literary inheritance. Yet a repulse is also an implicit acknowledgment of attractive force: in the lines quoted immediately above, personified nature certainly does seem alive and responsive to the misery of the poet. This illusion is soon shattered, but it is sustained long enough to prompt a recollection of occasions when, through their own surviving harps, 'universal nature did lament' the deaths of mighty poets.

4

On its first appearance, then, the Aeolian harp in *Dejection* is both an actual wind harp responding to the impulses of external nature, and a metaphor for a 'distempered' sensibility which, registering every kind of sensory and emotional shock at all moments of consciousness, gives utterance to that experience. Taken at the literal level, what the harp metamorphoses into music are gusts of wind.

Taken at the metaphorical level, what the harp utters is, or seems to be, the poem itself. Clearly, the 'dull sobbing draft' of line 6 is not the wind of inspiration, i.e., an extraordinary, even super-natural, visitation. Yet we might at first suppose that such a sensibility as this—the perfect passive medium—would also be accessible to Pythian afflatus: we might even suppose that lines 15–20 are a prayer for that to happen:

> And oh! that even now the gust were swelling,
> And the slant night-shower driving loud and fast!
> Those sounds which oft have raised me, whilst they awed,
> And sent my soul abroad,
> Might now perhaps their wonted impulse give,
> Might startle this dull pain, and make it move and live!

But as John Hayden has suggested in his trenchant study of *Dejection*, an 'Eolian visitation' would betray everything that Coleridge says about the nature of perception and creative vision in the rest of the poem.[27] So long as he is describing his own state of numb misery in Stanzas I–III, we can accept the opening convention of the Aeolian harp as a metaphor for the poet (who 'better far were mute') compulsively writing descriptive or diagnostic verse when he can no longer write poetry. We can conveniently forget about the convention when we come to the visionary stanzas in praise of Joy, and suppose that Coleridge has forgotten about it as well—until Stanza VII, when the Aeolian harp image reappears briefly only to be overturned by a crucial shift of imagery. Agent then supersedes instrument, the wind-as-harpist replaces the wind harp as Coleridge's figure for the poet:

> I turn from you, and listen to the wind,
> Which long has raved unnoticed. What a scream
> Of agony by torture lengthened out
> That lute sent forth! Thou Wind, that rav'st without,
> Bare crag, or mountain-tairn, or blasted tree,
> Or pine-grove wither woodman never clomb,
> Or lonely house, long held the witches' home,
> Methinks were fitter instruments for thee,
> Mad Lutanist! who in this month of showers,
> Of dark brown gardens, and of peeping flowers,
> Mak'st Devils' yule, with worse than wintry song,
> The blossoms, buds, and timorous leaves among.
> Thou Actor, perfect in all tragic sounds!

Thou mighty Poet, e'en to Frenzy bold!
What tell'st thou now about?

What happens, in Professor Hayden's words, is that, after using the Aeolian harp in its 'traditional and logical manner' in Stanza I, in Stanza VII Coleridge, 'collapses' the image and thus turns 'an image of passivity into one of activity.'[28] It is as simple and basic as that, but it is a point that deserves all the prominence Professor Hayden gives to it.

However, I cannot entirely agree with his reading of Stanza I or with what I take him to mean when he refers to 'the traditional image of the aeolian lute'. I can best explain my disagreement by showing what that traditional image was, in so far as it was a figure for creativity generally and poetic inspiration particularly. Students of English Romanticism will quickly recognize my indebtedness in what follows to M. H. Abrams' important and well-known essay 'The Correspondent Breeze: A Romantic Metaphor'.[29] It is a real debt but one that I try to repay by extending his analysis of Coleridge and Wordsworth.

Coleridge wrote one important poem about the physical characteristics and analogical possibilities of the Aeolian harp, and that poem was, of course, the poem which took its title from the instrument. In it the Aeolian harp is (as logically it must be) a metaphor for passive reception of the influxes of thought, feeling and sensation:

Full many a thought uncall'd and undetain'd,
And many idle flitting phantasies,
Traverse my indolent and passive brain,
As wild and various as the random gales
That swell and flutter on this subject Lute!

This looks very like Hartley's 'Mechanism' or like Priestley's redaction of Hartley. In attempting to construct a theory of the human mind after the model of Newtonian mechanism, pioneer psychologists like Hartley were not much concerned with the special case of artistic creativity. And neither is Coleridge overly concerned with it in *The Eolian Harp*. The young trespasser is after game at once bigger and smaller than 'My shaping spirit of Imagination':

Or what if all of animated nature
Be but organic Harps diversely fram'd,
That tremble into thought, as o'er them sweeps

> Plastic and vast, one intellectual breeze,
> At once the Soul of each, and God of all?

This cosmic metaphor, which is offered only to be immediately retracted in the famous palinodia 'But thy more serious eye . . .'.— this metaphor opens up a possibility that Coleridge exploits in a later poem, *The Nightingale* (1798). The possibility, namely, that the true poet is a person who is more than usually open to the influxes of nature and thus able to share in 'Nature's immortality'. But in *The Eolian Harp* Coleridge is preoccupied not with the creative human individual but with the cosmic relationship between God the Creator and the whole of his Creation. As formulated in lines 44—48, quoted above, that relationship involves the strictest determinism, as, minute by minute and impulse by impulse, the Creator sustains and governs his creatures. These surely are 'shapings of the unregenerate mind', as Coleridge himself admits in a rebound of Christian humility. But he might have pointed to clear parallels in the writings of such devout theists as Boehme, Hartley and Akenside. Indeed, one of the great attractions of the Aeolian harp metaphor doubtless was that it offered young Coleridge the possibility of momentarily 'harmonizing' favourite but quite different thinkers by stressing a common pantheistic element in their imagery. We should bear in mind, however, that antecedent uses of the wind harp as a cosmic metaphor are important here less because they influenced *The Eolian Harp* than because they suggested models of the creative artist which turned out to be irreconcilable with pantheism or any other form of determinism.[30]

Much the most striking of the possible 'sources' of Coleridge's central metaphor in *The Eolian Harp* was pointed out many years ago by Stallknecht.[31] He quotes extensively from several passages in Boehme's *The Signature of All Things* which are certainly very like lines 44—48 of *The Eolian Harp*. I give the same passages in an abbreviated form:[32]

> The creation is . . . a platform or instrument of the Eternal Spirit, with which he melodises; and it is even as a great harmony of manifold instruments which are all tuned into one harmony . . . as an organ of divers and various sounds or notes is moved with one only air, so that each note, yea every pipe has its peculiar tune, and yet there is but one manner of air or breath in all notes, which sounds in each note or pipe according as the instrument or organ is made.

The voice (or breath) of God continually and eternally brings forth its joy through the creature, as through an instrument . . . wherewith the Eternal Spirit plays or melodises.

> . . . the signature or form is no spirit, but the receptacle, container, or cabinet of the spirit, wherein it lies; for the signature stands in the essence, and is as a lute that liest still, and is indeed a dumb thing that is neither heard or understood. . . . Thus likewise the signature of nature in its form is a dumb essence; it is as a prepared instrument of music, upon which the will's spirit plays; what strings he touches, they sound according to their property.

The Aeolian harp did not exist during Boehme's lifetime, and he built his analogies out of such materials as were available: the organ or lute served him perfectly well, and neither is essentially different from Coleridge's Aeolian harp. One essential difference between Coleridge's and Boehme's metaphors is that the Eternal Spirit in Boehme's usage is the Third Person of the Christian Trinity and not 'At once the Soul of each, and God of all'. That is, in Boehme's cosmogony the First Person remains distinct from his Creation as Coleridge's 'one intellectual breeze' does not. A second difference, though only of degree, is that Boehme does not descend to the level of particularity from which Coleridge's analysis starts, i.e. the individual mind and sensibility. Had Boehme carried his metaphor to that level, it is difficult to see how he could have preserved any illusion of individual free will. Boehme is thus less pantheistic and less deterministic than Coleridge, but tendencies in those directions are clearly built into the extended cosmic metaphors which both writers use.

A third and (from the standpoint of the present study) more interesting difference is that, unlike Boehme's, Coleridge's deity is depersonalized to the extent of being 'Plastic and vast, one intellectual breeze'. Boehme's is the personalized God of Judaeism and Christianity who feels jealousy and love and joy, and about whom it is possible to say, 'The voice (or breath) of God continually and eternally brings forth its joy through the creature, as through an instrument. . .'. The perfect instrument of such a Creator, participating in and expressing his joy, might well be considered an attractive model for the Poet. That, I think, is Coleridge's position in The Nightingale. On the other hand, in a crisis of doubt about one's relationship with God and the rest of

God's creation, one might swing to the other extreme and re-structure the cosmic metaphor, taking the Creator himself rather than his instrument as the model of the poet. And that is Cole-ridge's position in *Dejection.*

To put the matter thus schematically is to risk a crude over-simplification of any poet's—let alone Coleridge's—mental proces-ses as he seeks to understand himself and his art in relation to the universe. But it may at least help us to see what potentialities the Aeolian harp held in store for the poet who would take it seriously as a cosmic metaphor which (so to speak) 'contained' a built-in subsidiary metaphor of poetic inspiration. These poten-tialities existed in the first place because of the classical traditions relating to Pythian afflatus, and the Biblical traditions relating to the Holy Spirit. Boehme was always aware of the linked analogies of Eternal Spirit, Wind, Breath, Voice, and Word. In *The Treatise of the Incarnation,* for instance, he cites *Genesis* and the Royal Harper as his authorities for saying that[33]

. . . God's breath is the *Air-spirit* upon which the Holy Ghost rides, as *David* saith, *The Lord rideth upon the Wind: and Moses* saith, *The Spirit of God moveth upon the Waters....*

A similar awareness is to be found in eighteenth-century poets like Akenside or Smart or Novalis who used the Aeolian harp or its equivalent as a cosmic metaphor.[34] After all, the activating wind was primary. It was a natural (or supernatural) force rather than a contrivance of man. Moreover, the wind and its traditional literary analogues offered greater resources of meaning and imagistic colouring than did the Aeolian harp and its analogues. To say so is not to deny the latent riches of the Aeolian harp symbol. I have already pointed out that by easy extension the analogues of the wind harp came to include the harp of the dead Orpheus, and I might note here that (according to a Talmudic tradition known to eighteenth-century commentators) the harp of David was often played by the wind while he slept. Such associations invested a relatively modern musical novelty with the glamour and power of two great myths from two great cultures. Such associations could be exploited by a poet who knew what he was about. Nonetheless, the wind as symbol was still more primitive, more potent. The Pentecostal wind had tongues of flame: it needed no intermediary mechanism to extract sounds from its rushes hither and thither.

There was one poet who responded to the power of the ancient metaphor of inspiration and who at the same time contributed largely to the literature of the Aeolian harp; who tried to find a sane compromise between the extremes of passive instrument and projective God-like creator; who as a formative influence on Coleridge was perhaps more important than Bowles or Hartley, and (Coleridge's later claims notwithstanding) was certainly more important than Boehme. This was Mark Akenside, one of the most precocious and, in the end, disappointing poets England has ever produced. At the close of the eighteenth century every young literary gentleman knew Akenside's *The Pleasures of Imagination* in its two (1744 and 1770) versions. Coleridge went much further. In *Elegy* (1794) he imitated (rather badly) Akenside's third Inscription, quoted from *The Pleasures of Imagination* on numerous occasions,[35] projected an edition of Akenside,[36] and spoke warmly of *The Pleasures of Imagination* as evidence that a 'metaphysical' poem could be good poetry.[37] Though Coleridge appears to have lost interest in Akenside after the winter of 1796–7, I believe that was because Wordsworth was a very satisfactory 'Akenside-substitute' and much more besides.

The important, and lasting, influence of Akenside on Coleridge was exerted early, then; and as John Danby has observed,[38] it is especially apparent in *The Eolian Harp*, which surely owes much to these celebrated lines from Book I of *The Pleasures of Imagination*:[39]

> For as old Memnon's image long renown'd
> By fabling Nilus, to the quivering touch
> Of Titan's ray, with each repulsive string
> Consenting, sounded through the warbling air
> Unbidden strains; even so did Nature's hand
> To certain species of external things,
> Attune the finer organs of the mind:
> So the glad impulse of congenial powers,
> Or of sweet sounds, or fair proportion'd form,
> The grace of motion, or the bloom of light,
> Thrills through imagination's tender frame,
> From nerve to nerve: all naked and alive

> Hence the breath
> Hence the green earth, and wild resounding waves....

> Of life informing each organic frame,

They catch the spreading rays; till now the soul
At length discloses every tuneful spring,
To that harmonious movement from without
Responsive.

Since Akenside wrote *The Pleasures of Imagination* several years before the Aeolian harp was known in England, he had to use a more recondite instance of an instrument played not by man but by the forces of nature. But commentators from Christopher Smart onwards regularly referred to Memnon's harp and the Aeolian harp in the same statement, making virtually no distinction between them. This was not insensitive of them, since Akenside himself regularly links light and wind in his metaphors of creation. No great mental leap, scarcely any leap at all, had to be made by Coleridge from Akenside's light harp to his own wind harp. It is true that Akenside's God is not 'Plastic and vast, one intellectual breeze', but an independent Person like Boehme's God. In other words, Akenside avoids the determinism and pantheism of *The Eolian Harp* by cutting the umbilical cord that connected God with His Creation. Akenside's world is charged with the glory of God, but it is not God. However, in spite of these very fundamental differences, it is difficult to believe that Coleridge's 'organic Harps diversely fram'd' are unrelated to Akenside's 'breath / Of life informing each organic frame'. What is ultimately more important, Akenside's description of the sensitive receptivity and openness of the mind ('all naked and alive . . . the soul . . . discloses') anticipates the receptive posture of *The Eolian Harp*:

> And thus, my Love! as on the midway slope
> Of yonder hill I stretch my limbs at noon,
> Whilst through my half-clos'd eye-lids I behold
> The sunbeams dance, like diamonds, on the main,
> And tranquil muse upon tranquillity;
> Full many a thought uncall'd and undetain'd,
> And many idle flitting phantasies,
> Traverse my indolent and passive brain. . . .

Here again, one has to emphasize the difference as well as the similarity: both poets emphasize openness, but openness for what? There is nothing 'indolent and passive' about the quick responses of the mind in Akenside's description.
In Book III of *The Pleasures of Imagination* Akenside follows

up his earlier description of God 'informing each organic frame' with 'the breath / Of life' by depicting his poet thus:[40]

> Lucid order dawns;
> And as from Chaos old the jarring seeds
> Of nature at the voice divine repair'd
> Each to its place, till rosy earth unveil'd
> Her fragrant bosom, and the joyful sun
> Sprung up the blue serene....

> Then with Promethéan art,
> Into its proper vehicle he breathes
> The fair conception....

As the maker of a particular work of art, Akenside's poet is a wholly active, God-like creator.[41] However, in his relationship with the Nature which nourishes his genius, the poet both gives and receives:[42]

> What then is taste, but these internal powers
> Active, and strong, and feelingly alive
> To each fine impulse....

> This, nor gems, nor stores of gold,
> Nor purple state, nor culture can bestow;
> But God alone when first his active hand
> Imprints the secret bias of the soul.
> He, mighty Parent! wise and just in all,
> Free as the vital breeze or light of heaven,
> Reveals the charms of nature.

The grammar of the last three lines is perfectly clear: 'Free' is the third in a series of adjectives listing the attributes of God, and to that adjective is firmly attached the modifying adverbial clause 'as [is] the vital breeze or light of heaven'. But that is not the way we respond to these lines if we read them as poetry rather than as versified aesthetics. The imagery of creative light and breath—'the vital breeze or light of heaven'—also functions asyntactically to usher in the predicate: 'Reveals the charms of nature'. For there is a submerged metaphor here, of wind and light breaking through a cloud to reveal a landscape. Thus the life-endowing breath/breeze of God and Promethean maker is associated with, almost becomes a metaphor for, the feeling perception of Nature.

Coleridge moved closer to Akenside when Wordsworth moved to Alfoxden, even though it was about then that he stopped making frequent references to *The Pleasures of Imagination*. I am thinking here especially of *The Nightingale*, which was written towards the end of the *annus mirabilis* as a public acknowledgment of the value of Wordsworth's teaching. Its point of departure is a repudiation of the pathetic fallacy enshrined in *Il Penseroso* and his own tamely derivative *To the Nightingale* (1795). It goes on to state his new poetic faith in terms which echo the passive receptivity of *The Eolian Harp* but now, as in Akenside's poem, involve a strategic surrender to the created forms of nature rather than to a controlling 'intellectual breeze':

And many a poet echoes the conceit;
Poet who hath been building up the rhyme
When he had better far have stretched his limbs
Beside a brook in mossy forest-dell,
By sun or moon-light, to the influxes
Of shapes and sounds and shifting elements
Surrendering his whole spirit, of his song
And of his fame forgetful! so his fame
Should share in Nature's immortality,
A venerable thing! and so his song
Should make all Nature lovelier, and itself
Be loved like Nature!

The poet might become like the joyous nightingale rather than a man-made harp. When Coleridge in ecstatic headlong verse imitates the rush and precipitation of the bird's music, we perceive that the nightingale is indeed being tried out as a new paradigm. But really it is the old one made wonderfully alive and particular:

and oft, a moment's space,
What time the moon was lost behind a cloud,
Hath heard a pause of silence; till the moon
Emerging, hath awakened earth and sky
With one sensation, and those wakeful birds
Have all burst forth in choral minstrelsy,
As if some sudden gale had swept at once
A hundred airy harps.

As in Akenside, light and wind are paired in the creative process. But Coleridge does not develop this idea in *The Nightingale* as he does in *Dejection* and, still later, in the 'one Life' passage which

121

he added to *The Eolian Harp* in 1817. A poem which advises the would-be poet to be 'of his song / And of his fame forgetful' cannot theorize at length about such matters.

Between *The Nightingale* and *Dejection* lay, among other things of moment, the mighty fragment of Wordsworth's 'poem for Coleridge', the nearly completed Books I and II of *The Prelude*. Since Abrams and others have already observed how Book I seems to anticipate *Dejection* in action and imagery, Book II in doctrine and phrasing, I shall take these points of resemblance for granted but without supposing that Wordsworth's reworking of such traditional philosophical problems and metaphors necessarily taught Coleridge anything new. It is more helpful to see *The Prelude* and *Dejection* in relation to each other as contributions to a poetic dialogue which began in 1797 and did not effectively end until ten years later in *To William Wordsworth*. On this view, the points of resemblance are precisely where we should expect to discover subtle but crucial points of difference. Rather than bearing the 'burthen of my own unnatural self' which Wordsworth with the help of external nature is able to throw off in the 'glad preamble' of *The Prelude*, Coleridge has somehow stolen 'From my own nature all the natural man'. Not a temporary undesired addition, that is, but a permanent loss. As for the wind imagery in the two poems, the 'sweet breath of Heaven' without and 'corresponding mild creative breeze' within are a Wordsworthian variant of the ancient metaphor of inspiration, but Coleridge hopes in Stanza I that the 'sounds' of the wind will send his 'soul abroad' and make his pain (the only feeling he has left to 'correspond' with) 'move and live' in unison with the storm. In Stanza VII the release does apparently occur when the poet turns and *listens* to the wind: his soul joins it (not the other way round) and his pain is enabled to move and live, externalized as art, in a series of imagined tragic scenes 'told' by the poet-wind.

Unfortunately, it is by no means clear how this release was affected in the first place. For at the beginning of this climactic stanza, Coleridge combines violent rhetorical gesture with cryptic allegory in a way that is mutually obfuscating:

> Hence, viper thoughts, that coil around my mind,
> Reality's dark dream!
> I turn from you, and listen to the wind,
> Which long has raved unnoticed. What a scream

Of agony by torture lengthened out
That lute sent forth!

Since it is more openly personified, the lute is now even more closely identified with the speaker than it was in Stanza I. But with that 'scream / Of agony' the lute has fulfilled its purpose as a metaphor for the distempered sensibility. Something has happened to 'startle this dull pain'—it is no longer 'dull'—and with that qualitative shift occurs the crucial shift in the wind/lute-poet metaphor. The pain can now 'move and live', and does so throughout the rest of the stanza. An important part of the transition must be the poet's willed turning outward ('I turn from you, and listen . . .'), but to say so is not to suggest that the external stimulus of the sounds of the wind 'startles' his pain, as he hoped it would in Stanza I. The argument of Stanzas II–V makes that reading impossible. The stimulus must be internal and it can scarcely be unconnected with the tortured self-analysis of Stanza VI. My own view is that the dramatic 'Hence, viper thoughts . . .' at the beginning of Stanza VII registers a profound shock of self-discovery: that the self-analysis at the end of Stanza VI is yet another self-fascinated, self-destructive act of 'abstruse research'. It is this discovery that startles the pain and at the same time energizes the soul to move outward. That some kind of purgation also takes place is strongly suggested by the outward movement that occurs not only in Stanza VII but especially in the concluding stanza. Of course the release is no epoch-initiating experience such as that recorded in the 'glad preamble' of *The Prelude*: the line '''Tis midnight, but small thoughts have I of sleep' forbids us to suppose that. But Stanza VII of *Dejection* has a dramatic function closely analogous to that of Wordsworth's preamble, which is yet another reason to read Coleridge's poem in the light of Wordsworth's reworking of the traditional metaphors of creative wind and the wind harp.

The shift within the major metaphor of the wind/lute-poet signalizes a major shift in Coleridge's world view, from the Hartleyan Mechanism of his early years to the Idealism of his later years. That shift had been in the making for some time, of course, and he had never been a simple believer in simple Mechanism. But in spite of the disclaimer at the end of *The Eolian Harp*, it is obvious that up to 1800 the wind harp did seem to him an adequate or at least very agreeable figure for the human mind and sensibility. The Aeolian harp became very personally associated with, indeed a sort of personal emblem of, Coleridge the poet. From the winter of 1800–1 onwards he was obliged to search for a new metaphor for the human mind and sensibility in its relations with God, Nature, and Art. For the purposes of *Dejection*, the wind-as-harpist was such a metaphor—and all the better for containing an implicit rejection of the central metaphors of poems like *The Eolian Harp* and *The Nightingale*. Another advantage of this metaphor was that, through its traditional associations, it vivified the metaphors in the key phrases 'genial spirits' and 'shaping spirit of Imagination'. A poem in which the poetic imagination is likened not merely to the wind but to the Holy Spirit has left eighteenth-century Necessitarianism far behind.[44]

My discussion of the musical metaphors in *Dejection* has centred thus far on the Aeolian harp and especially on the way that favourite toy of the Age of Sensibility became a major figure for poetic inspiration, posing the most fundamental questions about the relationship between poet, Nature, God and poem. But *Dejection* is not a poem about poets only, and, as we have seen, the cosmic harp metaphor developed explicitly in *The Eolian Harp* and implicitly in *Dejection* is ultimately inclusive of the entire Creation. Certainly it includes the Lady, herself apparently no poet. Like the poet, however, in her relationship with Nature she is a performer or animator rather than an instrument; she possesses the primal human creativity without which all of a poet's acquired skills are useless:

> And from the soul itself must there be sent
> A sweet and potent voice, of its own birth,
> Of all sweet sounds the life and element!

> O pure of heart! thou need'st not ask of me
> What this strong music in the soul may be!

> . . . .

> Joy is the sweet voice, Joy the luminous cloud—
> We in ourselves rejoice!
> And thence flows all that charms or ear or sight,
> All melodies the echoes of that voice,
> All colours a suffusion from that light.

. . . .
Joy lift her spirit, joy attune her voice:
To her may all things live, from Pole to Pole,
Their life the eddying of her living soul!

This is not the place to discuss the post-Newtonian theories of perception which lie behind these lines and particularly behind the apparent interchangeability of their sound and sight images. Here I must rather direct attention to a very much more ancient 'background' theme—that of World Harmony or World Music, the great traditional principle of cosmic unity which Coleridge and Wordsworth associated with 'Joy'. A summary review of what the doctrine of World Harmony meant should clarify the musical metaphors in Stanzas IV, V, and VIII of *Dejection* and anticipate several of the major points I shall make in the following chapter about the connexion between 'Joy' and Imagination.

Music was central to Hellenic civilization before the Pythagoreans determined that the universe was governed by the same mathematical ratios observed in Greek harmony. Essential to religious ritual and as accompaniment of both secular and sacred poetry, it was credited with mysterious but largely beneficent powers in myths such as those of Orpheus and Amphion. Perhaps the greatest poetry in praise of music ever written was composed by Pindar, in the first Pythian ode, a full century before a metascientific basis for the power of music was first fully expounded in the *Timaeus*. Based on Pythagorean cosmology, Plato's proved to be the definitive formulation of the doctrine of World Harmony.[45] Elaborated or popularized during the next two thousand years by a host of writers ranging in intellectual stature from St. Augustine to Nahum Tate, World Harmony constantly accompanied Neoplatonic speculations on the cosmos and man's relation to it. Consequently, any—even the most casual—student of the classical philosophers and rhetoricians, the Church Fathers, the Caballists or the Renaissance poets was certain to have encountered it in several versions. Of Coleridge this was unquestionably true. What were the basic tenets of the system?

A basic premise (and one of enormous importance to the Renaissance Platonists and the author of *Dejection*) is that the human soul stands in microcosmic relation to the body as the World Soul (or Holy Spirit) to the entire created Universe (figuratively the lyre of Apollo, Boehme's organ, etc.). 'Scientifically' speaking, the whole cosmos, from the highest spheres in their revolutions down to the central earth with its seasonal cycles, is governed by a mathematical harmony which produces music (principally sphere music) inaudible to human ears but of which our earthly music is an image. Boethius discriminates between (1) *musica mundana* or the cosmic harmony of the macrocosm; (2) *musica humana* or the harmony between body and soul and within the soul; (3) *musica instrumentalis* or what we should normally consider 'real music'. To these kinds of music may be added a fourth, heavenly or *prima musica*, of which the others are copies. What are the qualities or powers associated with each level?

The *prima musica* is associated with the divine *Logos* and original act of Creation, as in Dryden's *A Song for St. Cecilia's Day*:[46]

From harmony, from heavenly harmony
This universal frame began:
When Nature underneath a heap
Of jarring atoms lay,
And could not heave her head,
The tuneful voice was heard from high,
Arise, ye more than dead.

The *musica mundana*, which constantly informs the motions and structures of the universe, is at its most ravishing as sphere music; but in certain Christian variants, which combine the Graeco-Roman World Harmony tradition with that of the Hebrew Psalms, all the 'voices' of the Creation join in a concert of praise. The greatest example in English is the Morning Hymn in *Paradise Lost*; another and lesser is Coleridge's *Hymn before Sun-rise, in the Vale of Chamouni*. As for *musica humana*, the soul is in harmony with the body (particularly the senses), with Nature and with God, only when it is 'attuned' or 'well-tempered'; indeed, *musica humana* is a matter of 'temperament', and as Professor Hollander says, the notion of temperament 'was made to apply almost from the beginning of its linguistic history both to the tuning of strings and to the tempering of various parts of the human soul, thoughts, feelings . . .'.[47] The lowest kind of music, *musica instrumentalis*, though but a faint copy of the higher kinds, has remarkable powers to move the listener, to cure a distempered mind, to elevate the soul and make it receptive to religious or amorous experience, etc. The lore associated with the power of 'ordinary' music (and which as we have seen continues to be associated with Aeolian harp music) is given its most famous expressions in English in the *Romeo and Juliet* passage quoted earlier in this chapter and in Dryden's *Alexander's Feast*. We come full circle with the observation that Neoplatonists account for the power of *musica instrumentalis* by explaining that it reminds the soul of the celestial music which the soul forgot as a result of incarnation; a Christian Neoplatonist like Milton, adapting the tradition to *Genesis*, maintains that Adam and Eve were able to hear the *prima musica* before the Fall and that even now 'solemn music' can sometimes, as it were, momentarily return the soul to an Edenic state.

This summary merely hints at the richness of a tradition which was still, though barely, available to Coleridge and Wordsworth at the beginning of the nineteenth century. Its commonplaces, substantially unchanged since the Hellenic era, had gradually ceased to carry general conviction during the seventeenth and eighteenth centuries; they could be adapted to the Christian world-view but not to the one charted by mathematical physics and sensationalist psychology. Conservative souls there were, however, who still heard the old World Music, and the chief among these was certainly Milton, whose magnificent reshaping of the topic in a number of poems probably did more than anything else to keep it alive in eighteenth-century poetry and literary aesthetics. Another and closely related force for conservation were the Cambridge Platonists and their early eighteenth-century successors—ranging in seriousness and originality from Berkeley and Shaftesbury to Addison and Akenside—whose theories of perception all owed something to the intellectual tradition which nurtured Milton and Shakespeare's belief that a man has, or ought to have, a responsive 'music in himself'. It was principally through these channels, I believe, that the World Harmony doctrine was transmitted to Wordsworth and Coleridge, critically to affect their own shared doctrine of creative 'Joy' and to help prevent Coleridge from ever becoming a complete Hartleyan. Of course there is more to Coleridgean-Wordsworthian 'Joy' than can be convincingly referred to this one tradition, but among many 'sources' it was most ancient and probably most influential both directly and indirectly through the various eighteenth-century writers I shall examine in the following chapter.

If Coleridge's claim in the *Biographia* to have studied Plato, Plotinus and Ficino at an early age is accurate, then he may have had comparatively little to glean from Cudworth's vast *True Intellectual System of the Universe* (1678) beyond the few striking phrases and images which have been recently noticed by Professors Coburn and Schrickx.[48] For Cudworth is important in the history of English philosophy less as an original thinker than as a reviver and adapter of Plato's and especially Plotinus's thought in opposition to the atheistical tendencies of Hobbes's materialism and Descartes' dualism. On the other hand, Cudworth was derivative in the service of the same Christian cause that Coleridge wished to serve, and, as Professor Willey has pointed out, in Cudworth's restatement of the Neoplatonist theory of knowledge, 'we have some of the materials for a theory of the "imagination" akin to Coleridge's'.[49] Therefore, without maintaining that Cudworth was the primary source of any of Coleridge's ideas, we may describe him as a thinker and mine of images congenial to young Coleridge and other Platonistically inclined writers of the eighteenth century.

Cudworth follows Plato and Plotinus as well as Christian Neoplatonists in arguing that the world is governed by Harmony:[50]

. . . the ancient mythologists represented the nature of the universe by *Pan* playing upon a pipe or harp, and being in love with the nymph *Echo*; as if nature did, by a kind of silent melody, make all the parts of the universe every where dance in measure and proportion, itself being as it were in the mean time delighted and ravished with the re-echoing of its own harmony.

As formulated here, the cosmic metaphor of World Harmony makes no provision for the various 'parts of the universe' to move of their own volition; it is no less deterministic than the corresponding metaphor in lines 44–48 of *The Eolian Harp*. However, it is very far from Cudworth's intention to suggest that human beings have a merely passive relationship with the World Harmony. On the contrary, he thinks of the human mind as microcosmic, and therefore essentially active, as this later development of the metaphor makes clear:[51]

Now there is yet a pulchritude of another kind; a more interior symmetry and harmony in the relations, proportions, aptitudes and correspondencies of things to one another in the great mundane system, or vital machine of the universe, which is all musically and harmonically composed; for which cause the ancients made Pan, that is, nature to play upon an harp; but sense, which only passively perceives particular outward objects, doth here, like a brute, hear nothing but mere noise and sound and clatter, but no music or harmony at all; having no active principle and anticipation within itself to comprehend it by, and correspond or vitally sympathize with it; whereas the mind of a rational and intellectual being will be ravished and enthusiastically transported in the contemplation of it; and, of its own accord, dance to this pipe of Pan, nature's intellectual music and harmony.

Insisting as he does that the mind of man 'hath an inward and active participation of the same divine wisdom that made it', Cudworth clearly agrees with Milton's conception of a 'meeting soul' responding actively and 'vitally' to music.[52] Such a view of the human intellect also perpetuates the Neoplatonic theory of mind which underwrites Sidney's and later Shaftesbury's and Akenside's image of the poet as a second, Godlike, Maker.

Indeed, Cudworth's passionate belief in the dignity of man's mind was such that, while readily accepting the modern (Galilean and Cartesian) Atomist thesis that the properties of an object registered by the senses (such as colour, heat and sound) were 'secondary' and essentially unreal because not 'in' the object itself, he was able to turn even this drastic contraction of our field of secure knowledge into an occasion for pious rejoicing:[53]

. . . from those different modifications of the small particles of bodies . . . there are begotten in us certain confused *phasmata* or *phantasmata*, apparitions, fancies and passions, as of light and colours, heat and cold, and the like, which are those things, that are vulgarly mistaken for real qualities existing in the bodies without us; whereas indeed there is nothing absolutely in the bodies themselves like to those fantastick idea's we have of them; and yet they are wisely contriv'd by the author of nature for the adorning and embellishing of the corporeal world to us.

As we shall see, it was only a short step, soon taken by Addison, to a notion of the creative power of the imagination (or senses) which was to reappear in Akenside and Edward Young and eventually find its way into *Tintern Abbey and Dejection*.[54]

In describing the effects of the World Music on Pan or a human 'auditor', Cudworth uses such phrases as 'delighted and ravished' and 'ravished and enthusiastically transported'. It was a commonplace of the Neoplatonic (Plotinist) tradition that not merely contemplation of the *musica mundana* but listening to certain kinds of humanly composed music could cause the soul to be 'ravished' or 'transported', sometimes literally out of the body, into union with the One; in Christian adaptations, the soul was 'elevated' to a vision of the Heavenly Kingdom.[55] A less exalted state, yet still recognizably a trance-like 'ecstasy', is described by Dante: 'Music draws to itself the human spirits which are, as it were, mainly vapours of the heart, so that they almost cease from any action of their own, so undivided is the soul when it listens to Music; and the virtue of all the spirits is, as it were, concentrated in the spirit of sense which receives the sound' (*Convivio* II, 14).[56] For Dante, then, the rapture caused by ordinary music is a state of supreme inner-unity and undivided attention. For young Milton and the many other Christian writers who shared the heightened Platonism of the Renaissance with him, the musical ecstasies of the microcosm were far more elevating. By listening to 'solemn music' which echoed the celestial 'song of pure concent', they might hope, in the familiar words of *Il Penseroso*, for such combinations of word and sound[57]

> As may with sweetness, through mine ear,
> Dissolve me into extacies,
> And bring all Heav'n before mine eyes.

The same topic is developed, at greater length, magnificence and complexity, in *At a Solemn Music*:[58]

> Blest pair of sirens, pledges of Heav'n's joy,
> Sphere-borne harmonious sisters, Voice and Verse,
> Wed your divine sounds, and mix'd power employ
> Dead things with inbreath'd sense able to pierce,
> And to our high-rais'd phantasy present
> That undisturbed song of pure concent,
> Ay sung before the saphir-colour'd throne
> To him that sits thereon
> With saintly shout, and solemn jubilee....

Of course no committed Christian could suppose that the earthly music even of His Elect was 'undisturbed' by Original Sin, that first violation of the 'pure concent' which once characterized the Creation, and Milton goes on to explain how 'disproportioned sin. . . . / Broke the fair music that all creatures made / To their great Lord . . .'. This is an aspect of the subject to which I must return shortly, since it has important reverberations in later poetry and particularly in *Dejection*, but let us now consider briefly how the tradition of the musical ecstasy reappears, less modified than might be expected, in the poetry of Coleridge and Wordsworth.

In *The Power of Sound* (1828) Wordsworth wrote a long and elaborate ode in praise of music which not merely echoes *L'Allegro* and Dryden's *Song for St. Cecilia's Day* but exhibits a comprehensive knowledge of the World Harmony tradition. As Hutton remarks, this anachronistic poem of Wordsworth's old age must surely be among the last of its kind.[59] Whether the younger Wordsworth was so well versed in the lore of *musica mundana* may perhaps be doubted, and certainly he avoided the formal conventions of a St. Cecilia's Day ode. Yet there are many lines in the early poetry, especially in *The Prelude*, which suggest a more than passing acquaintance with the tradition, and there is at least one important passage in *Tintern Abbey* which may remind us of Dante and the Renaissance Platonists:

> —that serene and blessed mood,
> In which the affections gently lead us on,—
> Until, the breath of this corporeal frame
> And even the motion of our human blood
> Almost suspended, we are laid asleep
> In body, and become a living soul:
> While with an eye made quiet by the power
> Of harmony, and the deep power of joy,
> We see into the life of things.

Not by listening to music but by seeing the 'beauteous forms' of the Wye Valley does Wordsworth begin the journey from sensory perception to ecstatic vision. Those forms, to an eye made as 'quiet' as the sky (line 8), are instead an inaudible music and no less effective. It would be somewhat misleading to say that Wordsworth 'hears' the *musica mundana*; much more so to discover the World Harmony system (in any of its avatars) perfectly intact in *Tintern Abbey*. Wordsworth has much more faith in 'the language of the sense' than is characteristic of the tradition and correspondingly less desire to leave this world behind; his visions afford him a glimpse 'into the life of things' but do not 'bring all heaven before' his eyes. Nevertheless, the recollections of the World Harmony tradition are unmistakable both in his descrip-

131

tions of the 'blessed mood' and in his phrasings. (Perhaps the most memorable line in his poetry, 'The still, sad music of humanity', derives from it.) His method, and that of Coleridge, is to select and adapt those parts of the doctrine which, for him, are still alive and meaningful nearly a century after the system as a whole had ceased to inspire belief. One critical variation is that the 'joy' which results from mystical union or vision in Neoplatonist accounts is here paired with Harmony as a 'power' or cause of the mystical experience. This means that one must have both 'joy' within and 'harmony' without to achieve the experience: no problem in 1798 for the happy trio—William, Dorothy and Coleridge—secure in the knowledge that Nature repaid joy with joy and thus ensured an unfailing store of Joy and Harmony within:

thy mind
Shall be a mansion for all lovely forms,
Thy memory be as a dwelling-place
For all sweet sounds and harmonies. . . .

Coleridge's poems of the *annus mirabilis* are equally secure in the faith that 'Nature never did betray / The heart that loved her.' Of *The Nightingale*, another poem which participates in the World Harmony tradition, this is obviously true; and we need only quote the closing lines of *The Dungeon* (1797) to see how wholeheartedly he then embraced both the tradition and Wordsworth's optimism:[60]

With other ministrations thou, O Nature!
Healest thy wandering and distemper'd child:
Thou pourest on him thy soft influences,
Thy sunny hues, fair forms, and breathing sweets,
Thy melodies of woods, and winds, and waters,
Till he relent, and can no more endure
To be a jarring and a dissonant thing,
Amid this general dance and minstrelsy;
But, bursting into tears, wins back his way,
His angry spirit heal'd and harmoniz'd
By the benignant touch of Love and Beauty.

As parallels in phrasing, imagery and idea in *This Lime-Tree Bower My Prison* demonstrate, Coleridge also knew and even anticipated the expression of 'that serene and blessed mood' recorded in *Tintern Abbey*. To be sure, the 'ecstasies' in both poems take their departure from visual rather than auditory experience, but, as suggested earlier, the World Music is not limited to what can be heard. Coleridge's poem does conclude with an auditory image of a rook which

> when all was still,
>
> Flew creeking o'er thy head, and had a charm
> For thee, my gentle-hearted Charles, to whom
> No sound is dissonant which tells of Life.

In the 'concert' of World Harmony—of all things that share in what Coleridge and Wordsworth were to call 'the one Life'—all sights and sounds which in isolation might be dissonant are reconciled and achieve their own peculiar beauty. Indeed, in the terms of Coleridge's metaphor—which is also that of the World Harmony tradition—only a thing which is divorced from the great concert, the one Life, is truly dissonant.

When after the *annus mirabilis* the anxieties characteristic of poets of Sensibility reasserted themselves, the Nether Stowey interlude of Edenic harmony with man and nature, by confirming traditionary possibilities of joy believed in but never fully experienced before, must have given a corresponding lived reality to the no less traditionary experience of dissonance or deprivation which ensued. As for the literary tradition itself, the literature of Sensibility was haunted quite as much by recollections of lost powers and ecstasies as by premonitions of suicide and madness, and I believe that the World Harmony tradition contributed something to this deep and recurrent sense of loss.

From as early as Hellenistic times the claims made for the powers of earthly music were frequently said to apply only to the old music, which men no longer knew how to make, and not to the degenerate music of 'modern' times: a *topos* taken up with surprising conviction in Collins's ode *The Passions* and, modified yet still recognizable, in the closing stanza of *Kubla Khan*:

> Could I revive within me
> Her symphony and song,
>   To such a deep delight 'twould win me,
> That with music loud and long,
> I would build that dome in air,
> That sunny dome! those caves of ice!

In Neoplatonic versions of the theme the loss was of access to the celestial music enjoyed by the soul before incarnation; in

133

Christian versions the loss came after the Fall. This was a favourite topic of the younger Milton (e.g. in *At a Solemn Music* and *On the Morning of Christ's Nativity*, ix–xiv) and one which eighteenth-century admirers like Collins and Gray translated into aestheticist hyperbole, portraying Milton himself as last or alone of humankind to hear the celestial music: [61]

> With many a vow from Hope's aspiring tongue,
> My trembling feet his guiding steps pursue;
>   In vain—such bliss to one alone,
>   Of all the sons of soul was known,
> And Heaven, and Fancy, kindred powers,
> Have now o'erturn'd th'inspiring bowers,
>
> Or curtain'd close such scene from every future view.

Ancient as was the association of priest and poet, religious ecstasy and vatic inspiration, no writer before the eighteenth century could have put 'Heaven and Fancy' on an equal footing as 'kindred powers'. By doing so and linking loss of poetic powers with the Fall, Collins helped to create the myth of doomed genius which dominated the Age of Sensibility. For although Collins's ode was concerned more with the perils and frustrations of aspiring to an unattainable 'godlike gift' than with the inevitability of its loss, his introduction of the Fall or lost Golden Age into an allegory of poetic ambition inevitably reminds one of the fate of such trespassers as Satan, Adam and Prometheus. [62] So true is this—and so powerful are the echoes of the conclusion of *Paradise Lost* in Collins's own conclusion—that the *Ode on the Poetical Character* lingers in the mind as a fable at once of great individual aspiration and (for poets) equally great communal loss. Small wonder that Collins's ode 'inspired & whirled' young Coleridge 'along with greater agitations of enthusiasm than any the most *impassioned* Scene in Schiller or Shakspere'! [63]

For Milton the Elect who might still catch an echo of the heavenly music were Reformed Christians, for Collins the Elect were poets of genius. Wordsworth and Coleridge have their own spiritual Elect who are in tune, not with the celestial harmony, but with something more like the *musica mundana*: the babe Hartley laughing silently at the moon; the Idiot Boy listening, rapt, to the thunder of the waterfall; Dorothy experiencing 'wild ecstasies' on her solitary walk; Wordsworth himself out-growing such experiences but beginning to feel a 'presence' in nature which dis-

134

turbs him with the 'joy / Of elevated thoughts; a sense sublime', whose dwelling is also 'in the mind of man'. And finally, of course, there is Sara from whose soul is sent

A sweet and potent voice, of its own birth,
Of all sweet sounds the life and element!

Of the varieties of 'Joy' experienced in Coleridge and Wordsworth's poetry I shall have more to say later; here I wish to notice rather the kind of souls, the Coleridgean–Wordsworthian Elect, who are able to experience it in some form. Broadly speaking, all may be said to be, like Milton's 'Saints' or Adam and Eve before the Fall, closer to Heaven or the Neoplatonic source of life than is the generality of mankind. For the Wordsworth of *Tintern Abbey* this does not mean that they are morally superior or more artistically creative; on the contrary, though favoured spirits, they appear to be morally and intellectually unripe. They could not be great poets. Tempting though it may be to think of the change from this state of 'aching joys' and moral simplicity as a Fortunate Fall, it is necessary to insist on the absence of any sense of guilt and therefore on its remoteness from the Christian model which is so important for Coleridge.

When Coleridge says in *Dejection* that the 'strong music in the soul' is 'Joy' denied to 'the sensual and the proud' and given only to 'the pure, and in their purest hour', his epistemological and theological premises are close to those of Cudworth and Milton. And it is very much in the spirit of Renaissance (as well as eighteenth-century) Neoplatonism that he rejects the passive wind harp in favour of the wind-as-harpist metaphor; that, in the *Letter* version, he speaks of the 'Temper' (later 'habit') of his soul; and that, without trying to revive an obsolete picture of the physical universe, he reaffirms the truth of the microcosmic–macrocosmic view of man's relationship to God and Nature as imaged in the World Harmony tradition. It is specifically as a *Christian* Neoplatonist that, unlike Wordsworth in *Tintern Abbey*, he associates a decline in his creative relationship with Nature with a decline in his creative powers as a poet—and associates both with a prior loss of the 'Joy that ne'er was given, / Save to the pure, and in their purest hour'.[64] As we shall see, his estrangement from Nature and Nature's Music is also prefigured in Milton. However, it is inconceivable that Milton would have

135

come at the root problem—estrangement from God—in the same way. Only a poet born and educated after the Renaissance would have approached it as Coleridge does by insisting that sometimes Nature did indeed 'betray the heart that loved her'. And so it is to his eighteenth-century predecessors that we should turn our attention again.

NOTES

1. Charles Dibden, *The Professional Life of Mr. Dibden* (London, 1803), IV, 317. I owe this reference to Robert Bloomfield's 'Nature's Music', first published in 1808 and collected in *The Remains of Robert Bloomfield* (London, 1824), I, 97–143. Much of the lore of the Aeolian harp is stored in this work, which Coleridge perhaps knew, and further gleaned by writers whose work Coleridge could not have known: Georges Kastner, *La Harpe d'Eole* (Paris, 1856) and Geoffrey Grigson, *The Harp of Aeolus* (London, 1948), 24–45. For further background, see John Hollander, 'Spenser and the Mingled Measure', *English Literary Renaissance*, I (Autumn 1971), 226–38, and 'Wordsworth and the Music of Sound', *New Perspectives on Coleridge and Wordsworth: Selected Papers from the English Institute*, ed. Geoffrey H. Hartman (New York, 1972), 60–67.

2. This is Walter Kaufman's translation of lines 25–28 of the Dedication in *Faust* (New York, 1961).

3. See Note 1.

4. That 'harp' and 'lute' refer to the same instrument is clearer in *The Eolian Harp*, where, in lines 12 and 43, it is referred to as 'that simplest Lute' and 'this subject Lute'.

5. *The Castle of Indolence*, Book I, Stanzas XXXIX–XLII. Anderson, IX, 229.

6. *Il Penseroso*, 164–65, and *L'Allegro*, 133–34; *Essay on Criticism*, I, 143–45, 152–53. Anderson, V, 156, 154; VII, 34. The allusion to *L'Allegro* is noted by A. D. McKillop in his edition of *The Castle of Indolence and Other Poems* (Lawrence, Ka, 1961), 191.

7. *The Merchant of Venice*, V, i, 79–87. Quoted from *The Plays of Shakespeare* (London, 1785), III, 250–51.

8. *L'Allegro*, 135–50. Anderson, V, 154.

9. James Beattie, *Essays* (Edinburgh, 1776), 456–57. James Mason Cox, *Practical Observations on Insanity* (London, 1804) 166.

10. Christopher Smart, 'Inscriptions on an Aeolian Harp', Anderson, XI, 182.

11. *Ibid.*

12. *The Works of Robert Burns*, I, 42.

13. Mary Wollstonecraft, *Letters Written During a Short Residence in Sweden, Norway, and Denmark*, 71.

14. William Lisle Bowles, *Elegiac Stanzas Written During Sickness at Bath*,

15. *December 1795* (Bath, 1796), 5–6. Bowles provides a footnote to make absolutely clear that these lines do refer to the Aeolian harp.

Letters, I, 155, dated 10 March 1795, to George Dyer. The image is borrowed from an important passage in Akenside's *The Pleasures of Imagination* (1744), I, 109–24, which I shall discuss shortly. One of the two statues built by King Memnon at Memphis contained a hidden stringed instrument which according to Pausanias and Juvenal burst into music when the light of the morning sun rested upon the statue.

16. *Introduction to the Tale of the Dark Ladie* (1799) and *To the Snow Drop* (1800).

17. 'The Ignorant Book-Collector', *Lucian* (Loeb: New York, 1921), III, 188–91. Ovid, *Metamorphoses*, XI, lines 50–52.

18. Virgil, *Georgics*, IV, 454–527.

19. See Note 1.

20. *The Works of Edmund Spenser: The Minor Poems*, ed. Osgood and Lotspeich (Baltimore, 1947), lines 603–16. In this case I have preferred a modern restoration to an eighteenth-century edition of Spenser's poems, because the original spelling is an important feature affecting both meaning and pronunciation. Cf. *Anderson*, II, 570–71. *Anderson*, V, 159.

21. *Ode on the Death of Mr. Thomson*, lines 5–12. *Anderson*, IX, 530.

22. *The Castle of Indolence and Other Poems*, 206.

23. *The Works of Ossian* (London, 1765), I, 65, 110, 236, 370. The image crops up, on these pages, in four of Ossian's 'poems': *Temora, Fingal VI, Dar-thula, and Berrathon.*

24. *The Works of Ossian* (London, 1765), I, 65, 110, 236, 370. The image crops up, on these pages, in four of Ossian's 'poems': *Temora, Fingal VI, Dar-thula, and Berrathon.*

25. Schiller, *On Naïve and Sentimental Literature* (1795).

26. There is one passage in the 1796 draft of *The Destiny of Nations*, lines 9–12, in which Coleridge uses the wind-played harp precisely as Macpherson does on several occasions, i.e. imagining that the winds that plucked the harp strings are departed spirits soliciting notice.

27. John O. Hayden, 'Coleridge's "Dejection: An Ode"', *English Studies* (April 1971), 1–5.

28. *Ibid*, 3–4.

29. Collected in *English Romantic Poets*, ed. Abrams (New York, 1960), 37–54.

30. The reader will correctly infer that I mistrust any attempt to pin down a single or principal source for Coleridge's use of the Aeolian harp as a cosmic metaphor. Many possible sources have been suggested by scholars over the years, and I refer to those suggestions which seem both plausible and pertinent to the concerns of this chapter.

31. R. P. Stallknecht, *Strange Seas of Thought* (Durham, N.C., 1945), 106–7.

32. Stallknecht used the 1926 Everyman text of Boehme. I have gone back to the copy of *The Works of Jacob Behmen* used by Coleridge himself. The quotations are from *Works*, IV, 132, 134, 10.

33. *Ibid*, II, 26.

34. Smart's interest in the Aeolian harp is evident in his 'Inscriptions on an Æolian Harp' where he copies both Akenside and Thomson in an

35. Examples of his quotations from Akenside are *Letters*, I, 230 (22 August 1796) and 289 (26 December 1796), to Tom Poole; *Notebooks*, I, 123 (1795–96); epigraph to *Poems on Various Subjects*. There are many other instances, nearly all of them between 1794 and 1797.

36. *Notebooks*, I, 174 (14).

37. *Letters*, I, 215, dated 13 May 1796, to John Thelwall.

38. Cited in John Beer's *Coleridge the Visionary* (London, 1959), 316. Mr. Beer has an excellent brief discussion of Coleridge's use of the Aeolian harp as a metaphor, pp. 88–92.

39. *The Pleasures of Imagination*, I, 73–75, 109–24. *Anderson*, IX, 736. I quote from the 1744 version here and elsewhere, except in one or two instances when I specify the 1770 version. The former is much fresher and more daring than the later version, though I, 87–89 of the 1770 version was a favourite passage of Coleridge, and the unfinished Book IV contains the most striking premonitions of Wordsworth.

40. *The Pleasures of Imagination*, III, 398–403, 410–12. *Anderson*, IX, 749.

41. Cf. the famous passage in Shaftesbury, *Characteristics*, ed. Robertson (London, 1900), I, 136: 'Such a poet is indeed a second *Maker*; a just Prometheus under Jove.'

42. *Pleasures*, III, 515–17, 520–26. *Anderson*, IX, 750.

43. *The Prelude*, ed. de Selincourt and Darbishire (Oxford, 1959). I have also consulted Stephen Gill's edition of the 1805 *Prelude* (Oxford, 1970). For a recent detailed discussion of the dating of the 'Glad Preamble', see John Alban Finch's study, 'Wordsworth's Two-Handed Engine', in *Bicentenary Wordsworth Studies*, 1–13.

44. *Dejection* does not mark the burial of the Aeolian harp as a metaphor for poetic inspiration. In the posthumous *Confessions of an Inquiring Spirit* (London, 1840), 14, 32, 35–36, Coleridge employs familiar variations on this figure to argue against the theory that the authors of the Bible were divinely inspired throughout.

45. For the most wide-ranging account of the World Harmony tradition in Western thought and literature, see Leo Spitzer, 'Classical and Christian Ideas of World Harmony: Prolegomena to an Interpretation of the Word "Stimmung"', *Traditio*, II (1944), 409–64 and III (1945), 307–64. Standard for treatments of the theme in sixteenth- and seventeenth-century English literature is John Hollander's *The Untuning of the Sky* (Princeton, 1961), but for Milton Hollander's account must be supplemented by Spitzer and by James Hutton, 'Some English Poems in Praise of Music', *English Miscellany*, II (1951), 1–63. My discussion is particularly endebted to these studies. A more general and recent account of the Pythagorean cosmology *in toto* (not merely of its World Harmony aspect) studied in relation to Renaissance poetics is S. K. Heninger, Jr., *Touches of Sweet Harmony* (San Marino, 1974).

46. *Anderson*, VI, 168.

47. Hollander, 25. Cf. Spitzer, *Traditio*, III, 307–40, where *temperare* is related to its 'linguistic cluster'.

48. *Biographia Literaria*, II, 94. For a discussion of the (in my view inconclusive) evidence that Coleridge was an informed Neoplatonist, particularly well read in Plotinus, during his Christ's Hospital days, see L. Werkmeister, 'The Early Coleridge: His "Rage for Metaphysics"', *The Harvard Theological Review*, LIV (1961), 99–123. W. Schrickx, 'Coleridge and the Cambridge Platonists', *A Review of English Literature*, VII (1966), 71–91. Coburn, *Notebooks*, I, entries 174(16), 200, 201, 203–204, 208, 246–47. Coleridge borrowed the book twice from the Bristol Library: 15 May–1 June 1795 and 9 November–13 December 1796. Cf. Whalley, 'Bristol Library Borrowings', entries 55 and 90.

49. Basil Willey, *The Seventeenth Century Background* (1934; rpt. Doubleday Anchor Books: New York, n.d.), 161. Professor Willey's chapter (VIII) on the Cambridge Platonists is particularly suggestive to the student of Coleridge and should be read in conjunction with the excellent article by Schrickx. Also useful is R. L. Brett's account of Cudworth's place in the history of aesthetic theory in *Fancy and Imagination* (London, 1969), 21–27.

50. *The True Intellectual System of the Universe*, 2nd edn. (London, 1743), I, 160. The same passage is quoted by Schrickx, pp. 85–86, but for different purposes.

51. 'A Treatise Concerning Eternal and Immutable Morality', included in *The True Intellectual System of the Universe* (London, 1845), III, 600. This treatise was first published posthumously in 1731. It contains little if anything that is not either explicit or implicit in the *True Intellectual System*; Cudworth is nothing if not repetitive. But since the 'Treatise' is more narrowly concerned with epistemology than is the earlier work its restatement of basically identical ideas is occasionally more developed or pointed. I know of no evidence that Coleridge ever read the 'Treatise'.

52. 'Treatise', p. 601.

53. *True Intellectual System* (1743), I, 33. The same idea is further developed in the 'Treatise', p. 644, as follows: 'Though it was not the intention of God or nature to abuse us herein, but a most wise contrivance thus to beautify and adorn the visible and material world, to add lustre or embellishment to it, that it might have charms, relishes, and allurements in it to gratify our appetites....'

54. The source of this famous theory in *Spectator* No. 413 may be Hobbes, Cudworth's arch-enemy! Such is the contention of L. A. Elioseff, *The Cultural Milieu of Addison's Literary Criticism* (Austin, 1963), 179, but Cudworth's discussion seems a closer anticipation. That Addison knew Cudworth's *True Intellectual System* seems fairly likely, since Addison's admired Charterhouse Master Thomas Burnet was himself an admiring pupil of Cudworth. For an informed discussion of Addison's affiliations with Burnett, see Ernest Tuveson, *The Imagina-*

tion as a Means of Grace (Berkeley and Los Angeles, 1960), 101–102, 127.

55. For a full discussion of this topic, see G. L. Finney, 'Ecstasy and Music in Seventeenth-Century England', *Journal of the History of Ideas*, VIII (1947), 153–86. She quotes, among many apposite passages from Renaissance writers, this from Richard Hooker's *Of the Laws of Ecclesiastical Polity*, V, 38: there is that kind of music 'that carrieth as it were into ecstasies, filling the mind with an heavenly joy and for a time in a manner severing it from the body'.

56. Translation by W. W. Jackson in *Dante's Convivio* (Oxford, 1909), 110. Cited by Hutton, p. 22, who also refers to a parallel passage in *Purgatorio* II, 116–9. In a Notebook entry of December 1802 (*Notebooks*, I, 1296) Coleridge describes 'A Harmony so divine that a crash of discordant sound by accident did not at all affect the *aloofened* mind'.

57. *Il Penseroso*, lines 161–66, *Anderson*, V, 156.

58. *At a Solemn Music*, lines 1–9, *Anderson*, V, 166.

59. Hutton, p. 62. I also owe to Hutton the perception that the phrase 'still, sad music of humanity' derives from the World Harmony tradition. For a more general discussion of 'harmony' as theme and metaphor in Wordsworth's poetry, see Jonathan Wordsworth, *The Music of Humanity* (London, 1969), 245–58. Much the fullest and most informed discussion of Wordsworth's auditory imagery and its background is in Hollander, 'Wordsworth and the Music of Sound'.

60. For references to music in Coleridge's writings, see Marshall Suther, *Visions of Xanadu* (New York, 1965), 269–71 and *passim*. There is an excellent brief account of the role of 'harmony' in Coleridge's thought in John Beer's *Coleridge the Visionary* (London, 1959), 88–93. These treatments are usefully amplified in a very uneven book, sometimes impressively original and sometimes derivative and over-simplifying, by George H. Gilpin, *The Strategy of Joy* (Salzburg, 1972), 180–89. Professor Gilpin makes the connexion between Joy, Neoplatonic World Harmony and Imagination; his discussion, though valuable as far as it goes, is generalized and unconcerned with the provenance of this cluster of ideas.

61. *Ode on the Poetical Character*, lines 70–76, *Anderson*, IX, 523. Collins refers unmistakably to the celestial music in lines 64–66 and seems to be echoing *At a Solemn Music* in lines 32–34.

62. In assigning a Promethean character to the poet, Shaftesbury is careful to describe him as a 'just Prometheus under Jove' rather than an overreacher certain to be punished. Cf. Note 41 and the passage cited earlier in which Akenside also makes the connexion between poet and Prometheus.

63. *Letters*, I, 279, dated 17 December 1796, to John Thelwall.

64. Two further references by Coleridge to the World Harmony tradition should be noted. One, written a little over a year after *Dejection*, recalls the traditional 'tempering' and ethical powers of music, and projects a poem describing a triumphant reversal of the sickness of soul described in *Dejection*: 'Ode to Music—the thought I lost was

that perhaps Music bringing me back to primary Feelings did really make moral regeneration'. (*Notebooks*, I, 1505.) The second reference occurs much later, in the *Biographia* (II, 14), but is so pertinent to the present discussion as to require citation: ''The man that hath not music in his soul'' can indeed never be a genuine poet . . . the sense of musical delight, with the power of producing it, is a gift of imagination; and this together with the power of reducing multitude into unity of effect, and modifying a series of thoughts by some one predominant thought or feeling, may be cultivated and improved, but can never be learned'. God's World Harmony is the ultimate example of 'the power of reducing multitude into unity of effect'.

4

The All-Animating Joy Within

for in all things
I saw one life, and felt that it was joy
—Wordsworth, *The Prelude* (1805)

The favoured good man in his lonely walk
Perceives them, and his silent spirit drinks
Strange bliss which he shall recognize in heaven.
And such delights, such strange beatitudes
Seize on my young anticipating heart
When that blest future rushes on my view!
For in his own and in his Father's might
The Saviour comes! While as the Thousand Years
Lead up their mystic dance, the Desert shouts!
Old Ocean claps his hands!

—Coleridge, *Religious Musings*

1

To discuss 'Joy' and 'Imagination' as these concepts were inherited and modified by Coleridge is to venture out upon the high seas of intellectual and spiritual history. That this is true in the case of 'Imagination' must be patent to every student of literature. 'Joy' seems less awesomely problematic, but only, I suspect, because it has been less exhaustively converted by literary and intellectual historians. For if we seek to discover what lay behind Coleridge and Wordsworth's use of it and its near-relation 'Pleasure', we shall find not merely Hartley's Christian hedonism but the World Harmony tradition as well; the rhapsodic *Freude* of Schiller and even the *Joi d'Amour* of the Troubadours. Seeking to define what 'Joy' meant to Wordsworth, Donald Davie has discovered a precedent as far afield as the *Admiratio* (English Renascence 'Wonder')

142

THE ALL-ANIMATING JOY WITHIN

of Aristotelian and post-Aristotelian literary theory.[1] I have no wish to pursue this quarry, or 'Imagination' either, any further than is necessary for the purposes of this study, and fortunately only the crucial conjunction of these two concepts demands detailed attention here.

That they are conjoined is perhaps the main point of *Dejection*, as it was not the main point of earlier poems about 'Joy', or, still less, of Coleridge's later theoretical statements about 'Imagination'. The latter in particular belong to a period (probably not before 1804) when he had experienced the full impact of German Idealism and learned to see the problem of creativity from a rather different perspective. Lovejoy somewhat assiduously remarked of attempts to read *Dejection* as a 'Kantean' poem:[2]

... "joy" was *not* one of the *a priori* categories of Kant; and there is not even a formal parallel between Coleridge's psychological observation and Kant's theorem, since "the mind" which Kant makes the source of the *a priori* percepts (space and time) and the categories is the generic mind, identical in all men and unmodified by circumstances, while Coleridge is insisting upon the *differences* between the aesthetic reactions of individual minds—and specifically, of his own mind (at the moment) and Wordsworth's—and even of the same mind in different moods.

Yet in denying that *Dejection* is a 'philosophical poem' in the tradition of Kant, Lovejoy also seems to deny that it belongs to any intellectual tradition at all: it is a poem rather of 'psychological observation' than of 'ideas'. This is to overstate a valid point. *Dejection* was written out of intense personal suffering by a brilliantly gifted psychological observer who had previously experienced periods of intense happiness and creativity. Nonetheless, Coleridge's experience of dejection did conform to the expectations of eighteenth-century literary psychology; likewise, his theory of joyous creativity was one held before the glorious confirmation of the *annus mirabilis* or the desolating negative proof of the winters of 1800–1 and 1801–2.

One difficulty that has to be faced at the outset is terminological muddle. In Coleridge's earlier writings 'joy' does not always mean 'Joy', and 'Pleasure' seems sometimes to be 'a two-syllabled word for Joy' and sometimes not.[3] We may begin with a relatively minor problem. In *Tintern Abbey*, Wordsworth writes:

143

While with an eye made quiet by the power
Of harmony, and the deep power of joy,
We see into the life of things. . . .

In *This Lime-Tree Bower My Prison*, Coleridge writes:

                    So my friend
Struck with deep joy may stand, as I have stood,
Silent with swimming sense; yea, gazing round
On the wide landscape, gaze till all doth seem
Less gross than bodily; and of such hues
As veil the Almighty Spirit, when yet he makes
Spirits perceive his presence.

'Joy' clearly refers to a radiant moment of transensory vision which
approaches a condition of mystical union with the divine Spirit,
experienced usually—but not invariably—through the agency of
Nature. This was an experience which Wordsworth seems to have
known early and abundantly, the recollection of which was to
overflow into some of the greatest passages of *The Prelude* and
the *Immortality* ode. But was this the experience described in
Coleridge's schoolboy poem *To the Evening Star*?[4]

O meek attendant of Sol's setting blaze,
I hail, sweet star, thy chaste effulgent glow;
On thee full oft with fixed eye I gaze
Till I, methinks, all spirit seem to grow.

O first and fairest of the starry choir,
O loveliest 'mid the daughters of the night,
Must not the maid I love like thee inspire
Pure joy and calm Delight?

Both in style and paraphrasable content these lines are an odd
combination of the adolescent and the mature Coleridge. While the
experience recorded as '*Pure joy and calm Delight*' does appear to
be what he and Wordsworth were to write about later in identical
language, my guess is that the eighteen-year-old author of *To the
Evening Star* did not, as he was later to do, use that language deliberately as a special language inherited from various, chiefly
Christian mystical sources. Or to put it another way: the experience was described, but probably not understood, in traditional
terms—those terms being, as well, among the most common English words for states of pleasure or happiness of all kinds. This

seems the more likely because *To the Evening Star* is so uniquely anticipatory, and because Coleridge evidently thought so little of the poem that he never bothered to publish it.

What persuades us that the experience of 'Joy' described in *To the Evening Star* is the same as, or very like, the experience described in *Tintern Abbey* and *This Lime-Tree Bower My Prison*, is that it seems so unearthly, so mirthless. But it is not always thus in their writings. In *The Nightingale* Coleridge speaks of a 'tipsy Joy that reels with tossing head', while in a letter to Poole he says, '*My whole Being* so yearns after you, that when I think of our meeting, I catch the fashion of German Joy, rush into your arms, and embrace you—'.[5] In Wordsworth's *The Idiot Boy*, Johnny's mother

> kisses o'er and o'er again
> Him whom she loves, her Idiot Boy;
> She's happy here, is happy there,
> She is uneasy everywhere;
> Her limbs are all alive with joy.

> She pats the pony, where or when
> She knows not, happy Betty Foy!
> The little Pony glad may be,
> But he is milder far than she,
> You hardly can perceive his joy.

Wordsworth is not embarrassed to associate his own quiet mystical Joy with the frenzied maternal Joy of Betty, or even to point with not unkind amusement to the 'undignified' contrast between her palpitations and the reserved animal gladness of the pony. Neither is Coleridge embarrassed to write of his child.[6] 'Hartley is the same Animal as ever—he moves & lives,

> As if his Heritage were Joy
> And Pleasure were his Trade.

As it turns out, 'Joy' denotes not one but seemingly a whole host of experiences, animal as well as human, comic as well as solemn, frenetic as well as calm. To be sure, Coleridge and Wordsworth make discriminations by attaching epithets ('deep', 'tipsy', 'solemn', for example) or by coupling 'Joy' with words which convey somewhat more precise and limited meanings (for instance, 'glee', 'mirth', 'bliss'). But these qualifying words merely enforce the impression conveyed by *Dejection* that they came to believe in a generic Joy which, manifesting itself variously, acted as the great unifying and animating principle of the universe.

The difficulty is to find a really clear theoretical formulation of such a principle anywhere in their early writings. Later formulations there are, and at least one, dated 1819, which reads like an abstract of *Dejection* as it might have been written in later life:[7]

In joy individuality is lost and it therefore is liveliest in youth, not from any principle in organization but simply from this that the hardships of life, that the circumstances that have forced a man in upon his little unthinking contemptible self, have lessened his power of existing universally. . . . To have a genius is to live in the universal, to know no self but that which is reflected not only from the faces of all around us, our fellow creatures, but reflected from the flowers, the trees, the beasts, yea from the very surface of the [*waters and the*] sands of the desert. A man of genius finds a reflex to himself, were it only in the mystery of being.

As we shall see, what sounds like an echo of the Psalms in the imagery and diction of the closing sentences is really that, and not by accident. For young Coleridge and his predecessors regularly associated the Psalms with Joy and a creative, personifying involvement with nature. The problem, however, is not to gloss *The Philosophical Lectures*, but to decide how far we can make use of them or other later works to gloss a poem written seventeen years earlier. In my view, we should use them very cautiously and then only to confirm our reading of the earlier texts. And so, it seems to me, we have to return to 1802 and years preceding, and try as best we can to penetrate the obscurities of statements which belong to the period of Joy and great poetry. One reason we do not find clearer statements from that period is that the theory of Joy was not a stable 'given' of eighteenth-century philosophy, but was rather something partly inherited and partly worked out together by two men whose experiences of Joy and Grief were not identical before they came together and shifted constantly in different directions during the years that followed. These conditions scarcely lent themselves to the crystallization of transparent theoretical pronouncements, especially when there was a much greater need for a community of feeling which such pronouncements might disrupt.

This, a truism that applies to much more than the theory of Joy, is borne out, notoriously, by the discrepancy between the Preface to the *Lyrical Ballads* and Coleridge's various comments on it. Nonetheless, the community of mind they supposed themselves to have achieved was not a mere fond illusion. What Wordsworth said about 'Pleasure' in the Preface was, doubtless, not exactly what Coleridge would have said in 1802. Not exactly; but search as we may through their works, I believe we shall find no statement about Pleasure or Joy more pregnant or communal than the following one. The need for poetry to produce immediate pleasure he says, in an addition of 1802:[8]

is an acknowledgement of the beauty of the universe . . it is a task light and easy to him who looks at the world in the spirit of love: further, it is a homage paid to the native and naked dignity of man, to the grand elementary principle of pleasure, by which he knows, and feels, and lives, and moves. We have no sympathy but what is propagated by pleasure: I would not be misunderstood; but wherever we sympathise with pain, it will be found that the sympathy is produced and carried on by subtle combinations with pleasure. We have no knowledge, that is, no general principles drawn from the contemplation of particular facts, but what has been built up by pleasure, and exists in us by pleasure alone.

In spite of its immediate opacity, this passage is uniquely informative both because it is echoed in several of Coleridge's writings (including *Dejection*) and because it yokes together in a peculiarly Wordsworthian–Coleridgean combination ideas from sources as divergent as Aristotle, the Gospels, and David Hartley.

The connexion with Aristotle requires but little comment here. A reference to the *Poetics* in his previous paragraph prepares us for passing allusions to the doctrine of catharsis and to the familiar opening proposition (*Poetics*, IV) that learning is a source of the liveliest pleasure. This point has been noted and taken probably as far as it can be by Donald Davie in his fascinating argument that the rapt Glee or Joy of the *Lyrical Ballads* has a precedent in the pleasure and awe-producing 'Wonder' which Aristotle links with learning in the *Metaphysics* and the *Rhetoric*. In Professor Davie's hands this argument is a powerful instrument for fundamental analysis of Wordsworth's achievement in the *Lyrical Ballads*, but, as will become evident shortly, it is an approach which could not give us access to the full meaning of Joy in *Dejection*. So far as this essay is concerned, Wordsworth's glancing allusions to Aristotle are important chiefly as a reminder of the great antiquity of the pleasure principle in systematic studies of human and animal behaviour.

Hartley's presence is felt throughout this passage but perhaps especially when Wordsworth seems most Aristotelian: 'wherever we sympathise with pain, it will be found that the sympathy is produced and carried on by subtle combinations with pleasure'. The enthusiasm for Hartley, shared latterly by Wordsworth, was of course one of the great intellectual passions of Coleridge's young manhood, and traces of Hartley are to be found scattered throughout his early writings. In particular, I believe Hartley's use of the key terms 'Pleasure' and 'Joy' tended to regulate Coleridge's from 1794 until 1797 and probably years thereafter. Hartley's presence can be felt, for instance, in the following passage from *Lines to a Friend in Answer to a Melancholy Letter* (1795?):

> Wild, as the autumnal gust, the hand of Time
> Flies o'er his mystic lyre: in shadowy dance
> The alternate groups of Joy and Grief advance
> Responsive to his varying strains sublime!

The poem as a whole preaches a fatalism which seems to stem from Hartley's admission that his system of Mechanism 'destroys the notion of a particular providence altering the course of nature so as to suit it to the actions of men'.[9] According to that system life is essentially the mechanical pursuit of pleasure and flight from pain, and the human passions are divided into those two opposing camps, each 'grateful' passion having its opposite, 'ungrateful' passion, as in Coleridge's poem. The 'grateful' opposite of 'Grief', says Hartley, is 'Joy', and he takes some care to define these terms: 'Joy and grief take place when the desire and aversion, hope and fear, are at an end; and are love and hatred, exerted towards an object which is present either in a sensible manner, or in a rational one, i.e. so as to occupy the whole powers of the mind, as sensible objects, when present, and attended to, do the external senses'.[10] Though Hartley's 'grief' is quite unlike the desolated grief of the *Dejection* ode, his definition of 'Joy' as the consummation of love necessitating the presence of the beloved object (whether person or divine Spirit), is one that Coleridge and Wordsworth could have accepted even after they abandoned the rest of the Hartleyan system.

However, there is more in Wordsworth's 'grand elementary principle of pleasure' than can be easily referred to the philosophies of Aristotle or David Hartley, and that something more is the distinguishing feature of 'Joy' in *This Lime-Tree Bower My Prison* and *Tintern Abbey*, and in the poems which both poets wrote in 1802. The phrase 'by which he knows, and feels, and lives, and moves' is derived from *Acts*, 17: 24–28:

24.   God that made the world and all things therein, seeing that he is Lord of heaven and earth, dwelleth not in temples made with hands;

25.   Neither is worshipped with men's hands, as though he needed any things, seeing he giveth to all life, and breath, and all things;

26.   And hath made of one blood all nations of men for to dwell on all the face of the earth, and hath determined the times before appointed, and the bounds of their habitation;

27.   That they should seek the Lord, if haply they might feel after him, and find him, though he be not far from every one of us:

28.   For in him we live, and move, and have our being; as certain also of your own poets have said. . . .

This passage was a special favourite of Coleridge's, but it recommended itself to both poets as an expression of divine immanence of the Holy Spirit in Nature. Wordsworth does not say that 'Pleasure' is the Holy Spirit, but he strongly implies that it is through the instrumentality of Pleasure that the Holy Spirit works. Vague though Wordsworth's formulations are, it seems not unreasonable to infer from them that men and especially poets are most like, and interact with, the Holy Spirit when they most rejoice. Elsewhere in the Preface, he says that the poet is[11]

a man pleased with his own passions and volitions, and who rejoices more than other men in the spirit of life that is in him; delighting to contemplate similar volitions and passions as manifested in the goings-on of the Universe, and habitually impelled to create them where he does not find them.

All of these ideas are prefigured in brief passages describing his son Hartley in letters Coleridge wrote on 17 and 22 September 1800:[12]

Hartley is the same Animal as ever—he moves & lives,
As if his Heritage were Joy
And Pleasure were his Trade.

—he moves, he lives, he finds impulses from within & from without—he is the darling of the Sun and of the Breeze! Nature seems to bless him as a thing of her own! He looks at the clouds, the mountains, the living Beings of the Earth, & vaults & jubilates!

So the genial touches of sunbeam and breeze bless Hartley, who, as Nature's own child, finds quickening impulses of Joy from within and from without. This passage seems to anticipate the Preface and echo the 'glad Preamble' of *The Prelude* in its phrasing and imagery, which are here made more insistently religious in character by the allusion to *Acts*. In this context the 'Breeze' is inescapably linked with the 'breath' of *Acts*, 17:25; the passage as a whole, which was written partly as Coleridge's explanation why he would not have Hartley christened, is an affirmation of Verse 24, that the 'Lord of heaven and earth, dwelleth not in temples made with hands'. Though Hartley was not christened in 1800, Joy was —albeit in a non-conforming spirit.

The passages I have taken from Wordsworth's Preface and Coleridge's letters demonstrate that before the spring of 1802 they were in very close accord over the meaning of 'Joy'/'Pleasure' as a creative principle. The evidence indicates that the doctrinal leader at this stage was Coleridge; that in linking Joy with the operations of the Holy Spirit they were advancing by reverting to a position close to the one Coleridge held before he joined forces with Wordsworth. Close, but not the same: as *The Nightingale* testifies, it was the Wordsworths who convinced Coleridge that 'In Nature there is nothing melancholy'—a principle which his 1800 description of Hartley reaffirms emphatically, even while it carries the 'mystification' of Joy a stage further than it had gone in *Tintern Abbey* or *This Lime-Tree Bower My Prison*. It is carried still further in *Dejection*, at the same time that Coleridge finds himself obliged to reject the long-cherished belief that the Divine Spirit is immanent in, and accessible through, Nature.

That rejection, so central to the poem, makes it seem strange indeed that, at the end of Stanza I, Coleridge again alludes to Chapter 17 of *Acts*. The sounds of the gust and night-shower, he hopes,

> Might now perhaps their wonted impulse give,
> Might startle this dull pain, and make it move and live!

In previous adaptations Wordsworth and Coleridge spoke of Joy (or Pleasure) as the animating spirit of nature as well as man, while the Pauline text itself lent apparent support to the idea of a divine presence in nature. To invoke *Acts* in the radically altered circumstances of *Dejection* is therefore the most painfully ironic twist possible and the true measure of his desperation. This becomes especially clear and poignant if one juxtaposes the passage from *Dejection* with his two descriptions of Hartley in 1800: in them all is motion, joyous impulses from within and from without, and 'blessings' of creative breeze and sunlight; in the other, stasis, the forlorn hope that a violent impulse from without might awaken a 'corresponding' violent yet creative impulse within. As in his earlier adaptations of *Acts* 17:28, what is stressed is the power or lack of power to 'move'—'Animal' and 'inanimate' are key terms—and it is surely significant that when, in Stanza VII, the momentary feeling reunion with nature does occur, it is inaugurated by an internally willed movement: 'I turn from you, and listen to the wind'. In moving outward, the pain appears to be modified by an admixture of pleasure, such as Wordsworth claims is always present in our acts of creative sympathy. In this case the pleasure would seem to be that which traditionally belongs to tragic or elegiac art, as noted by Aristotle in the *Poetics* or by Spenser in *The Ruins of Time*:[18]

> Sorrowing tempered with deare delight,
> That her to heare I feele my feeble spright
> Robbed of sense, and rauished with ioy,
> O sad ioy made of mourning and anoy.

This interpretation is incomplete—it leaves unexplained what happens *between* Stanzas VI and VII—but as far as it goes it is consistent, I believe, with the statements about Joy which Coleridge and Wordsworth made during the years immediately preceding *Dejection*.

As I have already indicated, however, the 'mystification' of Joy in *Dejection* went beyond anything Coleridge and Wordsworth had arrived at together by 1802. To judge from some passing comments by scholars, this tendency has caused a measure of embarrassment or bafflement among his later readers. I do not know how else to account for E. H. Coleridge's explanation of what his grandfather meant by 'Joy', or for the survival of this explanation as authoritative or at least adequate:[14]

He called it joy, meaning thereby not mirth or high spirits, or even happiness, but a consciousness of entire and therefore well being, when the emotional and intellectual faculties are in equipoise.

We have seen that Coleridge did sometimes mean 'mirth or high spirits' when he spoke of Joy, and he meant it even in *Dejection* when he wrote:

With light heart may she rise,
Gay fancy, cheerful eyes....

More seriously misleading, though, is E. H. Coleridge's emptying Joy of its 'metaphysical' or 'mystical' content and fobbing us off with a 'psychological' interpretation which, though not positively wrong, defrauds the psychological experience of its Christian meaning—the meaning, that is, that made the experience seem worth writing about in the first place. In the pages that follow I shall offer a very different reading of Coleridge's mature theory of creative Joy, identifying its origins in an unusual constellation of Christian thinkers, mainly English and mainly eighteenth-century, whose works he knew before he made the fateful journey to Germany. As I see it, the principal antecedents were Hartley, Akenside, Young, Addison, and Milton: thinkers not equally important to or equally approved by Coleridge, but each contributing essential ideas or metaphors to an eventual Coleridgean synthesis. This approach will serve, I hope, to elucidate Stanzas IV and V of *Dejection* especially. Though an integral part of *Dejection*, these stanzas have a radiant visionary character and a metaphorical life of their own; their omission would destroy the ode, but they could be brought together with little alteration to form an independent poem.

2

Among Coleridge's many early references to Mark Akenside is one which couples his name with that of William Lisle Bowles. This occurs in a letter of late 1796: 'I have room enough in *my* brain to admire, aye & almost equally, the *head* and fancy of Akenside, and the *heart* and fancy of Bowles. . . .'[15] That he conceived himself to be a poet who, at least potentially, united the respective strengths of Akenside and Bowles, is suggested by a statement in the same letter:

I feel strongly, and I think strongly; but I seldom feel without thinking, or think without feeling. Hence tho' my poetry has in general a *hue* of tenderness, or Passion over it, yet it seldom exhibits unmixed & simple tenderness or Passion. My philosophical opinions are blended with, or deduced from, my feelings: & this, I think, peculiarizes my style of Writing.

What this blending of strong thought and strong feeling was supposed to achieve is illustrated strikingly if not very successfully in Coleridge's earlier (1794–6) sonnet *To the Rev. W. L. Bowles*:[16]

My heart has thank'd thee, BOWLES! for those soft strains
Whose sadness soothes me, like the murmuring
Of wild-bees in the sunny showers of spring!
For hence not callous to the mourner's pains
Thro' Youth's gay prime and thornless paths I went:
And when the *darker* day of life began,
And I did roam, a thought-bewilder'd man!
Their mild and manliest melancholy lent
A mingled charm, such as the pang consign'd
To slumber, though the big tear it renew'd;
Bidding a strange mysterious PLEASURE brood
Over the wavy and tumultuous mind,
As the great SPIRIT erst with plastic sweep
Mov'd on the darkness of the unform'd deep.

This can be read as a basically 'Hartleyan' poem on the Pleasures of Imagination in which the final Genesis image is a bombastic ornament, i.e. a vehicle grossly disproportionate to the 'scientific' tenor. Equally possible, and in my opinion more likely, Hartley is the reassuring prop in a poem inspired—whatever Coleridge says about Bowles—by a passage in *The Pleasures of Imagination*:[17]

Know then, the sov'reign spirit of the world,
Though, self-collected from eternal time,
Within his own deep essence he beheld
The bounds of true felicity complete;

The idea that the Creation was an outward expression of the joy which the divine Spirit experienced from contemplating the un-created forms of things is a recurrent one in Akenside: [18]

Then liv'd the almighty One: then, deep-retir'd
In his unfathom'd essence, viewed at large
The forms eternal of created things;
The radiant sun, the moon's nocturnal lamp,
The mountains, woods, and streams, the rolling globe,
And wisdom's mien celestial. From the first
Of days, on them his love divine he fix'd,
His admiration; till in time complete,
What he admir'd and lov'd, his vital smile
Unfolded into being.

Related to this passage is one which at a couple of points antici-pates the thought and phrasing of *Dejection*: [19]

Mind, mind alone, (bear witness earth and heaven!)
The living fountains in itself contains
Of beauteous and sublime: here hand in hand,
Sits paramount the Graces: here enthroned,
Celestial Venus, with divinest airs,
Invites the soul to never-fading joy.

Clearly, a Creator such as this Neoplatonic 'Mind' of Akenside's, if he made poets in his own image, made them very like the young bard of *To the Rev. W. L. Bowles*. When Akenside argues for the divine inspiration of poets, [20]

From Heaven my strains begin; from heaven descends
The flame of genius to the human breast,
And love and beauty, and poetic joy
And inspiration. . . .

inspiration is paired with 'poetic joy'. I should add that (contrary to the impression conveyed by this passage) Akenside is too good a Newtonian to think of 'inspiration' as involving a direct super-natural visitation. For him as for Coleridge it was rather a matter of divine attributes being passed down to mankind and poets in

---

Yet by immense benignity inclin'd
To spread around him that primeval joy
Which fill'd himself, he rais'd his plastic arm,
And sounded through the hollow depth of space
The strong, creative mandate.

particular. Coleridge must have responded enthusiastically to Akenside's grandiose conception of the creative imagination allied with divine 'Joy'. Neither Bowles nor Hartley entertained such a lofty view of the poetic enterprise, though the humbleness of the one ('the only *always natural* poet in our language') and the scientific caution of the other carried their own powerful recommendations.[21] If Coleridge fancied himself for a time as the uniter of all their gifts, no wonder that he was so quick to recognize the genius of Wordsworth, who really did unite them.

Akenside was twenty-two years old when he completed *The Pleasures of Imagination*, which must surely rank among the most precocious poems in the language. He makes no secret but rather a display of his indebtedness to a host of ancient and modern thinkers; and indeed the great virtue of his poem is a catholicity which never shatters into complete incoherence though it enforces many a transition at a considerable cost in logic. In the passages I have quoted his chief modern source is certainly Shaftesbury, but his classical erudition was rich and might well have included the principal ancient Neoplatonists.[22] The other modern thinker who contributed largely—much more, indeed, than did Shaftesbury—to the shaping of *The Pleasures of Imagination* was Joseph Addison. Many of Akenside's most striking passages are little more than versifications of Addison's *Spectator* papers on 'Chearfulness' (Nos. 381, 387, 393) and the 'Pleasures of Imagination' (Nos. 411–21). That Akenside succeeds (more or less) in making Shaftesbury and Addison lie down peacefully together seems at first glance a most remarkable achievement, since we rightly think of Shaftesbury as a notable antagonist and Addison as a famous champion of the New Philosophy of Newton and Locke. Yet whatever their epistemological incompatibilities, they had common ground in an optimistic temperament and a rhapsodic appreciation of nature as an expression of the Divine Spirit. That common ground counted for more with young Akenside than any mere epistemological chasm: which was doubtless as it should have been, and very much in the Addisonian spirit of gentlemanly reconciliation of modern thought with classical–Christian values. Though it was perhaps in Akenside's poem that Coleridge first admired them, Addison's influential contributions to eighteenth-century ideas about the relationship between Joy and creativity deserve to be given in his own words.

Addison's thesis in his papers on Chearfulness is that God so framed nature and man as to produce (given the right outlook) 'a Satiety of Joy, and an uninterrupted Happiness'.[23] As for nature,[24]

If we consider the World in its Subserviency to Man, one would think it was made for our Use; but if we consider it in its natural Beauty and Harmony, one would be apt to consider it was made for our Pleasure.

That was exactly what Addison felt about nature, as numerous passages in his writings glowingly testify. Unfortunately, nature was no longer what she seemed: Newton and Locke had seen through her appearances to the quantifiable reality of weight, motion, and extension, and Addison was a man of too much honesty and too much mode not to look again, through the lenses of the New Philosophy:[25]

We may further observe how Providence has taken care to keep up this Chearfulness in the Mind of Man, by having formed it after such a manner, as to make it capable of conceiving Delight from several Objects, which seem to have very little use in them, as from the Wildness of Rocks and Desarts, and the like grotesque Parts of Nature. Those who are versed in Philosophy may still carry this consideration higher, by observing that if Matter had appeared to us endow'd only with those real Qualities which it actually possesses, it would have made but a very joyless and uncomfortable Figure; and why has Providence given it a Power of producing in us such imaginary Qualities as Tastes and Colours, Sounds and Smells, Heat and Cold; but that Man, while he is conversant in the lower Stations of Nature, might have his Mind cheared and delighted with agreeable Sensations? In short, the whole Universe is a kind of Theatre filled with Objects that either raise in us Pleasure, Amusement or Admiration.

This theory, which first appeared in Cudworth's *True Intellectual System*, is restated with embellishments in the third of the *Spectator* papers on the Pleasures of Imagination (No. 413), where Addison 'chearfully' concludes:[26]

In short, our Souls are at present delightfully lost and bewildered in a pleasing Delusion, and we walk about like the Enchanted Hero of a Romance, who sees beautiful Castles, woods and

THE ALL-ANIMATING JOY WITHIN

Meadows; and at the same time hears the warbling of Birds, and purling of Streams; but upon the finishing of some secret Spell, the fantastick Scene breaks up, and the disconsolate Knight finds himself on a barren Heath, or in a solitary Desart.

It is difficult for a twentieth-century reader not to ask himself what Edmund Spenser or Herman Melville would have made of such a guileless vision.

Now there are obvious and ironic resemblances between the anti-Lockean position reached by the despairing Coleridge of *Dejection* and the neo-Lockean position adopted by the happy Addison of the *Spectator* papers on Chearfulness and Imagination. I shall argue that these resemblances are important even if (from another point of view) 'superficial'. But I do not wish to underestimate the width of the epistemological and temperamental gulf between the two men. First, repudiating the mechanistic philosophies of Newton and Locke was an essential intellectual step in the gestation of *Dejection*.[27] Second, an essential emotional step was the failure to experience what the constitutionally optimistic Addison said was readily available from nature: 'He [God] has given almost every thing about us the Power of raising an agreeable Idea in the Imagination: So that it is impossible for us to behold his Works with Coldness or Indifference, and to survey so many Beauties without a secret Satisfaction and Complacency'.[28] This second point of dissent leads to a further distinction. When Coleridge laments, 'I see, not feel how beautiful they are', and goes on to say,

> And would we aught behold, of higher worth,
> Than that inanimate cold world allowed
> To the poor loveless ever-anxious crowd,
> Ah! from the soul itself must issue forth,
> A light, a glory, a fair luminous cloud
> Enveloping the Earth—

he is not talking about a theory of sensory perception, creative or otherwise. He is talking about a power of the soul at once to endow and apprehend ('feel' as 'Beauty') a spiritual quality in nature which is beyond the capacity of the senses, however inventive, to experience.

Yet for all these important differences of theory and temperament, the affinities are real. Coleridge is obliged to use meta-

157

phorical language to describe a 'joyous' relationship with nature, and many of his metaphors of light, glory, cloud and garment are precisely those used by Addison and Akenside, to clothe the 'very joyless and uncomfortable' universe of primary qualities:[29]

> . . . we discover imaginary Glories in the Heavens, and in the Earth, and see some of this Visionary Beauty poured out upon the whole Creation; but what a rough unsightly Sketch of Nature should we be entertained with, did all her Colouring disappear, and the several Distinctions of Light and Shade vanish?

> and whence the robes of light
> Which thus invest her with more lovely pomp
> Than fancy can describe?

For although Coleridge is concerned with the presence (or absence) of a transensory quality in nature, which gives divine life rather than colour or sound to an otherwise 'inanimate cold world', that quality of life is fused with the 'sensible' qualities of nature and therefore cannot be apprehended apart from them. And while the coldness of his 'inanimate cold world' could have no place in Addison's universe of primary qualities, that world is surely akin to the 'very joyless and uncomfortable' world which gives Addison a quick shiver. More important still, Addison so transmogrifies Locke that what is beheld in nature—'imaginary Glories in the Heavens' and 'Visionary Beauty'—has supersensory qualities that argue a divine origin: when the Heavens proclaim the glory of God, they do so through man himself involuntarily giving to nature and receiving again what he has previously received from God. That is Coleridge's position in *Dejection*. In fairness to Addison, I should note too that he does not suppose that the pleasures of nature are available at all times to all men: according to *Spectator* No. 381, the atheist or the impenitently guilty man cannot enjoy them. Clearly, he did not think there were many such exiles from the feast of life. Coleridge could have taught him much about the degrees and snares of guilt, and also about the difficulty of bearing up under 'Pain and Sickness, Shame and Reproach, [and] Poverty', which Addison thought did 'not deserve the Name of Evils'.[30]

I cannot leave Mr. Spectator without remarking two curious and moving results of his theorizing about the relationship between 'Chearfulness' and Imagination in a Newtonian world. In No. 393, the third of the essays on Chearfulness, he gives full rein to his love of nature, in phrases that go echoing down the eighteenth century:[31]

Such an habitual Disposition of Mind consecrates every Field and Wood, turns an ordinary Walk into a Morning or Evening Sacrifice, and will improve those transient Gleams of Joy, which naturally brighten up and refresh the Soul on such Occasions, into an inviolable and perpetual State of Bliss and Happiness.

The 'transient Gleams of Joy' are what Addison, following Milton, calls 'Vernal Delight': a natural springtime experience which the reverent mind will 'improve' into a transcendent Christian experience. Addison's description of 'Vernal Delight' is worth quoting:[32]

In the opening of the Spring, when all Nature begins to recover herself, the same Animal Pleasure which makes the Birds sing, and the whole Brute Creation rejoice, rises very sensibly in the Heart of Man. I know none of the Poets who have observed so well as *Milton* these secret Overflowings of Gladness which diffuse themselves through the Mind of the Beholder, upon surveying the gay Scenes of Nature. . . .

He goes on to quote from *Paradise Lost*, IV, lines 148–56:

Blossoms and Fruits at once of golden hue
Appear'd, with gay enamel'd colours mixt:
On which the Sun more glad impress'd his beams
Than in fair evening Cloud, or humid bow,
When God hath showered the earth, so lovely seem'd
That Lantskip: And of pure now purer air
Meets his approach, and to the heart inspires
Vernal delight and joy able to drive
All sadness but despair, &c.

The malaise described in *Dejection* is something less than 'despair', but these passages from Addison and Milton have a clear anticipatory relevance not only to *Dejection* but to *The Rainbow* and the *Immortality* ode: fruits, all of them, of what William Heath has called the 'Elegaic Spring' of 1802. Let me cite one further passage from *Spectator* No. 393 for the sake of the perhaps penumbral light it sheds on Wordsworth and Coleridge and the spotlight it fixes on two of Addison's own, very remarkable and very pertinent, 'odes':[33]

The Creation is a perpetual Feast to the Mind of a good Man, every thing he sees chears and delights him; Providence has im-

159

printed so many Smiles on Nature that it is impossible for a Mind which is not sunk in more gross and sensual Delights to take a Survey of them without several secret Sensations of Pleasure. The Psalmist has in several of his divine Poems celebrated those beautiful and agreeable Scenes which make the Heart glad, and produce in it that Vernal Delight which I have before taken notice of.

Addison's poetry is usually and rightly considered inferior to his prose, but it too was the work of a full and inventive mind. The two odes I wish to consider here were, in all likelihood, a sort of by-blow of the speculations published in Nos. 387, 393, and 413. The first of these is a sing-song paraphrase of the Twenty-third Psalm which begins:[34]

> The Lord my Pasture shall prepare,
> And feed me with a Shepherd's Care;
> His Presence shall my Wants supply,
> And guard me with a watchful Eye;
> My Noon-day Walks he shall attend,
> And all my midnight Hours defend.

No one is likely to prefer this to the King James version. But Addison gives his paraphrase a twist which unobtrusively brings David up to date:[35]

> Tho' in a bare and rugged Way,
> Through devious lonely Wilds I stray,
> Thy Bounty shall my Pains beguile:
> The barren Wilderness shall smile
> With sudden Greens and Herbage crown'd,
> And streams shall murmur all around.

If I read these lines correctly, the 'bare and rugged Way' is none other than the 'very joyless and uncomfortable' world of primary qualities which we have already encountered in *Spectator* No. 387 and which there as here is transformed miraculously by the bounty of God working through the perceptual faculties of men. Perhaps Addison's description of nature communicates little of the 'Vernal Delight' he claims to have discovered in the Psalms, but there can be no doubt that he was deeply responsive to natural beauty and felt strongly that it was, in some sense, a revelation of the Godhead. At the same time, as we have seen, he accepted the contemporary scientific view of the natural universe which removed not only all 'sensible' qualities from it but also all supernatural causation. It is true that the very men responsible for this view, Locke and Newton, staunchly maintained that Nature itself was the most eloquent witness to the existence of God. But theirs were essentially reaffirmations of the old arguments from Design and necessary First Cause; whereas Addison, in reaffirming with the Psalmist that the Heavens declare the glory of God, was thinking of that half-aesthetic, half-religious experience of 'Vernal Delight'. Addison's solution has the gratifying effect of magnifying the dignity and power of man in the very act of humble worship and appreciation, but it has the frightening consequence of making what we receive from nature strictly dependent on our own physical and spiritual conditions. A 'good Man' is able to feast at nature's board and hear the Heavens declare the glory of God, but how 'good' (and healthy) do we have to be to enjoy this gift? While admitting the problem, or part of it, Addison seems to have had slight difficulty in returning an optimistic answer. His testimony is in his beautiful ode, inspired by Newton and the Nineteenth Psalm:[36]

I

The Spacious Firmament on high,
With all the blue Etherial Sky,
And spangled Heav'ns, a Shining Frame,
Their great Original proclaim:
Th'unwearied Sun, from day to day,
Does his Creator's Pow'r display,
And publishes to every Land
The work of an Almighty Hand.

II

Soon as the evening Shades prevail,
The Moon takes up the wondrous Tale,
And nightly to the listning Earth
Repeats the Story of her Birth:
Whilst all the stars that round her burn,
And all the Planets, in their turn,
Confirm the Tidings as they rowl,
And spread the Truth from Pole to Pole.

III

What though, in solemn Silence, all
Move round the dark terrestrial Ball?

What tho' nor real Voice nor Sound
Amid their radiant Orbs be found?
In Reason's Ear they all rejoice,
And utter forth a glorious Voice,
For ever singing, as they shine,
'The Hand that made us is Divine'.

Coleridge probably knew this poem, so like *Dejection* in many of its rhymes and phrasings, because it became a popular Protestant hymn later in the eighteenth century.[37] If he did, he would have noted that the Reason which can hear the *musica mundana* is not the Reason of the soundless, voiceless Newtonian universe. It must be an inspired, creative faculty in man, himself growing more potent and more vulnerable as the colours, the voices, and the glory fade out of heaven.

4

Mrs. Barbauld relates a tradition that one of Akenside's chief aims in *The Pleasures of Imagination* was to combat the gloom of Edward Young's *Night Thoughts*,[38] and certainly Young's serial poem was gloomier before than after the publication of Akenside's youthful masterpiece in 1744. But no one who has read Young with any care is likely to take Mrs. Barbauld's gossip seriously; for his work is not uniformly or even typically melancholy. As I suggested in Chapter Two, Young's view of man is traditionally Christian, but with the traditional contrasts of exaltation and debasement, ecstasy and despair, made more abrupt and frequent than usual:[39]

How poor, how rich, how abject, how august,
How complicate, how wonderful, is man!

. . .

Helpless immortal! insect infinite!
A worm! a god!

Admittedly, this is Young in a delirium of exclamatory antitheses; his flights up or down are usually more extended and poetically effective. The passages I shall be quoting are the upward flights, and it should therefore be borne in mind that they are balanced by passages which detail the ills and evils that ensue from the Fall. Unlike Akenside, whose 1744 version of *The Pleasures of Imagin-*

ation stands in relation to the 1770 version much as the 1805 version of *The Prelude* does to that of 1850, Young was a seasoned and orthodox Christian who steered well clear of pantheism and the more secret shoals of Neoplatonism. The Rector of Welwyn wanted very badly to be made a bishop.

Praise of 'Joy' and 'Pleasure' is scattered throughout Young's writings, but reaches its climax in Night VIII. It would be rash to assert that he used these words with quite the same shades of meaning that Wordsworth and Coleridge were to use them a half-century later. But there is surely small difference between the 'Pleasure' of the following passage and the 'great elementary principle of pleasure' in Wordsworth's Preface:[40]

What mortal shall resist, where angels yield?
Pleasure's the mistress of etherial powers;
For her contend the rival gods above;
Pleasure's the mistress of the world below;
And well it was for man, that *pleasure* charms;
How would All stagnate, but for *pleasure's* ray!
How would the frozen stream of action cease!
What is the pulse of this so busy world?
The love of *pleasure*: That, thro' ev'ry vein,
Throws motion, warmth; and shuts out death from life.

It is pointless to enquire whether Young joined Hartley and Aristotle in Wordsworth's mind when he dedicated a paragraph to this topic. Hartley himself *might* have been influenced by Young's enormously successful poem, and Young very probably was influenced by Aristotle. What matters here is that in restating this not only 'elementary' but also very ancient 'principle of pleasure', Wordsworth could have found it formulated with considerable force in the very poem from which he had recently borrowed a key idea for inclusion in *Tintern Abbey*—a matter to which I shall return shortly.

Much of what Young says about 'Joy' (as distinct from the broader principle of 'pleasure') in Night VIII is said more succinctly in two stanzas of a later poem, *Resignation*:[41]

Joy is our duty, glory, health;
    The sunshine of the soul;
Our best encomium on the power
    Who sweetly plans the whole:

163

Joy is our Eden still possess'd:
    Be gone ignoble grief!
'Tis joy makes gods, and men exalts,
    Their nature, our relief. . . .

The identification of 'Joy' with prelapsarian innocence is crucial to Young's conception in Night VIII (as it is to Coleridge's in *Dejection*):[42]

Who forms an instrument, ordains from whence
Its dissonance, or harmony, shall rise.
Heav'n bid the soul this mortal frame inspire;
Bid virtue's ray divine inspire the soul
With unprecarious flows of vital joy. . . .

Young is so carried away with this vision that he nearly forgets that, after all, this is also a Vale of Tears and Trials for fallen man. It is at this point that Addison enters the poem as a stabilizing influence. Young is a man of emotional extremes (such at least is the effect of his rhetoric), whilst Addison is for the mean even in 'Chearfulness': 'Those are often raised into the greatest Transports of Mirth, who are subject to the greatest Depressions of Melancholy. On the contrary, Chearfulness, tho' it does not give any Depths of Sorrow.' 'Chearfulness,' he assures us, 'is of a serious and composed Nature, it does not throw the Mind into a Condition improper for the present State of Humanity'.[43] Young develops the same apt admonishment in the following way:[44]

What cause for *triumph*, where such ills abound?
What for *dejection*, where presides a Power,
Who call'd us into being to be blest?
So grieve, as conscious, grief may rise to joy;
So joy, as conscious, joy to grief may fall.
Most true, a wise man never will be sad;
But neither will sonorous, bubbling mirth,
A shallow stream of happiness betray:
Too happy to be sportive, he's serene.

This part of Night VIII abounds with such wholesome counsel to the improvident, and is indeed highly relevant to (though not necessarily an 'influence' on) both *Dejection* and *Resolution and Independence*. It is noteworthy, however, that Addison and Young do not single out poets as especially vulnerable.

Addison's influence is also apparent in the famous passage from Night VI which inspired an even more famous one in *Tintern Abbey*:

> Therefore am I still
> A lover of the meadows and the woods,
> And mountains; and of all that we behold
> From this green earth; of all the mighty world
> Of eye, and ear,—both what they half create,
> And what perceive. . . . [45]

Young's version: [45]

> In senses, which inherit earth, and heav'ns;
> Enjoy the various riches *nature* yields;
> Far nobler! *give* the riches they enjoy;
> Give taste to fruits; and harmony to groves;
> Their radiant beams to gold, and gold's bright fire;
> Take in, at once, the landscape of the world,
> At a small inlet, which a grain might close,
> And half create the wond'rous world they see.
> Our *senses*, as our *reason*, are divine.
> But for the magic organ's powerful charm,
> Earth were a rude, uncolour'd chaos still.

Here we recognize again the theories of Cudworth and Addison, which probably descended directly to Wordsworth and Coleridge but certainly descended indirectly through both Akenside and Young. Addison's ideal of 'Chearfulness' was transmitted through the same channels. Yet it must be evident from the passage just cited that Young, much more than Akenside, transcendentalized Addison and rubbed off most of the Augustan polish. So true is this that MacLean has identified Young as a very rare bird indeed: an eighteenth-century poet who escaped the broadcast influence of Locke.[46] Commenting on the passage just quoted and on Young's *Conjectures on Original Composition*, Fairchild gives a truer perspective: 'This conception of the divine creativeness of both the senses and the higher reason is much more significantly "romantic" than Young's melancholy . . . both the theory of genius and the more obviously religious transcendentalism of *Night Thoughts* are parallel to cognate developments from the type of Christianity which Young inherits. Historically regarded both express, in their different spheres, the sense of inward freedom, goodness, and power which is felt by the "elect Christian".[47] Evidence to support this interpretation is scattered throughout Young's later writings. In his earlier years as a fashionable satirist and companion of Addison and Pope, he imbibed notions and values which he never abandoned entirely. But these benevolized rather than supplanted the old-fashioned Protestantism of the Inner Light which seems to have been handed down to him by his father, seventeenth-century Dean of Sarum.

This is also to say that, English as he is, Young has real affinities with various European, and especially German, Protestant writers, e.g. Coleridge's beloved shoemaker mystic Jacob Boehme, whose influence in England, though different in kind, was comparable in scope to that of Young in Germany. This is not the place to enter upon a discussion of Boehme and his influence, but I may note in passing that the *Aurora* which Coleridge claimed to have read in school contains passages linking 'Joy' and creativity which remind one of both Young and Coleridge:[48]

God the Holy Ghost . . . proceeds from the Father and the Son, and is the holy moving Spring or Fountain of Joy in the whole Father.

The holy Angels were made to be Creatures from God, that they should *praise, sing*, sound forth and jubilate before the Heart of God, which is the Son of God, and *increase* the heavenly Joy.

Where else should the Father place them, but before the Gate of his Heart? Does not all Joy of Man, which is in the *whole* Man, arise from the Fountain of the Heart?

There are equally striking and pertinent passages in Boehme's *The Signature of All Things.*[49] I stress what at first might seem improbable or peripheral, the points of contact between Young's and Boehme's ecstatic mysticism in the Protestant tradition, partly because these are also points of contact with Coleridge, but also because they may help to account for much of Young's appeal to Herder and Klopstock and, through them, the youthful Goethe. Klopstock, who revered Young as a master and corresponded with him, belonged to the comparable tradition in Germany.[50] Though Goethe's *Autobiography* suggests that *Night Thoughts* was important to him and other young Germans chiefly as a dispenser of English melancholy, I think that Young's influence on *The*

Sorrows of Young Werther is apparent (if anywhere) in Werther the enthusiast, creating worlds about him but paying no attention to the cautionary wisdom which calls for 'serious joy'.

I believe that Myra Reynolds was the first of many scholars to notice that the passage in Night VI which helped shape the thought and phrasing of *Tintern Abbey* also had a strong parallel with the theory in *Dejection* that 'we receive but what we give'.[51] This is true, though as I have shown, Coleridge might have found the same ideas in other writers; and it was Akenside that he seems to have known by heart during the crucial Bristol–Nether Stowey period of collaboration with Southey and Wordsworth. However this may be—and who can suppose there was only a single source for such ideas?—Coleridge certainly studied Young's *Works* in the Spring of 1795 and, sixteen years later, affirmed that Young's 'love of point and wit had often put an end to his pathos and sublimity; but there were parts in him which must be immortal. He (Mr. C.) loved to read a page of Young, and walk out to think of him'.[52] That Coleridge held such a high opinion of Young in 1811 helps to confirm that he might have been affected by him at a much earlier date. But more important for the purposes of the present study is the fact that he was absorbing some of Young's ideas as early as 1795. One passage that might have struck him at the time occurs in Letter III ('On Pleasure') of *The Centaur Not Fabulous*:[53]

He, as well as they, has his parks, gardens, grottos, cascades, statues, paintings &c. but enjoys them more. Not because his are better than theirs, but because he is better than they. His paintings have beauties unborrowed from the pencil; and his statues in *his* eyes appear, like *Pygmalion's*, to live; though *mere* marble in *theirs*. His all-animating joy within gives graces to art, and smiles to nature, invisible to common eyes. Objects of sense, and imagination, for the greater power of pleasing, are indebted to the goodness of his heart. For as the sun is itself the most glorious of objects, and makes all others shine, so virtue itself is the greatest of pleasures, and of all other pleasures redoubles the delight.

This paragraph from the author of *Night Thoughts* sums up much of the meaning of 'Joy' in *Dejection*. Coleridge readily agreed with Young that 'unprecarious flows of vital joy' were freely available, in Coleridge's words, ' . . . to the pure, and in their purest hour'.

And, of course, was the rub. Coleridge felt guilty about many things done and (especially) not done, including his failure to make better use of his 'all-animating joy within' when he had it. Irony upon irony, that failure was later turned into an argument against taking Werther's way out:[54]

Call to mind what you were!

I gave you innocence, I gave you hope,
Gave health, and genius, and an ample scope.
Return you me guilt, lethargy, despair?
Make out the invent'ry; inspect, compare!
Then die—if die you dare!

5

No other line in *Dejection* has quite so much resonance as the short one that opens Stanza III: 'My genial spirits fail...' I have already pointed out that this line sadly, ironically recalls not only Milton's original phrase in *Samson Agonistes* (l. 594) but also Wordsworth's confident echo of Milton in *Tintern Abbey* (l. 113). Effective as these echoes are and as this line is in its entirety, we may feel that a part of it—the single word 'genial'—is still more wonderfully effective in the way it concentrates meaning. All possible connotations of that word and all that I have said about the relationship between Joy and Imagination seem to be compressed here—thanks to the unique context created by the poem as a whole. Yet we have to be cautious about the connotations we discover in this particular usage of the word, lest they prove historically improbable or even impossible. We seem to be on safe ground to begin with if we seek possible meanings of 'genial' in Dr. Johnson's *A Dictionary of the English Language* (1755):

GENIAL: adj. [genialis, Lat.]
1. That contributes to propagation.
    Higher of the genial bed by far,
    And with mysterious reverence I deem.   *Milton.*
    Greater Venus, *genial* pow'r of love,
    The bliss of men below and gods above! *Dryden.*
2. That gives cheerfulness, or supports life.
    Nor will the light of life continue long
    But yields to double darkness nigh at hand;
    So much I feel my *genial* spirits droop. *Milton.*

3. Natural; Native.
    It chiefly proceedeth from natural incapacity,
    and *genial* indisposition.
                                                Brown's Vulg. Errors.

Used as Coleridge uses it in *Dejection*, the word must carry with it nearly the full burden of its history. Milton's primary meaning, as defined by Johnson, seems to be (approximately) Coleridge's primary meaning as well. The sexual overtones implicit in *genialis* are ones we might have missed in Coleridge's use of 'genial', though perhaps not in Milton's. And Johnson's third category, 'Natural', appears to be a perfectly compatible secondary meaning of 'genial' in both Milton and Coleridge.

So far, so good. But I believe that most of us will feel that something is missing from this cluster of meanings that is part of the meaning of 'genial' in *Dejection*—namely, the connotations of 'genius' in the relatively modern sense of creative genius. It is easy enough to find biographical and other reasons why this meaning was not recorded by Samuel Johnson in 1755. The problem arises when, turning to the *OED*, we find that 1825 is the date of the first recorded instance of 'genial' used in the sense 'Of or pertaining to genius; characterized by genius (chiefly after Ger. *genial, genialish*)'. Did the word not mean that before Carlyle used it to translate Goethe in 1825? The problem becomes greater when we note that the *OED* corrects Johnson's third category of 'Natural' (*OED*: 'pertaining to "genius" or natural disposition') and going on to suggest that 'in the later echoes of Milton's phrase *genial spirits*, the adj. is prob. taken in' the sense of 'cheering, enlivening,' or 'sympathetically cheerful, jovial, kindly'. An initial reaction is likely to be—it was so in my own case—that the learned compilers of the *OED* have got things wrong all along the line. It is true that Johnson's 'That gives cheerfulness, or supports life' is more an impressionistic paraphrase of 'genial spirits droop' than it is a precise definition of 'genial' itself; or, if you like, Johnson's definition crowds two distinct meanings into a single category. This may be poor lexicography, but at least it does not do violence to the meaning of words as they are used, with astonishing connotative richness and subtlety, in two of the greatest poems in English.

Here, I think, we have a classic case of a conflict of interest between poets and lexicographers. Most of the time poets use a wide range of language with a sharp denotation which makes their work a treasure trove for lexicographers; in turn, the lexicographers' work becomes indispensable to students of poetry—and indeed to writers of poetry. However, as Fred C. Robinson explains in connexion with the meanings of words in Old English poetry:[55]

the lexicographer can unwittingly blind his reader to denotations and allusions which are important to a full understanding of the specific work in which they occur. Another kind of lexicographical obfuscation results when the dictionaries conceal from the reader the full force of the poetic style and particularly of the figurative language used in the early texts. If a word occurs in a slightly unusual application, the lexicographer's tendency is to introduce into the dictionary entry a special meaning for the occurrence, a definition which will fit in a literal way the context in question. This propensity often leads lexicographers to flatten out figurative language and to resolve ineptly numerous intended ambiguities.

How much greater is the danger that this will happen in the case of post-medieval poetic usage! Many are the Renascence and modern poets who so control the context of a word or phrase, itself bearing a context of historical usage, that its various secondary meanings are almost as important as its primary meaning—if indeed it is possible to decide what the primary meaning is. To take an extreme but highly apposite example: in *Gerontian* T. S. Eliot turns such possibilities into a poetic method which seems ultimately to empty language of meaning by deliberately forcing it to yield too many meanings. What, for instance, is the 'primary' or 'literal' meaning of any of the first four nouns in the following passage?[56]

Think now

History has many cunning passages, contrived corridors
And issues, deceives with whispering ambitions,
Guides us by vanities. Think now
She gives when our attention is distracted
And what she gives, gives with such supple confusions....

When 'History' suddenly turns into a whore in the last lines, we are left to puzzle over a passage which can be said to enact part of its own meaning—namely, that the historical development of language has given words so many meanings that none of them may mean what it appears to mean in a particular usage. Are the 'cunning passages' vaginal, textual, or territorial? And if territorial, are they actions or things? Whatever they are, they are not the stuff out of which dictionaries can be made.

In the case of Milton, the lexicographer's problem is more difficult because the poetic method is not one of systematic obscurantism; Milton's prose and verse supply the *OED* with many of its most lucid examples. But in those rare moments—'genial spirits' is one of them—when the full lexical resources of a word are hinted at by its rhythmic, figurative and syntactical contexts, the lexicographer may be the last person able to do justice to its meaning even while he is the first to supply the means of judging his own inadequacy. For if we look at the examples given by the *OED*, we find that Milton used 'genial' in several senses, including 'generative' and 'festive'. In those circumstances, and in the circumstances of Samson's victimization by Dalila, we must surely recognize sexual failure in the imagery of

So much I feel my genial spirits droop,
My hopes all flat, nature within me seems
In all her functions weary of herself;
My race of glory run, and race of shame,
And I shall shortly be with them that rest.

And in the dragging rhythms we surely feel something the opposite of 'festive'. Poets do not lock the different meanings of words into separate compartments in their minds, and Milton was notably sensitive, even among poets, to the possibilities of controlled ambiguity, of puns on an ancient Latin or Hebrew root, or of adroit allusions to memorable uses of the same word by earlier poets. In this use of 'genial' the secondary meanings of 'generative' and 'festive' are so nearly as important as the primary meaning of 'natural disposition' that to give the right primary meaning only is to give the wrong meaning. Here is a case where a fusion of old meanings creates what is virtually a new word.

This is what happens in *Dejection* as well. In the new context of Coleridge's celebration of 'joy', Milton's phrase does indeed acquire (as the *OED* maintains) a new stress on 'cheering, enlivening' or 'sympathetically cheerful, jovial, kindly'. At the same time, it seems in its new setting to lose most, though not all, of its sexual overtones: not all, because we cannot but be aware of the history of the phrase. The really new element, however, is the additional sense of 'pertaining to creative genius'. That it exists I have no doubt whatever, and I believe there is no real conflict between this claim and the claim by the *OED* that the word in this sense ('chiefly after Ger. *genial, genialisk*') makes its first quotable appearance in 1825. The sense of 'pertaining to creative genius' is an important secondary meaning of 'genial' in Coleridge's usage, but is never, I believe, its primary meaning. It is hard to say what influence German precedents might have had, since although Coleridge did of course know German by the time he wrote *Dejection*, the new fusion may well have occurred much earlier. When, in 1798, Wordsworth wrote,

Nor perchance,
If I were not thus taught, should I the more
Suffer my genial spirits to decay:
For thou art with me here upon the banks
Of this fair river

neither he nor Coleridge knew German, but they had developed their theory of the creative power of Joy:

While with an eye made quiet by the power
Of harmony, and the deep power of joy,
We see into the life of things.

Given such a theory, it was almost inevitable that 'genial' should acquire, for them and, through their poetry, for us, a secondary meaning of 'pertaining to creative genius'.

What is a little surprising is that it took the adjective so long to catch up with the noun in English, since 'genius' in the modern sense had been current for nearly a century before Wordsworth wrote *Tintern Abbey*. Both noun and adjective have the same Latin root, and down to the beginning of the eighteenth century their meanings in English seem to have run parallel courses, never departing very far from the complex of meanings that had accrued around the Latin 'genius'. In retrospect, the modern (creative) 'genius' appears to have been implicit in the Latin word, as is suggested in the late C. S. Lewis's discussion of a definition of 'genius' given by St. Augustine:[57]

We have here a pretty clear distinction between what may be called Genius A (the universal god of generation) and Genius B (the δαίμων, tutelary spirit, or 'external soul' of an individual man); and it is plain, as Augustine points out, that while there is but one Genius A, there are as many Genii BB as there are men. It is with these latter that the modern reader is familiar; they are brothers to the δαίμων of Socrates, ancestors of the Guardian angels in Christian pneumatology, and have dwindled by a natural metaphor into the 'genius' of a modern novelist or painter.

Why, then, did the same dwindling not take place in the adjective at about the time it did in the noun? Why did it have to wait for Wordsworth and Coleridge? My guess is that there are earlier occurrences of 'genial' which bear a secondary sense of creative genius, but that they are difficult to recognize and nearly impossible to demonstrate. (I have spent more than a few hours trying to do both.) However this may be, it is certainly true that after Milton the adjective came increasingly to mean 'festive', 'cheering', 'jovial', while the noun came to mean, more often than not, the modern creative 'Genius'. In effect, 'genial' carries forward—to the gradual exclusion of other associations—the festive associations of the Hymenal Genius A; and 'genius' carries forward, as Lewis explains, the 'daemonic' associations of Genius B. In the circumstances of eighteenth-century literary biography—of Savage and Collins, Burns and Chatterton and the rest—what had the new 'Genius' in common with the well-established sense of festivity and cheer in 'genial'? The creative theory of Coleridge and Wordsworth was large enough to accommodate nearly all of the original associations and subsequent offshoots of Augustine's 'genius'. Their use of 'genial' did temporarily restore—and even augment—the original richness that English inherited from Latin. But that restorative effect is now available only as a nuance to students of their poetry. For 'genial' in the German sense employed by Carlyle has never been naturalized in English, and at least two of the senses recorded by Johnson were beginning to disappear during his own century.

So far as the present essay is concerned, the last gloze on 'genial' has to be left to Wordsworth in *Resolution and Independence*. When he speaks of '. . . genial faith, still rich in genial good', we have no apparent reason to connect 'genial' as it is used here with creative genius. But when he goes on in the next stanza to speak

Of him who walk'd in glory and in joy
Behind his plough upon the mountain side;
By our own spirits are we deified:

We Poets in our youth begin in gladness;
But thereof comes in the end despondency & madness . . .

the 'spirits' of the third line certainly seem to be the same as the 'genial spirits' of Tintern Abbey and Dejection, here unmistakably linked with the figure of the Promethean poet. We may be sure that the man who wrote these lines understood how in Coleridge's use of the phrase 'genial spirits', the word 'spirits' controls and mirrors the meanings of 'high spirits', tutelary spirit, and Holy Spirit with its own analogous creative breath and wind. This is to affirm that Wordsworth, not greatly less than Milton and Coleridge, was a scholar-poet, and that the poetry under discussion here is learned poetry—however unstudied and genial it might seem.

NOTES

1. 'Dionysus in Lyrical Ballads', Wordsworth's Mind and Art, ed. A. W. Thomson (Edinburgh, 1969), 110–39. Following Beer, Gilpin offers a kind of shorthand 'mythic' interpretation of 'Joy' as essentially Dionysian (The Strategy of Joy, 16–36). Though incomplete and ahistorical in approach, this is the best interpretation to date.

2. A. O. Lovejoy, 'Coleridge and Kant's Two Worlds', ELH, VII (December 1940), 348–49. For a recent assessment of the very inconclusive evidence concerning the influence of German Idealism on Coleridge before 1804, see G. N. G. Orsini, Coleridge and German Idealism (Carbondale, 1969), 43–56.

3. The phrase and perception are Marshall Suther's in The Dark Night of Samuel Taylor Coleridge, 80.

4. Geoffrey Grigson, The Harp of Aeolus, 34–35, points out the precocious nature of this poem.

5. Letters, I, 490, dated 6 May 1799.

6. Letters, I, 623–24, dated September 1800, to James Webbe Tobin.

7. The Philosophical Lectures, ed. Kathleen Coburn (London, 1949), 179. Cf. as well 168, 412, and 413.

8. Wordsworth, Preface to Lyrical Ballads (1802), ed. Paul M. Zall, Literary Criticism of William Wordsworth (Lincoln, Neb., 1966), 51. Further citations are from this edition of the 1802 Preface.

9. Observations on Man (London, 1834), I, 319.

10. Ibid, I, 234.

11. Preface to the Lyrical Ballads (1802), 48–49.

12. Letters, I, 623–24, to Tobin, and 625, to Godwin.

13. Works, II, lines 319–22. Anderson, II, 568.

14. E. H. Coleridge, 'The Lake Poets in Somersetshire', Transactions of the

15. *Royal Society of Literature*, Second Series, XX (London, 1899), 120. This definition was given modern currency by I. A. Richards in *Coleridge on Imagination* (2nd edn, 1950), 150.

15. *Letters*, I, 279, dated 17 December 1796, to John Thelwall.

16. *Poems* (1796), 45.

17. *The Pleasures of Imagination*, II, lines 307–15. *Anderson*, IX, 742.

18. *Pleasures*, I, lines 64–73. *Anderson*, IX, 736.

19. *Pleasures*, I, lines 481–86. *Anderson*, IX, 739.

20. *Pleasures*, I, lines 56–59. *Anderson*, IX, 736.

21. The quotation is from *Letters*, I, 278, dated 17 December 1796, to John Thelwall.

22. Cf. the famous passage in Shaftesbury, *Characteristics*, ed. Robertson (London, 1900), I, 136: 'Such a poet is indeed a second *Maker*; a just Prometheus under Jove. Like that sovereign artist or universal plastic nature, he forms a whole, coherent and proportioned in itself, with due subordinacy of constituent parts'.

23. *The Spectator*, ed. Donald F. Bond (Oxford, 1965), III, No. 387, p. 454.

24. *Spectator*, p. 452.

25. *Spectator*, p. 453.

26. *Spectator*, No. 413, pp. 546–47.

27. See *Letters*, II, 675–703, written in February and March 1801.

28. *Spectator*, III, No. 413, p. 546.

29. *Spectator*, *Ibid*; *Pleasures*, III, 485–87. *Anderson*, IX, 750. The phrase 'a very joyless and uncomfortable universe' is from *Spectator*, III, No. 387, p. 453.

30. *Spectator*, No. 381, p. 431.

31. *Spectator*, No. 393, p. 476.

32. *Spectator*, p. 474; the passage quoted by Addison is from *Paradise Lost*, IV, 148–56.

33. *Spectator*, p. 475.

34. *Spectator*, IV, No. 441, p. 51.

35. *Ibid*.

36. *Spectator*, IV, No. 465, pp. 144–45.

37. Cf. H. N. Fairchild, *Religious Trends in English Poetry* (New York, 1939), I, 182.

38. Introduction to *The Pleasures of Imagination* (London, 1794).

39. Quoted from Night III by Fairchild in *Religious Trends* (New York, 1942), II, 143.

40. Edward Young, *The Works of the Author of Night Thoughts* (London, 1774), III, Night VIII, p. 245.

41. *Anderson*, X, 145.

42. Young, *Works*, III, Night VIII, p. 250.

43. *Spectator*, III, No. 381, pp. 429, 430.

44. Young, *Works*, III, Night VIII, p. 253.

45. *Ibid*, III, Night VI, p. 155.

46. Kenneth MacLean, *John Locke and English Literature of the Eighteenth Century* (New Haven, 1936), 14, 160.

47. Fairchild, *Religious Trends*, II, 148.

48. See *Letters*, IV, 750–51, dated 3 July 1817, to Tieck. I quote from Coleridge's copy of the William Law edition of *The Works of Jacob Behmen, The Teutonic Philosopher* (London, 1764), I, 36, 56.

49. *Ibid*, IV, 132, 134. See also my discussion of Boehme in the previous chapter.

50. See, for instance, F. H. Adler, *Herder and Klopstock* (1913), 213–14, where Klopstock's use of *freude* is traced to the German mystics.

51. *The Treatment of Nature in English Poetry* (Chicago, 1909), 120–21.

52. George Whalley, 'The Bristol Library Borrowings of Southey and Coleridge, 1793–8', *Transactions of the Bibliographical Society—The Library* (September, 1949), 119. See also *Notebooks*, I, 33–36. Recorded by Sir John Taylor Coleridge, 20 April 1811, *Coleridge's Miscellaneous Criticism*, ed. T. M. Raysor (London, 1936), 438.

53. The edition of Young's works which Coleridge was reading was that of 1774. The passage quoted can be found in Vol. IV, 166.

54. The Suicide's Argument', dated 1811.

55. 'Lexicography and Literary Criticism: A Caveat', *Philological Essays*, ed. James L. Rosier (The Hague, 1970), 105.

56. *Collected Poems 1909–1935* (New York, 1936), 44.

57. *The Allegory of Love* (London, 1936), 361.

The Greater Ode

The *Erigone* of *Eratosthenes* is a Poem, in which you cannot find a single Fault. Would you therefore say, that *Eratosthenes* is a greater Poet than *Archilochus*, because he is confus'd, and wants Order and Oeconomy in many of his Writings; a Fault he only slides into by reason of that Divine Spirit which hurries him away, and which he cannot command if he would? In like manner, as to *Lyrics*, had you rather be *Bacchylides* than *Pindar?* Or in Tragedy, *Ion* of *Chios*, than *Sophocles? Bacchylides* and *Ion*, 'tis true, make no false Steps, nor write any Thing but what is Elegant and Polite: Not so *Pindar* and *Sophocles*; for sometimes in the midst of their greatest Violence, while they Lighten and Thunder, if I may so express my self, their Fires suddenly become extinct, and they unhappily fall.

—Longinus, *On the Sublime* (trans. Welsted, 1712)

And may not I presume a little further, to show the reasonableness of this word *vates*, and say that the holy David's Psalms are a divine poem? . . . For what else is the awaking his musical instruments, the often and free changing of persons, his notable *prosopopeias*, when he maketh you, as it were, see God coming in his majesty, his telling of the beasts' joyfulness, and hills' leaping, but a heavenly poesy, wherein almost he showeth himself a passionate lover of that unspeakable and everlasting beauty to be seen by the eyes of the mind, only cleared by faith?

—Sidney, *Defence of Poesie*

1

Ode, Conversation poem, or verse letter *manqué?* There are good, obvious reasons for deciding that *Dejection* belongs to one or another of these familiar Romantic kinds. And that this is so is a pretty strong argument that it belongs to none of them, but that it is better classified (if at all) according to new principles based on new readings of the nineteenth-century lyric. M. H. Abrams has ventured such a classification, of what he calls 'the greater Romantic lyric'.[1] I believe that his essay in inductive generic description is sound as far as it goes, and that it is especially illuminating as a guide to the structural and thematic features which *Dejection* shares, on the one hand with the Conversation poems of the *annus mirabilis*, and, on the other, with a host of later poems ranging from *Stanzas Written in Dejection* to *A Prayer for my Daughter*. Such an approach avoids the procrustean tendencies of traditional generic criticism; it fastens our eye on the object rather than on a name, on the practice rather than on a theory. This is mostly to the good, and especially when, as in Professor Abrams' case, description based on induction also provides a focus for historical inquiry into the origins and development of the new literary kind. In this chapter I shall take my departure from his description of the greater Romantic lyric, and extend the historical search farther than he was willing to go.

What are the characteristics of the greater Romantic lyric?[2]

Some of the poems are called odes, while the others approach the ode in having lyric magnitude and a serious subject, feelingfully mediated. They present a determinate speaker in a particularized, and usually a localized, outdoor setting, whom we overhear as he carries on, in fluent vernacular which rises easily to a more formal speech, a sustained colloquy, sometimes with himself or with the outer scene, but more frequently with a silent human auditor, present or absent. The speaker begins with a description of the landscape; an aspect or change of aspect in the landscape evokes a varied but integral process of memory, thought, anticipation, and feeling which remains closely interwoven with the outer scene. In the course of this meditation the lyric speaker achieves an insight, faces up to a tragic loss, comes to a moral decision, or resolves an emotional problem. Often the poem rounds upon itself to end where it began, at the outer scene, but with an altered mood and deepened understanding which is the result of the intervening meditation.

As Professor Abrams notes, some of the poems in question are called odes, while his own nomenclature deliberately alludes to a distinction which was traditionally made between different types of odes: '*Faute de mieux*, I shall call this poetic type "the greater

Romantic lyric," intending to suggest, not that it is a higher achievement than other Romantic lyrics, but that it displaced what neo-classical critics had called "the greater ode"—the elevated Pindaric, in distinction to "the lesser ode" modeled chiefly on Horace—as the favored form for the long lyric poem'.[3] On this showing, the greater ode and the greater Romantic lyric are alike in that both, at best, are longer lyrics with 'lyric magnitude and a serious subject, feelingfully meditated'. The differences between them are primarily procedural: the speech in the greater Romantic lyric is a 'fluent vernacular', and the meditation is always 'closely intervolved with the outer scene'. The latter distinction suggests to Professor Abrams that the origins of the greater Romantic lyric are to be found, not in the eighteenth-century ode, but in the 'loco-descriptive' poem which takes its bearings from Denham's *Cooper's Hill* and develops in various ways down to Bowles' *Sonnets* of 1789. That there is a large element of truth in this genealogy is immediately apparent (once we have been shown where and how to look), and Professor Abrams is surely right to direct our attention to the loco-descriptive poem in the first instance.

Yet many of the characteristic procedures and thematic concerns of the greater Romantic lyric, as exemplified in the Conversation poems, *Dejection* and the *Immortality* ode, cannot be convincingly traced to the loco-descriptive tradition. Indeed, a little reflexion on these poems and Professor Abrams' abstract might well persuade one that any comprehensive inquiry into their generic origins must be a formidable task. For it would doubtless sift the influences not merely of the ode and loco-descriptive traditions but even of literary kinds as seemingly remote as the epistolary novel and Shakespearian soliloquy. Certainly one could not ignore the development, notably in *The Task*, of a meditative blank verse capable of rendering the sinuosities of thought and feeling, the movements from outer to inner and back again, which are usual in the greater Romantic lyric. (This same blank verse seems also to have provided a touchstone for the intimate, idiomatic voice even in poems, like *Dejection*, which abandon the appearance of connectedness and seamless meditative flow in favour of an irregular stanzaic pattern which openly requires the reader to supply his own transitions and perceive that much of the action of the poem occurs between and around fragments of verse.) Nor is this all. But to explore all or even many of the possible generic tributaries is as far beyond the practical limits of my own as it was of Professor Abrams' inquiry, and I must follow his example of tracing a single major branch—that of the eighteenth-century ode—which I take to be no less of an influence than the loco-descriptive poem on the greater Romantic lyric. I shall argue that something more specific and informative than 'lyric magnitude and a serious subject, feelingfully mediated' was intended, at least by the first generation of Romantic poets, when the authors of greater Romantic lyrics called them 'odes', and that even when called 'Lines' or 'Stanzas' this kind of poem was structurally and stylistically indebted to the eighteenth-century ode.

Thus to argue is certainly not to deny that the blurring and breakdown of generic categories during the eighteenth century was a phenomenon at least as important and extensive as the attempts, by poet after poet, to master the ancient literary kinds—to bend the bow of Ulysses. But no study which ignores that ambition can come fully to terms with the poetry written by men who grew up during the eighteenth century and were educated by scholars like James Bowyer. In spite of his tales of 'effusions' and the opium muse, Coleridge was a deliberate artist who discovered freedom within the constraints of inherited literary conventions. Quite as warmly as other learned poets before him—Jonson, Milton, Gray—Coleridge responded to the standing challenge presented by the great traditional kinds: Osorio, The Ancient Mariner and such fine sonnets as To Asra and Work Without Hope are among his obvious responses to this challenge.[4] No traditional kind fascinated young Coleridge so much as the 'greater ode'. He wrote odes in English, odes in Greek; plagiarized odes from the German; parodied odes on various occasions; and used the irregular 'Pindaric' strophe with clear emblematic intent in three poems about poetic power and its loss—Monody on the Death of Chatterton, Kubla Khan and Dejection: An Ode. And yet until very recently commentators have generally ignored what I take to be the first and most basic piece of information about Dejection: that it is called 'An Ode' and is in fact a variant of the eighteenth-century English greater ode.[5]

That little has been made of the kind of poem Dejection proclaims itself to be is perhaps not so surprising after all, since the apparently spontaneous, confessional nature of the poem—an appearance strongly reinforced by de Selincourt's discovery of the 'original' letter version—does not square very well with our notions of neoclassical imitation. Nor is the difficulty merely sentimental. Coleridge the critical theorist, which is to say the later Coleridge, is partly to blame for our initial reluctance to read the poem as an ode. For even if we do not accept (or fully understand) his theory of the Imagination, we do generally accept several of its organicist corollaries. Surely we all agree that 'there is a difference between form as proceeding, and shape as superinduced;—the latter is either the death or the imprisonment of the thing;—the former is its self-witnessing and self-effected sphere of agency'.[8] This proposition was never meant to underwrite departures from poetic convention so radical as those in, say, Olson's *Maximus* poems, but it might well lead us to expect a high degree of improvisation in Coleridge's own poetry. Nor are we altogether disappointed. Not only did he cultivate the illusion of improvisation and spontaneity in his poetry—the Conversation poems depend on that illusion being sustained—but he used inherited forms with great freedom and inventiveness, and his discovery of the greater Romantic lyric, which occurred when he transformed 'Effusion 35' into *The Eolian Harp*, is a perfect example of 'form as proceeding'. He *did* sometimes improvise as well as create the illusion of improvisation. And we rightly feel that he would not have been a poet at all, certainly not a great and seminal poet, if his poems had been no more than brilliant rhetorical contrivances fulfilling the generic prescriptions of another age.

Nonetheless, the Schellingesque formulations of 1817 or 1818 can be seriously misleading about Coleridge's practice fifteen years earlier and generally about the characteristic strategies and expectations of the literature of Sensibility. For him as for his predecessors the greater ode was not merely a major neoclassical kind with various prescribed conventions: it was the neoclassical kind which prescribed imaginative departures from the logical, the regular and the mundane. It thus maximized (in theory, anyway) the creative tension between licence and order, innovation and tradition, that characterizes all successful art. In the case of *Dejection* there were the most compelling reasons, personal as well as literary, why this tension could not be relaxed.

I do not wish to suggest that *Dejection* is a greater ode (or, as Coleridge would have it, a 'sublimer Ode'') in the way that *France: An Ode* and *Ode to the Departing Year* so flamboyantly are. On the

181

contrary, to insist that *Dejection* is an ode is partly to insist on an ironic contrast with such poems. Coleridge himself did so, by implication, when he arranged for *France: An Ode* to be republished in the *Morning Post* on 14 October 1802, ten days after the first publication of *Dejection*. But a sad ironic contrast is only part, and not the largest part, of the story. For *Dejection* does utilize many of the strategies and thematic concerns which belong to the ode. And though we are not wrong to feel that the poem, whatever Coleridge called it, has more in common with *This Lime-Tree Bower My Prison* or even *Tintern Abbey* than it has with *France: An Ode*, we should not let the matter rest there. We should remember that, in a note of 1800 Wordsworth ventured to hope that *Tintern Abbey* had 'the principal requisites' of an ode. Evidently the ode meant more and other things to them than it does to us, and it behooves us to find out what elements of the ode they salvaged in creating the greater Romantic lyric.

Moreover, the greater Romantic lyric is but one major development in nineteenth- and twentieth-century lyric form which takes its departure from eighteenth-century poetics and practical experimentation—and from the 'neoclassical' ode especially because it so often provided both doctrine and *exemplum* for those poetics. The ode is thus central to our understanding not only of the literature of Sensibility but also of much subsequent poetry which cannot be helpfully described in Abrams' terms. *Dejection*, as the last great (and arguably greatest) poem in the eighteenth-century ode tradition, is a principal bridge between this tradition and extended lyrics as remote as *When Lilacs Last in the Dooryard Bloom'd* and *The Waste Land*.

2

At this point, it may be useful to outline the discussion which follows; for it covers extensive ground and not always by straight marches. As in previous chapters my approach to *Dejection* is to place one of its major aspects within an extended context of developing historical usage. Once again the emphasis is on the usage of the century in which Coleridge grew to maturity and wrote all of his great poems except *Dejection*. However, I also move backward in time to look at the chief classical models of the eighteenth-century ode. Because generic continuity and change can scarcely be understood in isolation, some notice must be taken of the changing social functions of literature as well. In this connexion I circle back to such earlier topics as the Neoplatonist tradition in eighteenth-century poetry and the exalted self-image of the poet as joyous harmonist and *poète maudit*.

Section 3 explains briefly how and why eighteenth-century theorists polarized lyric form into 'greater' and 'lesser' odes. Section 4, an analysis of the lesser ode and its Horatian model, works largely as a foil to section 5, a longer and more particularized account of Pindar and the English Pindaric tradition. After showing that, in several important features of theme, structure and especially characterization of the poet, the greater ode may be considered authentically Pindaric, I go on in section 6 to suggest that it transmits these features both to the Conversation poems and the 'Romantic' odes of Coleridge, Wordsworth and Shelley. However, in view of the unprecedented importance of landscape in the Conversation poems and *Dejection*, my discussion returns in section 7 to the eighteenth century to document the frequent unions of ode and topographical poem and the mediating influence of the Psalms.

3

Eighteenth-century critics devised various schemes of classification for the various subcategories of ode which, from Cowley and Dryden to Collins and Gray, dominated the field of English lyric poetry. Much the most useful for my purposes is also the most general, simple and customary one—of 'greater' and 'lesser' odes. This is the scheme adopted by Dr. Johnson for his *Dictionary* definition of 1755: 'the ode is either of the greater or less kind. The less is characterised by sweetness and ease; the greater by sublimity, rapture, and quickness of transition'. As we shall see, this definition perpetuates an ancient tendency to deal with the subject in bold dichotomous terms, making the distinction between 'greater' and 'less' intelligible by marking the extremes and omitting the middle. A more adequate (but scarcely dictionary-length) definition of what the ode meant to the Age of Sensibility would continue to reflect the felt dichotomy between major categories of ode while acknowledging the existence of ancient and modern odes, some of them among the finest ever written, which are characterized by neither 'sweetness' nor 'sublimity' but by something more akin to the Roman *gravitas* or Miltonic 'melancholy'.

A useful starting point is the scheme of classification devised by Hugh Blair for his frequently reprinted *Lectures on Rhetoric and Belles Lettres* (1783). Blair's scheme is based on relative elevation of 'matter' and 'character':[8]

All Odes may be comprised under four denominations. First, Sacred Odes; Hymns addressed to God, or composed on religious subjects. Of this nature are the Psalms of David, which exhibit to us this species of Lyric Poetry in its highest degree of perfection. Secondly, Heroic Odes, which are employed in the praise of heroes, and in the celebration of martial exploits and great actions. Of this kind are all Pindar's Odes, and some few of Horace's. These two kinds ought to have sublimity and elevation, for their reigning character. Thirdly, Moral and Philosophical Odes, where the sentiments are chiefly inspired by virtue, friendship, and humanity. Of this kind, are many of Horace's Odes, and several of our best modern Lyric Productions; and here the Ode possesses that middle region, which, as I observed, it sometimes occupies. Fourthly, Festive and Amorous Odes, calculated merely for pleasure and amusement. Of this nature, are all Anacreon's; some of Horace's; and a great number of songs and modern productions, that claim to be of the Lyric species.

That Blair and other eighteenth-century theorists considered sacred hymns at one end of the lyric scale and Anacreontic drinking songs at the other to be 'odes' at all might come as a surprise to readers whose expectations have been formed by reading the most famous English odes, including those of the eighteenth century. Strictly speaking, of course, 'ode' originally meant any kind of poem intended to be sung, chorally or monodically, and the greatest age of English Christian hymnody was not likely to permit that meaning to be lost. Certainly the theory and actual composition of the odes in Blair's second and third categories—the only kinds of lyric poem we should unhesitatingly call odes today—were influenced by eighteenth-century studies of the Psalms, and since this influence extended to Coleridge and Wordsworth as well I shall return to it in a later section of this chapter.

Though displaced by Christian piety from the first category, Pindar's odes were clearly 'Sacred' as well as 'Heroic' in matter and hence sublime as well as elevated in character. In them the eighteenth century perceived the prototypical greater ode and fit model for the treatment of any topic, from the King's birthday to a romantic chasm, that was supposed to be elevated and/or sublime. So far as the best poets of the period were concerned, the favoured theme of the greater ode was the authentically Pindaric theme of the power of music and poetry, and it was poems treating it—Dryden's *Alexander's Feast* preëminently, rivalled briefly by Gray's *The Bard*—which were generally reckoned to be the greatest of English greater odes. In comparison with such odes, all other lyric kinds (except sacred hymns, of course) had to be relegated to the category of lesser odes—lesser, though in some cases dignified by the rumour or reality of classical antecedents. However, a subcategory that ranges from grave moral rumination to drinking song is so extended as to be nearly useless, and we badly need Blair's narrower third category of 'Moral and Philosophical Odes'—lyric poems that occupy a 'middle region' and are exemplified by 'many of Horace's Odes, and several of our best modern Lyric Productions'. An earlier and more influential theorist than Blair, the poet Edward Young, described such odes by means of an eighteenth-century metaphorical commonplace adapted, as we shall shortly see, from Horace himself:[9]

> The Roman ode
> Majestic flow'd;
> Its stream divinely clear and strong;
>   In sense and sound,
>   Thebes roll'd profound;
> The torrent roar'd, and foam'd along.

Among the modern poems Blair probably had in mind were Gray's *Ode on a Distant Prospect of Eton College* and Collins' *Ode to Evening*. Though to the post-Wordsworthian temper of mind (which they helped create) these odes seem more truly elevated and sublime for not straining after these attributes and not dealing with gods and heroes, clearly they belong to a middle region in terms both of Blair's hierarchies and the claims they implicitly make for poetry and poets. At the same time, though they lack the sublime *frisson* essential to the greater ode, obviously they have more in common with that kind than with the slight 'Festive and Amorous Odes' of Blair's lowest category. Indeed, to eighteenth-century eyes these last appeared so humbly remote from the greater ode as scarcely to deserve the appellation 'ode', and in many discussions of the genre they seem to have been included only as an academic afterthought. In casual usage the word 'ode' tended increasingly to mean what we mean by it, while the distinction that mattered (partly because it wasn't always obvious) was between Pindaric greater odes and the *comparatively* lesser odes of Blair's third category.

When the distinction is made at a level of abstraction so high and with reference solely to subject matter and general 'character', its relevance to the history of poetry (rather than the history of literary theory) is perhaps not immediately apparent. Yet subsumed under these broad generic categories are many ancient and fundamental differences of poetic principle, rhetorical strategy and formal procedure which continue to matter to poets and serious students of poetry. And if the contrasts which the greater/lesser formula invites often strike us as over-bold and schematic, we may recall in extenuation that Horace himself provided model and partial sanction when he replied in these terms to a suggestion that he write a Pindaric ode in honour of Augustus:[10]

Pindarum quisquis studet aemulari,
Iulle, ceratis ope Daedalea
nititur pinnis, vitreo daturus
    nomina ponto.

monte decurrens velut amnis, imbres
quem super notas aluere ripas,
fervet inmensusque ruit profundo
    Pindarus ore,

laurea donandus Apollinari,
seu per audacis nova dithyrambos
verba devolvit numerisque fertur
    lege solutis . . .

multa Dircaeum levat aura cycnum,
tendid, Antoni, quotiens in altos
nubium tractus: ego apis Matinae
    more modoque,

grata carpentis thyma per laborem
plurimum, circa nemus uvidique
Tiburis ripas operosa parvos
    carmina fingo.

Whoever endeavours, O Iulus, to rival Pindar, makes an effort on wings formed of wax, by art Daedalian, about to communicate his name to the azure sea. Like a river, pouring down a mountain, when sudden rains have increased it beyond its accustomed banks; such the deep-mouthed Pindar rages and rushes on immeasurable; sure to merit Apollo's laurel, whether he rolls down *his* new-formed terms thro' the daring dithyrambic, and is born on in numbers exempt from rule. . . . A strong air elevates the Dircean swan, O Antonius, as often as he soars into the lofty regions of the clouds: *but* I, after the custom and manner of the Matinian bee, that laboriously gathers the grateful thyme, I, a diminutive creature, compose elaborate verses about the grove and the banks of the watry Tibur. (Trans. Christopher Smart.)

It is true that Horace is very misleading about Pindar's tumultuous irregularity and his own humble craftsmanship, but the historical interest and importance of his comparison are nonetheless great. The images developed in this ode, between aspiring Icarus and artful Daedalus, mountain torrent and calm Tiber, swan and bee, inspiration and toil, together form a paradigmatic and immensely influential expression of the rival views of poetic creativity which later theorists were to label Dionysian and Apollonian or Longinian and Aristotelian. In this connexion we may recall that Longinus' praise of Pindar (quoted as an epigraph to this chapter) also makes him the very prototype of the Icarian poet, soaring marvellously but at great risk—a comparison not likely to be overlooked by Coleridge or the other young writers of the Age of Sensibility who sought a poetic form adequate to their conception of poetic glory and fate. Thus associated with archetypal images of aspiration and sublimity, the *idea* of Pindar had the primitive appeal of myth to the eighteenth-century imagination and likewise the Gulliverish power of myth both to magnify and minimize distinctions—as for instance between the actual poetic practices of Horace and Pindar or between those of Pindar and his English imitators.

So much must be allowed, as also that the eighteenth century groped after Pindar in a dusk of philological, rhetorical and social historical misinformation. Yet it is true as well that the major English ode writers from Dryden to Coleridge (and especially Gray and his circle) were scholar-poets who understood Horace tolerably well and brought a poet's opportunistic insight to the task of understanding Pindar. As the recent case of Ezra Pound has demonstrated, such poets tend sometimes to 'improve' their originals out of recognition but also sometimes to intuit actual meanings and poetic manoeuvres in advance of philologists.[11] Therefore, while it is beyond the scope of this essay and of my own competence to gauge the precise margins of error in eighteenth-century readings of the Pindaric and Horatian texts, I shall venture to assume that poets like Gray and Collins discovered something more in them than their own reflections or the mythic images projected by Longinus and Horace himself. What, if we put aside these images in favour of formalistic analysis, are some of the more obvious traits of their ancient models which reappear with more or less consistency in eighteenth-century lesser and greater odes? What light is thrown on these traits by the vastly different social contexts in which the poems were written?

4

A professional poet who wrote in a cosmopolitan age, Horace enjoyed the literate as well as generous patronage of those at the centre of imperial power. He did many literary things superlatively well and transmitted to later ages a variety of poetic models ranging in style and function from verse epistles to a solemn choral ode commissioned for the Augustan revival of the secular games. There is no such thing as 'the Horatian ode'; rather, there are various kinds of odes written by Horace, chiefly in adaptation of Greek lyrics as different from each other as Anacreontic banquet songs and Pindarizing victory odes. The 'Matinian bee' visited many flowers besides the homely thyme and soared, when he chose, far beyond the Tiber valley. Yet without denying that diversity is an essential feature of Horace's achievement as of his influence on later poets, we can recognize certain attitudes and images, favourite strophic and structural patterns, as characteristic. The odes that English readers have tended to cherish as especially 'Horatian' are secular, Epicurean and intimate (though never confessional) in tone: an urbane voice from a leafy retreat. The typical movement of these odes is a suave linear progression towards a rhetorical goal which, if often not the one anticipated by the reader, is nonetheless reached by a clear path of moral suasion and familiar imagery. Good examples are the beautiful spring odes (I, iv and IV,

vii) which begin as joyful celebrations of the rebirth of vegetation but shift, suddenly yet smoothly enough, to darkened thoughts of human mortality and the need to live while we may, and then conclude wryly and almost inconsequentially as if deliberately to blur the boundary between our experience of the poem and our experience afterward. The general impression of compactness, elegant simplicity and control in Horace's odes is created partly by the (predominantly Alcaic and Sapphic) monostrophic pattern of four fairly short lines which occurs in a majority of them.

This summary description is highly selective to be sure, but it is not arbitrary in that it focusses on those elements of Horatian odes which are least 'Pindaric'. Although the elements they shared —such as a common indebtedness to the ancient forms of prayer —may have been of great structural or thematic importance in Horace's lyric poetry, these would have seemed less strikingly 'Horatian' to an age which was rediscovering Pindar. It was partly for this reason that the most purely Horatian of English odes written in imitation of Horace were those of seventeenth-century poets like Marvell, who wrote well before English taste and ambition in lyric poetry were reformed on a rich diet not merely of Pindar but also of Longinus, Shakespeare, Spenser, Percy's *Reliques*, and above all Milton. Yet the Horatian influence on eighteenth-century lyric poetry was no less pervasive for being strangely mixed. Horace himself had expanded the range and variety of Latin poetry by domesticating many Greek lyric forms, and eighteenth-century poets in their turn found him a congenial and accommodating model for lyric poetry of various 'levels'—levels extending upwards from drinking songs to the hymns of Addison and Wesley. Here, however, we are concerned with lyrics of the 'middle region', and I should like to comment briefly on the two famous odes I have already mentioned as among the 'modern Lyric Productions' Blair probably had in mind when he established this category.

As its title suggests, *Ode on a Distant Prospect of Eton College* (1742) is a poem more than commonly 'elevated' in tone and subject, and it shares with the greater ode (and other neoclassical genres) various stylistic devices—allegorical personifications, Latinisms, poetical diction of a certain kind—which were to be the objects of Wordsworth's censure. Are there any grounds of more than antiquarian interest for distinguishing it as a lesser rather than greater ode? The *Eton* ode is closely associated in form and theme with its immediate predecessor, *Ode on the Spring* (1742), which is unmistakably a spring ode in the Horatian tradition. Moreover, the *Eton* ode was written many years before Gray's Pindaric studies and differs radically from his own as well as other English greater odes. Unlike either the highly variable Cowleyan Pindaric or later attempts to imitate the regular tripartite sequence of strophe, antistrophe and epode, the *Eton* ode's ten strophes of ten short lines each are identical in metrical and rhyme pattern. Such symmetry, which affects both ear and eye, tells us at once that this is no bravura Christmas tree of a poem, as much visual bardic emblem and ornament as verbal construct. Closely related to the 'unaspiring' strophic shape of the ode is the strictly human scale of Gray's prospect on life; if the poem is 'Greek' at all, it is so in the way its sombre fatalism echoes that of the tragic choruses of Sophocles. The meditative *persona* of the *Eton* ode is not a poet celebrating the divine power of Musick and Poesy but a man moved to utterance by familiar human emotions of hope, disappointment and nostalgia:[12]

> Ah, happy hills, ah, pleasing shade,
> Ah, fields belov'd in vain,
> Where once my careless childhood stray'd,
> A stranger yet to pain!
> I feel the gales, that from ye blow,
> A momentary bliss bestow,
> As waving fresh their gladsome wing,
> My weary soul they seem to sooth,
> And, redolent of joy and youth,
> To breathe a second spring.

Here, fleetingly, Gray's imagery, tone and sentiment conspire to remind us of *Tintern Abbey*, the 'glad preamble' of *The Prelude* and still more of the several poems of 1802 in which Wordsworth and Coleridge arrived at their firmest reckonings of human limitation and loss. In most of these poems, including the *Eton* ode, we may also discern vestiges of the ancient *topoi* of the spring ode. The essential difference is that the joyful, then poignant, vernal landscapes of Horace—and even those of Gray—seem never to have been apparelled in celestial light.

Strophic regularity and human scale are equally characteristic of the *Ode to Evening*. That Collins' strophe is modelled on Milton's English version of the 'Pyrrha' ode (I, v) is certainly no accident but rather a very pointed hint that this is a lesser ode. Indeed, the more closely one examines the imagery and the strophic and syntactical patterns of *Ode to Evening* the more clear it becomes that this poem was designed to be an ideal antitype of the 'tumultuous' greater ode:

> Now teach me, *Maid* compos'd,
> To breathe some soften'd Strain,
> Whose Numbers stealing thro' thy darkening Vale,
> May not unseemly with its Stillness suit,
> As musing slow, I hail
> Thy genial lov'd Return!

Like his Evening, Collins' poem is very thoroughly 'composed'; its elaborate system of verbal recurrence and balance achieves an effect of artistic completeness and repose. If we think of this effect in architectural rather than musical terms, we can see more easily why there was no place in the poem for such 'sublime' pictures from Salvatore Rosa as these:[18]

> Then let me rove some wild and heathy Scene,
> Or find some Ruin 'midst its dreary Dells,
> Whose Walls more awful nod
> By thy religious Gleams.

These are scenes which might well appear in a greater ode (as they do in Stanza VII of *Dejection*) not merely because they are sublime but because the 'Ruin . . . Whose Walls more awful nod' is an architectural analogue of the variety of greater ode (like *Kubla Khan* and *Dejection*) which suggests arrested motion and composition still in process by being fragmentary and imperfectly finished.

Collins' excision of this passage raises more general questions concerning his principles of inclusion and exclusion in this poem. Why, in an ode to evening, does he leave out so many characteristic evening scenes—especially peopled scenes—that would have been altogether appropriate in a lesser ode? (He refers to 'Friendship,' in the closing lines, but no friends appear in the poem.) Why, in a 'descriptive' ode, are the scenes so little localized? The short answer to these questions is, of course, that the tone and descriptive procedures of *Ode to Evening* are derived from *Il Penseroso* and are radically unlike those of loco-descriptive poetry:

Milton's 'pensive Nun' Melancholy belongs to night and shade, Collins' 'calm votress' Evening is patroness of the 'Pensive Pleasures', and both goddesses lead the solitary poets through a series of scenes which are more contiguous in mood than space, which are rather 'objective correlatives' of a state-of-mind than particularized landscapes observed on a journey or from a local vantage-point.

In this respect, too, the procedures of these poems differ from the 'prospect' openings of the *Eton* ode and the typical greater Romantic lyric. Yet just as this distinction may remind us that, Horatian antecedents notwithstanding, lesser odes are not as like as peas in a pod, so it may warn us not to expect uniform effects from personal and literary causes so diverse as those which lie behind the early greater Romantic lyrics. In *Tintern Abbey* and *This Lime-Tree Bower My Prison* there is an affirmation of the power of the mind to transcend the immediate restrictive 'prison' of the bower or of a lonely room by recalling other more restorative or elevating scenes, and it would be difficult to say which takes precedence—the adjustment of image to mood or of mood to image. This balance is lost in *The Nightingale*, where Coleridge takes Milton's 'Most musical, most melancholy' as his text for a sermon against projections of indoor moods upon Nature and on behalf of the curative powers of natural images. In *Dejection*, on the other hand, the balance is tilted in the other direction, and his several allusions to Milton's companion poems are spiritually akin to those of Collins.

However, it is not my contention that *Ode to Evening* or any other lesser ode much affected the earlier poetry of Coleridge and Wordsworth either as model or channel of influence. On the contrary. To the Wordsworth of *Ode to Duty* as to the Keats of *Ode on a Grecian Urn* and *To Autumn* (though for somewhat different reasons) the 'composed' qualities of the lesser ode came to have a deep appeal. But in the expansive early years of their friendship, Coleridge and Wordsworth strove for quite different qualities in their poetry—ones that called for ballad metres, blank verse and the varied strophes of the greater ode. As for the patent anticipations of theme and device to which I have called attention, these are less important as straightforward 'influences' than as striking examples of ways a generically minded age sought to infuse new life in old forms. Though they had their own distinctive decorum and formal conventions, both lesser and greater odes readily assimilated other literary kinds (such as the epithalamion or pastoral elegy, distinguished by a special 'matter' rather than a special verse form) and appropriated organizational devices from various sources in poetry, prose and the other arts (such as the prospect, progress or excursion). Clearly, this process of grafting and cross-breeding cannot have escaped the notice of Wordsworth and Coleridge, but it was a characteristic of the literature of the age rather than of the lesser ode particularly. This being so, we have to expect 'influence' to flow through numerous and sometimes obscure channels. Though the second stanza of the *Eton* ode may well have been suggestive, the loco-descriptive tradition also exerted its influence directly through Dyer's *Grongar Hill* and, as Abrams maintains, indirectly through Bowles' River Itchin sonnets. So far as the spring ode is concerned, the possible models ancient and modern were legion, and for Coleridge the most recent and affecting instance of the kind—if we leave the *Immortality* ode out of account—must have been Perdita Robinson's *To Spring* (1800). On the other hand, the influence of *L'Allegro* and *Il Penseroso* on *Dejection* may have been direct:[14]

Might startle this dull pain

And singing startle the dull night   (*L'Allegro*, l. 42)

Or pine-grove whither woodman never clomb

      me Goddess bring
To arched walks of twilight groves,
And shadows brown that Sylvan loves
Of pine, or monumental oak,
Where the rude axe with heaved stroke
Was never heard   (*Il Penseroso*, ll. 132–37)

As for the 'Hence!' formula with which Coleridge opens his seventh stanza, who can say whether it derives from the Companion poems or from eighteenth-century imitations?

5

In nothing, indeed, are Collins, Gray and other poets of the Age of Sensibility so like the Coleridge of *Dejection* as in their constant awareness of the example of Milton. Here however I must reverse the current of my argument and point out that, pervasive as Milton's influence was, there was a particular literary kind—the greater ode—in which the hagiographical figure (as distinct from the poetic practice) of Milton loomed especially large. As patron saint and martyr of the English sublime, he was the exemplary hero of Collins' *Ode on the Poetical Character* (a poem which 'inspired & whirled' young Coleridge[15]) and the peer of Shakespeare and Pindar in Gray's *The Progress of Poesy*. It is in the context of this tradition that Coleridge's Miltonizing and other, perhaps more important, formal and thematic features of *Dejection* come into focus at last.

Many of the leading characteristics of the greater ode have already been noticed in the course of discussing the lesser ode. For eighteenth-century poets and theorists normally thought of these kinds of ode as paired elemental opposites, the one calling up the other by inevitable association and consequently with exaggerated emphasis on their differences rather than their likenesses. Longinus and Horace himself were largely responsible for this tendency and for what may be called the myth of 'Pindar' as the very type of the high-flying 'irregular' genius aspiring beyond mortal limits and therefore in constant danger of a fall. Influential as the myth was, however, it is my contention that eighteenth-century poets were not wholly blind to certain important formal and thematic elements in Pindar's odes and that these elements, together with some belonging to the myth, were eventually bequeathed to Romantic and Symbolist lyric poetry in England and America. What were these elements? What connexion, if any, is there between the social function of Pindar's odes and that of the major odes in the English Pindaric tradition?

Unlike those of Horace, the surviving odes of Pindar are all of one kind: choral odes which were accompanied by music and dance and performed in conjunction with the Panhellenic games held in honour of the principal Greek deities. Though deriving from and retaining many of the formal and thematic properties of cult hymns, the 'Pindaric' odes were basically secular poems commissioned by wealthy and often princely patrons as the traditional climax of their victory celebrations after the games. Eduard Fraenkel writes: 'Some kind of festival song had probably its fixed place in any such celebration, but it was a matter of chance, and depended in a large measure on the social and economic situation of the victor and his family, whether a famous poet could be induced to compose the ἐπινίκιον. However, whether great works of poetry or products of simple craftsmanship, the poems written for such an occasion formed an organic element in the life of the society which gave rise to their production'.[16] On such occasions there was a momentary community between poetry and music, religion, athletics, wealth and political power; and it was the poet as indispensable professional encomiast who made this moment occur. As the greatest and most courted professional of his kind, Pindar may have achieved a unique independence in his relations with his patrons and the rest of society. At any rate, it is as the frank counselor and efficacious priest no less than as the immortal and immortalizing poet-composer that he appears in his own odes. When eighteenth-century writers call him the 'prince of poets', the metaphor they use to indicate his qualitative rank among poets alludes also to his princely bearing and honoured position in the social order of his age.

Yet we must not forget that Pindar's was a public art of encomiastic poetry governed by rhetorical conventions which may have included, as certainly they would have been enforced by, a mask of haughty independence. Indeed, the social function and mode of presentation of Epinician odes might seem to belie much more than Pindar's independence. The late Elroy Bundy has argued that Pindar's art, by its very nature, 'is hostile to personal, religious, political, philosophical and historical references that might interest the poet but do nothing to enhance the glory of a given patron, hostile to abruptness in transitions, to gross irrelevance, to lengthy sermonizing, to literary scandals and embarrassments, hostile in short to all the characteristics of style and temper that we ascribe to Pindar'.[17] Whether Bundy overstates his compelling and revolutionary case is beside the point of the present inquiry. What does matter here is that while some of these characteristics of style and temper were doubtless ascribed to Pindar out of ignorance or wishful thinking and may now be seen to have no objective existence in the poetic texts or the cultural order of fifth-century Greece, others really were present either as individual traits or as generic conventions well understood by his audience. Among the latter are Pindar's seeming digressions and what R. W. B. Burton describes as the 'formulae of break-off and transition which have their counterpart, with variations of metaphor, not only in Pindar's own works but also in Bacchylides. . . ."[18] Such devices point, beyond the exigencies of encomiastic poetry, to the origin of such 'Pindaric' devices as the prophetic vision and concluding prayer, and perhaps too of the circular structure, which are to be found in many of the odes.[19]

How far Pindar's authority as encomiast depends on them and on the priestly character that goes with them may be observed in the first Nemean ode, well known to eighteenth-century readers through the translations of Gray's friend Gilbert West and the famous scholar-poet Sir William Jones. This ode, composed in honour of the veteran soldier Chromius of Aetna, opens with customary praise of the patron's homeland and victory and then deals somewhat more particularly with his hospitality and his capacity as a man of action. At this point, half way through the poem, Pindar shifts by means of a rapid yet plausible transition-by-association to the story of Heracles' birth and Tiresias' prophetic account of the demigod's subsequent exploits and wedding feast:[20]

> Then straight he calls th' unerring seer,
> Divine Tiresias, whose prophetic tongue
> Jove's sacred mandates from the Tripod sung;
> Who then to all th' attentive throng explain'd
> What fate th' immortal gods for Hercules ordain'd.

The different degrees of conviction with which they treat Tiresias' prophecy may perhaps be gauged by West's addition of a prop—the tripod—which Pindar found unnecessary. However, West is sufficiently inward with Pindar's art to recognize the unstated yet all-important parallels between Chromius and Heracles and likewise between Pindar and his fellow-Theban Tiresias. Without such a recognition the second half of the ode would necessarily seem something of a *non sequitur*; for the ode ends, most untypically, with the myth section and there are no further explicit references to Chromius or his achievements. Yet Pindar evidently expected his audience to draw the correct inferences; an expectation which implies that its members had a remarkably instructed grasp of the indirections and associative leaps usual in this kind of poetic discourse. Or perhaps he only expected many of them to be preoccupied with the spectacle or awed by the solemn ritualistic appeals to family, patriotic and above all religious feelings. In any event, by making Tiresias' prophecy his own, Pindar pays not only Chromius but himself a splendid compliment, and it is obviously essential to his encomiastic design that he be accepted by his audience in the dramatic character of infallible seer-priest.

I call attention to the source of a number of Pindar's structural and rhetorical devices, including the seer-priest *persona*, in order to stress their adaptability. To be sure, merely local conventions there were in the Epinician odes—such as the introductory naming of the victor or the formulary sequence of parts—which seem to have been developed to suit the needs or expectations of a particular, perishable audience and occasion. These have not travelled well and attempts to reproduce them, either in defiance or ignorance of major cultural variables, strike us today as very pedantically 'neoclassical'. The same may be said of attempts to replicate other potentially more naturalizable Pindaric devices too closely or too completely. However, the more serious aims of neoclassical imitation generally, and of English Pindaric imitations in particular, were opposed to this sort of anachronism. Stated simply and optimistically, imitation sought to re-embody constants of theme and form whose presence in ancient literature could alone explain its enduring power to move and instruct. This was an ideal based on the assumption that 'Nature' was 'One clear, unchanged, and universal light', only maybe rather clearer in the simpler 'happier days' of Homer or Pindar than in modern times.[21] In practice, poets of the eighteenth and late seventeenth centuries were frequently less optimistic about the possibility of successful imitation than we might suppose: partly because of their extensive experience of the difficulties of translating the Greek and Roman classics and partly because of their growing awareness of the cultural gap between modern and ancient civilizations. Dryden and Pope constantly and deliberately substituted felicities of their own for what seemed the inimitable graces of Virgil and Homer; scholars like West began the still-unfinished task of placing Pindar in his social context, accounting for at least some of his obscurities and apparent eccentricities by reference to customs and occasions long since disappeared from view. As for conditions in their own time, these might appear—depending on the social, political and religious perspectives of the authors concerned—both more and less favourable to imitation of the great classical models.

And of course the conditions, all sorts of conditions impinging on the writing of poetry, did vary enormously during the century and a half of the English Pindaric Revival. If we consider but one of them—the extent to which school and university education equipped poets from Cowley to Coleridge to scan or construe Pindar's odes with any accuracy—we shall begin to see why not one but several distinct versions of the Pindaric ode were current during this period. Indeed, Pindar doubtless commended himself as a model partly because he was not well understood and especially at the beginning of the Revival appeared a most heterogeneous mixture of measured public ceremony and incoherent subjective lyricism. Depending on temperamental and other needs as much as on the scope and refinement of their scholarship, English Pindarists tended in their imitations to develop real or imaginary *aspects* of their model rather than try to do everything that Pindar was alleged to do. In turn, these very partial versions acquired the status of models in their own right, and, because they did answer some of the abiding needs of English poetry and society, imitations of them flourished long after their infidelity to Pindar had been exposed.

The most notorious example of such persistence is the irregular 'Pindarique' ode originated by Abraham Cowley. Now, in fact, Cowley's Pindaric imitations are written in various verse forms and on various themes: perhaps the best of them, *The Extasie*, is a monostrophic poem of religious vision which reminds one that its author was a contemporary of Milton rather than of Dryden. Quite explicitly not a poem of public encomium, *The Extasie* does nevertheless represent Pindar's prophetic and visionary aspect as faithfully as could be desired of a mid-seventeenth-century English Pindarism is associated mainly with misreadings which led him to compose some of his odes in sequences of unlike strophes —a pattern or lack of pattern which seemed altogether in character with the Pindar of Horatian–Longinian myth. Although Cowley's mistake was corrected by Congreve in a well-known essay of 1706,[22] eighteenth- and early nineteenth-century poets continued to make use of a licensed irregularity which, besides being emblematic of gusty inspiration, gave them more expressive freedom (or at least more obvious expressiveness) than a more uniform pattern allowed. In the case of *Dejection* and possibly of *Kubla*

Khan we have also to bear in mind that the circumstances of writing did not lend themselves to perfect symmetry, but it would be difficult to say where accident ends and rhetoric begins in poems calculated to suggest spontaneity and composition still in progress.

English poets also had need of a vehicle for the praise of great men and events: what model for a poem on the occasion of the King's birthday more suitably royal than an Epinician ode? Greater odes of this category generally exude confidence in the excellence of contemporary British civilization and in the mutually fostering relationship between poetry and society. One that does and that I shall discuss in more detail later is Edward Young's *Ocean: An Ode* (1728), written in celebration of British naval and mercantile triumphs under George II. Protestant, nationalistic and warmly appreciative of the achievements of modern science, Young had no difficulty affirming the greatness and goodness of his age or the appropriateness of a Pindaric model for poems eulogizing its accomplishments. Not that the future friend of Richardson and author of *Conjectures on Original Composition* believed in slavish copying of the ancients; but, also the sometime protégé of Addison, he did believe in imitation as defined above and in judicious encomia upon the establishment.

To other observers, however, who were perhaps less content with the political-religious *status quo* or who might have experienced the hardships of Grub Street authorship, it sometimes appeared that the engrossing prestige of the mathematical and experimental sciences was rather threatening than otherwise and that there was an increasing tendency in English life to measure all things by the standards of the market economy. The very greatest poets writing during the first century of the Pindaric Revival wrote from a position of political retirement and felt spiritual exile during their declining years, and as the eighteenth century wore on a feeling that the times were out of sympathy with poetry grew widespread among authors who lacked the political grievances of Milton, Dryden and Pope. Commentators recalled the neglect of Dryden and Milton and the still more ghastly—if apocryphal—end of Otway, and certainly the incidence of destitution, suicide and madness among eighteenth-century poets argues that it was a period of uncommon disorientation and, not infrequently, despair for them. The 'pole-star of the ancients' seemed more than ever needful as a guide; yet often the most that seemed feasible was an ironic or wistful adaptation of the old devices and conventions to circumstances quite unlike those which had variously nurtured the geniuses of Pindar, Horace or, closer to home, Shakespeare and the younger Milton.

It is not surprising that in these circumstances many poets turned from the praise of 'great' men and their doings to encomiums of poets and the powers of poetry; nor that the Pindaric ode became the chosen model for poems seeking to revive the ancient prestige and morale of the dejected muse. For, as we have seen, the 'prince of poets' had made the highest possible claims for both poets and poetry, representing himself as an inspired prophet and poetry-wedded-to-music as a power in human affairs analogous to the divine power of harmony with which Zeus governed the universe. These topics were far from exclusively Pindaric in origin or provenance and had indeed a venerable history of usage in all the major literatures of Europe. But they were taken up with fresh conviction and/or rhetorical verve in a series of odes written for cantata performance at St. Cecilia's Day celebrations. Purcell wrote music for several of these odes, while Dryden, Addison and Pope contributed texts.[23] Of course Pindar would have found the musical harmonies of these Cecilian odes as strange to his ears as the words which made poetry-and-music and poet-composers both the means and object of eulogy. Yet these odes for music were his true progeny, and it is unfortunate that, excepting Dryden's, the best of them lack the poetic interest and power of two mid-eighteenth-century odes by Collins and Gray which treat the same topics but were not written for musical setting. In reading them, we should bear in mind that by 1746 and 1754, the respective dates of *Ode on the Poetical Character* and *The Progress of Poesy*, the cosmological basis of the World Harmony tradition had long since been exploded by the New Science, and the Spenserian–Miltonic idiom of both poems sounded decidedly archaic: the music we hear is of another age when—so the ancient and recurrent legend runs—poets were more skilled, poetry and music more potent.

The Progress of Poesy opens with a restatement (in places a translation) of Pindar's most famous celebration of the power of harmony in the first Pythian ode, and it is manifestly appropriate that an ode which both traces the progress of poetry and sings its praises as a heavenly boon to mankind should begin at the source of its own tradition. However, the real hero of Gray's poem, as of the earlier *Ode on the Poetical Character*, is Milton —the sublime, epic Milton, as might be expected, but also the visionary young lyricist of *At a Solemn Music* whose glimpse of 'the sapphire-coloured throne' in a musical ecstasy seems also to be a prevision of his later and ampler views of the same scenes in *Paradise Lost*. Gray's lines on, and in imitation of, Milton are perhaps the finest of any in his greater odes:[24]

Nor second he, that rode sublime
Upon the seraph-wings of ecstasy,
The secrets of th' abyss to spy.
He pass'd the flaming bounds of place and time:
The living throne, the sapphire-blaze,
Where angels tremble while they gaze,
He saw; but, blasted with excess of light,
Clos'd his eyes in endless night.

In a note of 1768 Gray remarks a parallel with Homer's blind minstrel Demodocus, and other models have been suggested. But who can doubt that, close student of Pindar that he was, he also had in mind the blind seer Tiresias? At all events, Gray's Milton is an English reincarnation of Pindar in his twin roles of prophet and harmonist; a source of knowledge ancient, true and elevated beyond the reach even of a Newton. Mediated variously by Longinianism, World Harmony *topoi* and the contemporary belief that Greek and Hebrew poetry were alike in spirit and technique, the conflation of Pindar and Milton joined the ancient and recent past of poetry and affirmed to the Enlightenment that, in Collins's words, 'Heaven and Fancy' were and ever would be 'kindred powers'.

Yet Gray's image of Miltonic transcendence is finally ambiguous and disturbing and does not augur well for the future progress of poetry. His 'presumptuous' Milton, 'blasted with excess of light', is an overreacher like Ovid's Tiresias or Longinus' Pindar but still more like Milton's own Satan. Registered here is an ancient perception which gained new force during the Age of Sensibility: that the visionary power ascribed to poets at their loftiest might sometimes prove too great to control, blinding or deranging them by its possession and devastating them by its loss. Gray claims no such power for himself but (alluding to Horace's praise of Pindar) settles for 'mediocrity':

But ah! 'tis heard no more—
Oh! lyre divine, what daring spirit
Wakes thee now? Though he inherit
Nor the pride, nor ample pinion,
That the Theban eagle bear
Sailing with supreme dominion
Through the azure deep of air:
Yet oft before his infant eyes would run
Such forms, as glitter in the Muse's ray
With orient hues, unborrow'd of the sun:
Yet shall he mount, and keep his distant way
Beyond the limits of a vulgar fate,
Beneath the good how far—but far above the great.

Fortunate were those eighteenth-century poets who aspired no farther—far enough it was, by any sane measure of human limits or the actual achievement of poets, Pope among them, who took Horace as their principal ancient model. As a personal conclusion, therefore, these final lines of *The Progress of Poesy* are modest yet assured and seemingly free of any taint of disappointed ambition. But they cannot be taken solely as a personal conclusion, because the historical 'progress' which Gray substitutes for Pindar's myth comes down as far as Shakespeare, Milton and Dryden, and then leaps abruptly to Gray himself, who is consequently a figure in the progress as well as a personal voice. The poem thus ends, as does Collins' great ode, with a deep sense of anticlimax for English poetry. The striking difference between the conclusions of the two poems is that in Collins' case the anticlimax is also felt as intensely personal frustration. Collins avows 'high presuming hopes' for himself; Gray avows nothing of the sort but instead ascribes presumption to the sublime—but perilous—hero-model of both poems.

To many readers—probably, in fact, to most readers of poetry since 1798—these odes of Collins and Gray seem too literary by half, their image of the poet-as-superman an alienating pretension as well as a dangerous stimulant for later poets. To such readers it must also seem that, anglicizing Pindar by Miltonizing him, these mid-century odes misrepresent both poets more or less seriously and open themselves to the charge of being neither Greek nor strictly English.

These objections cannot be dismissed as simply irrelevant, but they are less just or damaging than they appear to be at first sight. Allusiveness and bardic *hauteur* belonged to this kind of poetry from the start, and the contribution of Gray and Collins was to press brilliantly to its conclusion the tendency in English Pindarism to make poetry and poets the end as well as the means of encomium. What should the diction of such poetry be if not elegantly and elaborately unlike the 'language really used by men'? This is not to maintain that, with respect to diction and the 'character' of the poet, these odes provided sound models for youthful readers and poets. English poetry could go no farther in this vein without becoming self-intoxicated, morbid or merely bizarre—which it frequently did during the years between these poems and the early masterpieces of Coleridge and Wordsworth. But the greater odes of Collins and Gray also helped make those masterpieces possible by transmitting themes and topics as well as structural and rhetorical devices which were to be of major importance in and beyond the *Lyrical Ballads*. Or if 'transmitting' implies too much of direct influence (considering how frequently Wordsworth cites Gray as an example of how *not* to write), let me say instead that in their time and language they more than others preserved and renewed the currency of formal and thematic elements belonging to what may be called, for lack of a better term, the extended epiphanic lyric: i.e. the kind of poem which in European literary tradition is especially associated with the name and practice of Pindar.[25] From this lunar perspective on literature, we may see the more clearly that, far from being simply the 'heirs' of Collins and Gray, Coleridge and Wordsworth in their time had available a host of models, earlier and later as well as better and worse, than those provided by the eighteenth century. This is true and yet, closer to earth, it is also true that starting where they did they must have found the work of mid and late eighteenth-century poets generally both more and less 'available' to them than work from other periods and languages. We know what Wordsworth very deliberately (if not always carefully) rejected in the poetry of Gray. We can now infer a little more surely what the future author of *Dejection* found so moving in *Ode on the Poetical Character*. What might they have found suggestive in the work of much less original and challenging Pindarists of the intervening generation?

Among the odes that might be chosen in illustration is one by that great scholar but less than mediocre poet, Sir William Jones. In fact a ponderously playful epithalamion, *The Muse Recalled* (1781) mimes the gestures of a 'muse poem' with calculated obviousness. Following the example of the second Olympic and first Pythian (the two Pindaric odes which appear to have been most widely admired and imitated during the eighteenth century), Jones invokes his lyre:[26]

> Return! thy golden lyre,
> Chorded with sunny rays of temper'd fire,
> Which in Astraea's fane I fondly hung,
> Bold I reclaim: but ah, sweet maid,
> Bereft of thy propitious aid
> My voice is tuneless, and my harp unstrung.
> In vain I call—what charm, what potent spell
> Shall kindle into life the long-unwakened shell?

The 'spell', once the long-winded Jones gets round to casting it, is amusingly like the more concise and effective one which concludes *Kubla Khan*:

> While, with solemn voice and slow
> Thrice pronouncing thrice I trace
> On the silken texture bright,
> Characters in beamy light,
> Names of more than mortal power,
> Sweetest influence to diffuse;
> Names that from her shadiest bower
> Draw the soft reluctant Muse.

As may be inferred from this passage, there is more of *The Rape of the Lock* than of the second Olympic throughout much of the ode, and we need not dust Jones's lengthy sub-Popean descriptions of the fair maids and flowers that decked the 'bowers of Wimbledon' when Lord Viscount Althorp married Miss Lavinia Bingham. However, Jones grows more earnest and 'Pindaric' towards the end of the poem. After reflecting briefly on the bridegroom's public career in 'this voluptuous, this abandoned age', he moves in prophetic vision to the shores of North America:

> Beyond the vast Atlantic deep
> A dome by viewless genii shall be raised,
> The walls of adamant compact and steep,
> The portals with sky-tinctur'd gems emblazed:

There on a lofty throne shall Virtue stand;
To her the youth of Delaware shall kneel;
And, when her smiles rain plenty o'er the land,
Bow, tyrants, bow beneath the avenging steel!
    Commerce with fleets shall mock the waves,
    And arts, that flourish not with slaves,
Dancing with every Grace and ev'ry Muse,
Shall bid the vallies laugh and heav'nly beams diffuse.

She ceases; and a strange delight
    Still vibrates on my ravish'd ear:
What floods of glory drown my sight!
    What scenes I view! What sounds I hear!
This for my friend—but, gentle nymphs, no more
    Dare I with spells divine the Muse recall:
Then, fatal harp, thy transient rapture o'er,
    Calm I replace thee on the sacred wall.

Obviously these are the merest formulary verses by a learned poetaster, and the convention of inspiration makes them seem the more hackneyed and flat. But a less learned, more gifted writer would not employ the 'Pindaric' devices so deliberately and nakedly, and thus would illustrate my case less clearly. Here the prayer-prophetic vision is followed by a fresh gust of inspiration (in context, a digression) which is interrupted by the formulary break-off and transition, allowing the poet to conclude the poem emphatically by circling back to his opening image. Such devices are justified by the underlying convention that the poem is a momentary surrender to forces frankly recognized at the end as unruly and dangerous, obliging the poet to check himself and return to normality. In the hands of a poet with some understanding of psychological processes, this convention and its accompanying devices could be revived to mirror those processes and create a sense of dramatic immediacy.

6

Monody on the Death of Chatterton in its 1796 version is a poem in the greater ode tradition which shows how early Coleridge grasped these possibilities:

But dare no longer on the sad theme muse,
    Lest kindred woes persuade a kindred doom:

For oh! big gall-drops, shook from Folly's wing,
Have blacken'd the fair promise of my spring;
And the stern Fate transpierc'd with viewless dart
The last pale Hope that shiver'd at my heart!

Hence gloomy thoughts!

Thus in traditional rhetoric as well as theme and poetic *persona* this early experiment with the greater ode form is a rehearsal for *Dejection*. Although the contemporary *Eolian Harp* differs so widely in tone, diction and versification from the *Monody* as to make the two poems seem scarcely by the same author or of the same species, many of the 'Pindaric' devices reappear in it as well: the circular structure, the vision which is also a digression, the abrupt break-off and transition back to normality. No prayer or vision concludes *The Eolian Harp* as it does the *Monody* and many other epiphanic poems, but there is an equivalent injunction *not* to indulge in anything of the sort but rather to stick within the bounds of humble (and apparently mindless) piety and domesticity. In subsequent developments of the Conversation poem, the radiant moment of joyous vision is of course central and the concluding prayer is a major structural device. Here we have occasion to recall Wordsworth's declaration that *Tintern Abbey* was an ode in fact though not in name. Usually, and rightly, we think of it as a poem patterned after Coleridge's Conversation poems, but Wordsworth evidently recognized the lineaments of a more ancient form behind the novel features of *Frost at Midnight* and *This Lime-Tree Bower My Prison*. At any rate, he claimed to have the ode in mind as a model while he was writing *Tintern Abbey*: 'I have not ventured to call this Poem an Ode; but it was written with a hope that in the transitions and the impassioned music of the versification would be found the principal requisites of that species of composition'.[27] He does not mention the several other characteristic devices of odes in the Pindaric tradition which are present in this Conversation poem. But they are there, so completely integrated in the movement of Wordsworth's meditative blank verse, so perfectly adapted to his intimate tone of address, that they remind us scarcely at all of their acknowledged source.

To speak of Epinician odes, eighteenth-century greater odes and Conversation poems as 'extended epiphanic lyrics' is to maintain that they share important family likenesses. And although 'the epiphanic lyric' (extended or otherwise) is a mere abstraction, an ahistorical fiction of generic theory which exists only to help us perceive relations in and between actual poems, the historical connexions I have traced in this section make 'family' something more than a casual metaphor. Yet this is not to deny that the differences between the variants are equally or perhaps more important than the likenesses. A poem written in blank verse, the tone of which is conversational at first though rapturous or elevated in prayer by the end, would be quite unlike any Epinician or greater ode even if the formal and tonal differences did not point to vast differences also in the nature of the epiphanies and the relationships between the poet and other human beings. How should it be otherwise when the poems come from social and artistic *milieux* as remote from each other as those of ancient Thebes, England under the last Stuarts and the first Hanoverians, and England after the French Revolution and the rise of Unitarianism? And when the comparison is broadened further to include several of Walt Whitman's 'chants'? That any constants of theme or form survive through so much change is evidence at least of the persistence of religious and literary culture, if not necessarily of Jungian archetypes or 'universal human nature'. What these constants amount to may become clearer from a brief comparative *résumé* of the kinds of epiphanic lyric I have discussed so far, directing attention first to those aspects of poetry which are most immediately sensitive to changes in the social environment and thereafter to those of form which are normally less so because more constrained by the environment which literary tradition itself creates.

As we have seen, Pindar in his priestly character is both of and above his audience, and his prophecies and 'inspired' narrations of the Greek myths are grounded in the religious beliefs which he and they hold in common. On the other hand, few poems of any kind can be less communal than the greater odes of Collins and Gray, and even the Cecilian odes were written for a choice audience of sympathetic musicians and literati. They follow Pindar in their celebration of the priestly or godlike power of the poet to create *ex nihilo* and control the passions—their epiphanies are typically manifestations of this power: images of genesis as in *The Muse Recalled* or *Kubla Khan* or of astonishing manipulations as in *Alexander's Feast* or the many odes which invoke the Orpheus

207

myth. But this power is felt to be as isolating as it is highly privileged. By contrast, the epiphany of a Conversation poem is a moment of ecstatic insight 'into the life of things', of oneness with the 'one Life' of God, man and nature; it is not the special experience of the poet *qua* poet but is shared with or attributed to the person addressed by him. Although the experience is enjoyed only by a spiritual elect, nobody is excluded because of modest education, social status or intellectual endowment—and certainly not because of sex. The same may be said of the intended readership of these poems, which presumably corresponds in range roughly to the range of persons addressed in them, i.e. from the two Saras to Lamb and Wordsworth. As for the poet in a Conversation poem, he continues to perform priestly offices, such as looking into the future and praying for the welfare of others; but this role is domesticated (though never quite lost) in those of husband, father, brother or friend.

What these variants of the epiphanic lyric have chiefly in common, on this showing, is that the poet in them always retains a more than vestigial priestly character and that the moments of vision which occur through his instrumentality claim ultimate source and sanction 'from above'. A slightly more detailed summary would show as well that such poems frequently account for the visionary and harmonizing powers of the poet by appealing to the traditional lore and principles of World Harmony. Were leading features of style and structure added to the sketch, it would fill out to a recognizable abstract of the poems under discussion—i.e. poems of the secular life which appropriate rhetorical strategies and much else from sacred poetry, discovering a reassuring conformity or even resemblance between certain human and divine activities and invoking protection for the human actors. But even the few and highly generalized family likenesses which have emerged thus far may help us understand what has puzzled some readers of *Dejection*: how a poem felt to be so unified can be both a 'greater ode' and a 'Conversation poem', combining visions of the 'one Life' with a bardic vision in Stanza VII, the presiding kindly presence of the 'Friend' with a brief but commanding appearance by the 'mighty Poet'. The particular means Coleridge uses to prepare for the explosive entrance of the greater ode in Stanza VII are the stanzaic pattern (of a greater ode) and meteorological portents (of a Conversation poem) at the beginning. But the union of lyric kinds achieved in *Dejection* is possible because they are of the same poetic family.

The structural and stylistic devices characteristic of these lyrics are basically methods of framing and heightening which island the poetic experience from the flow of everyday reality and authenticate the moment of vision at its centre. Some of them, notably the prayer and circular structure, have remained culturally current since antiquity; but others, such as the accompaniments of music and dance, have had to be modified or replaced altogether. One important eighteenth-century development was that landscape, so central as the occasion and anchor of the poet's meditation in Conversations poems, also acquired the rhetorical function of framing and heightening the lyric action both of these poems and many earlier greater odes as well. The Snowdonian landscape of *The Bard*, for instance, although offering little else to mind or eye, provides a sublime staging for the bard's prophecies and suicide, raising them at once well beyond the grasp of a mere lowland mentality —such as that of the medieval English king addressed by the bard, or that of Gray's brow-beaten contemporary reader. By contrast, the variable landscapes of a Conversation poem, played on by the shifting lights of weather and memory, do not oblige a reader to scale the sublime heights at a single bound; but rather, with wonderfully flexible blank verse, they raise him gently and unawares. In other respects too the greater ode's is a more demanding rhetoric than those either of its successor, the Conversation poem, or of its supposed model, the Epinician ode. I say 'supposed' because, following his commentators quite as much as Pindar himself, the authors of greater odes often pressed the traditional means of dramatizing and validating the role of the poet as seer and harmonist to extremes of discontinuity which would have bewildered Pindar's audience even more than they did many eighteenth-century readers. Coleridge and Wordsworth moderated and in some respects countered this tendency in their Conversation poems and may be said in the process to have naturalized or, better, domesticated the greater ode in English. On the other hand, the poetics of the eighteenth-century greater ode were adopted in *Dejection* and, making ever greater demands on medium and audience, in the extended symbolist lyrics of the American poetic tradition.

The developments touched on in the preceding paragraph are

far-reaching in implication and complex in provenance. But while I cannot pursue the American fortunes of the greater ode in the present essay, I must say something further concerning the new and central role of landscape in extended lyric poems—the development which led to what Professor Abrams has called the greater Romantic lyric.

7

I have shown that *Tintern Abbey* does have at least some of 'the principal requisites' of an ode in the Pindaric tradition. Although an imitation and enlargement of Coleridge's Conversation poems, its opening is less 'conversational' and therefore closer in tone to the elevated openings of greater odes; its ejaculatory 'oh's' and impetuous transitions are more frequent and striking than those in, say, *This Lime-Tree Bower My Prison*. At the same time that it is closer to the greater ode, however, in its opening panorama *Tintern Abbey* is also much more patently a descendant of the 'prospect' or 'loco-descriptive' poem than is any of Coleridge's Conversation poems except possibly *Reflections on Having Left a Place of Retirement*. Both more of an ode and more of a loco-descriptive poem, *Tintern Abbey* so lends itself to generic analysis that one wonders whether Wordsworth himself, considering how to make use of Coleridge's discoveries in a more ambitious lyric of the same kind, carried out the same analysis. That he might have done so is suggested not only by the configuration of the poem and the note he appended to it but also by his later practice of sorting poems, his own and others, into various new and traditional generic categories. At all events, different as it is in several vital respects from any greater ode or loco-descriptive poem that I know, *Tintern Abbey* does appear to be a deliberate, but by no means unique, attempt to combine the two types of poem.

Although central to the Conversation poems, to *Dejection* and to the larger category of greater Romantic lyric which subsumes them and many later poems by other writers, a meditation involving or revolving around a landscape is no necessary feature of the ancient or modern ode. But neither has landscape ever been excluded from the major kinds of ode. Both Pindar and Horace manifest a strong attachment to particular places: Horace's references to his Sabine farm and surrounding countryside are frequent and loving; Pindar's complimentary notices and invocations of his victors' home towns or territories are infused with a strong feeling for the local. Gray doubtless had these precedents in mind when he wrote the most famous union of ode and prospect poem, *Ode on a Distant Prospect of Eton College*. Yet his interest in landscape as an object either of detailed observation or sustained contemplation is little more pronounced than that of Horace and Pindar. So far from being a 'Romantic precursor' in this respect, Gray is closer to Denham (who uses landscape for political allegory) than he is to Coleridge or Wordsworth—or to the painter-poet John Dyer. To be sure, no eighteenth-century poet responds to a landscape as do Coleridge and Wordsworth in the Conversation poems and the major odes of 1802. But in the *Eton* ode, despite fleeting premonitions of Wordsworth, Gray responds *only* as a moral allegorist. We shall have to look elsewhere for a combination of ode and loco-descriptive poem which is in any meaningful sense 'proto-Wordsworthian' or 'proto-Coleridgean'. We can begin with Dyer's *Grongar Hill* (1726).

In its familiar octosyllabic couplet form, *Grongar Hill* was the most widely loved prospect poem in English. Though scarcely so important in the history of poetry as *Cooper's Hill*, Dyer's poem gave the kind a new lease on life by making it more closely observant of nature and infused with a feeling which owes much to Milton and something to Shaftesbury. Wordsworth was one of its keenest admirers.[28] Since he admired Dyer's work particularly for its 'purity of style', we can be fairly certain that he did not admire, if indeed he was even aware of, the poem in its first published version as a greater ode. What concerns us here, however, is not whether he knew the two versions and might have considered one inferior to the other, but simply that this famous loco-descriptive poem first saw light as an ode. Why? And why did Dyer then proceed immediately to trim back the exuberant Pindaric foliage into neat rows of Miltonic couplets? A short answer to the first of these questions is that the provincial Dyer was probably deflected from his natural vein by the Pindaric enthusiasms of the London coterie which first recognized his literary talents and arranged to have his poems published alongside theirs. Richard Savage and the other leading member of this group, Aaron Hill, acclaimed both Cowley's Pindaric imitations and the landscape paintings of Claude Lorrain and of Dyer himself. Hill's

The Hundred and Fourth Psalm Paraphrased, for example, is a 'painterly' rendering of the Psalm in the form of a greater ode. Compare the Authorized version of Psalm 104: 25–26 with Hill's dilation of the same passage:[29]

So is this great and wide sea, wherein are things creeping innumerable, both small and great beasts.

There go the ships: there is that leviathan, whom thou hast made to play therein.

The *Sea's* wild Herds, as well as those, of *Land*,
Rough molded *Sons*, too, of thy formful Hand!
All *live*, and *move*, by thy *Command*.
That horrid Scene fatigues the aking Eye!
There canvass'd Ships the op'ning Depths defy;
There does *Leviathan* wide-wallowing, lie!
    And, while his Sports the finny Nations fly,
Th'unwieldy Monster sucks in Seas; and spouts 'em at the Sky.

Though Hill's version is charming in its way, he had none of Dyer's slender but distinguished talent for compact description and moralizing. But he was a knowledgeable and up-to-date man of letters whose example and precepts may well have suggested the initial form of *Grongar Hill*. If at first glance it seems strange to find the greater ode serving as the common solvent of Psalm and loco-descriptive poem, we should remember that the common element of the sublime in nature—actualized in some of the Psalms and potential in topographical poetry—must have cried out for a 'modern' Pindaric treatment. Moreover, as I shall explain shortly, there were (supposedly) venerable generic links between the Psalms and the odes of Pindar.

In one important respect the ode *Grongar Hill* is closer than the couplet version to *Cooper's Hill*. Both the ode and *Cooper's Hill* somewhat irreverently stress the primacy of the imagination:[30]

Nor wonder if (advantag'd in my flight,
By taking wing from thy auspicious height)
Through untrac'd ways and airy paths I fly,
More boundless in my Fancy than my eye. . . .

Thus Denham. Dyer, in keeping with the lofty character of the Pindaric bard, apostrophizes Fancy in the first stanza:[31]

Thou! that must lend Imagination Wings,
And stamp Distinction, on all worldly Things!

and returns to the same idea in his final stanza:

Here, while on humble earth, unmarked I lie,
I subject *Heav'n* and *Nature* to my Eye. . . .

Between *Cooper's Hill* and *Grongar Hill* lie, not merely the Long-inian and Pindaric revivals, but also the reactions of Cudworth, Shaftesbury and Addison to the New Philosophy. And so in spite of his finer and more sensuous relish for the things of Nature, Dyer goes much further than Denham in his claims for the active, creative role of the imagination in conferring value on 'humble earth'. Yet because the Promethean stance was an awkward and unaccustomed one for Dyer, his ode version of *Grongar Hill* is a medley of delicately observed particulars, such as 'Faint fairy Earthquakes' of the images reflected in streams, and prospects so generalized in their sublimity that the poet's eye comes to focus, at last, not on them but on its own activity:

And, gently changing into soft and light,
[The scene] Expands immensely wide, and leads the *journeying*
Sight.

Lacking any means of bridging the gap between observation and imagination, humble and sublime, Dyer is obliged—and doubtless relieved—to scale down his claims for the role of imagination in his poem:[32]

Now, while Phoebus riding high,
Gives lustre to the land and sky!
Grongar Hill invites my song,
Draw the landskip bright and strong;
Grongar, in whose mossy cells,
Sweetly musing quiet dwells;
Grongar, in whose silent shade,
For the modest Muses made. . . .

In forsaking Pindaric self-absorption for the 'modest Muses' of topographical verse, Dyer does not become a mere copyist number-ing the stripes of the tulip, but like Phoebus gives 'lustre' to the landscape and reveals its intrinsic interest:

Wide and wider spreads the vale;
As circles on a smooth canal:

> The mountains round, unhappy fate!
> Sooner or later, of all height,
> Withdraw their summits from the skies,
> And lessen as the others rise:
> Still the prospect wider spreads,
> Adds a thousand woods and meads;
> Still it widens, widens still,
> And sinks the newly-risen hill.

This and other descriptive passages added to the octosyllabic version have a freshness and accuracy only infrequently present in the ode, but it cannot have been these qualities that led Wordsworth to remark that 'In point of *imagination*, and purity of style, I am not sure he [Dyer] is not superior to any writer in verse since the time of Milton'.[33] Although this appears to be extravagant praise, a judgment passed casually in a letter to Lady Beaumont, Wordsworth took 'imagination' and 'purity of style' too seriously to speak of their possession *altogether* casually. And it is true that the 'modest' couplet version of *Grongar Hill* is much more 'imaginative' than its strutting predecessor in precisely the ways that Wordsworth would most have appreciated. A case in point is the ambiguous grammar of the last line quoted above: is it the prospect, its widening controlled by the rising eye, that 'sinks' the hill, or is it the hill that, intransitively, sinks? The ambiguity animates the landscape while at the same time celebrating the active role of perception—a balance which Wordsworth strove to maintain.

Another and more striking example of Dyer's imagination at work in the new version occurs in his revision of a passage quoted earlier:

> And, swelling to embrace the light,
> [The scene] Spreads around beneath the sight.

The landscape is not much more distinctly visualized here than it was before, but Dyer's personification of it is rich with implications which must have struck Wordsworth. For on this occasion the early eighteenth-century landscape artist does seem to wed Heaven and Earth and mediate between Pindaric transcendence and loco-descriptive earthboundness by the same figurative means that Coleridge and Wordsworth regularly use because of their belief in 'the one Life within us and abroad'.

For a moment, then, Dyer attained the sublime of nature to which both he and Aaron Hill aspired in their Pindaric assaults on Grongar and the 104th Psalm. Yet on the whole the feeling behind most of the personifications of nature in the received text of *Grongar Hill* is more akin to the old-fashioned affection for country scenes and manners that runs through *L'Allegro* than it is to Coleridgean or Wordsworthian 'Joy'. And this is in keeping with the retrenchment of mood and style which Dyer undertook as soon as he realized that the greater ode was no fit vehicle for loco-descriptive poetry. His models for revision were Horace and the Milton of the Companion poems, and Horatian epicureanism appears to have restrained any impulse towards Miltonic or, for that matter, Shaftesburian or Addisonian ecstasies in the new poem. Moreover, because he took the prospect convention to entail description almost exclusively of what was directly present to the eye, together with such moral reflections as were prompted by the scenes in passing, Dyer in effect also denied himself the elegant concision of a Horatian ode or the subtle adjustments of image to mood which are to be found in the Companion poems, *Ode to Evening* and even the *Eton* ode. I trust it will be evident that, in describing *Grongar Hill* thus negatively, my object is to define the limits of its likely influence rather than to complain that it does not do what, after all, it had no intention of doing. For in its best passages Dyer's poem does have the qualities of 'imagination' and 'purity of style' which Wordsworth claimed for his work. So far as the question of influence is concerned, the fact that this combination of qualities is so very Wordsworthian suggests to me that Dyer's example may have been more important than that of many a greater poet. One thing is sure: Wordsworth must have observed in *Grongar Hill* how advantageously loco-descriptive poetry could assimilate stylistic elements and rhetorical forms (e.g. the Horatian 'wish', originally a Pindaric prayer, of lines 129–32) from other kinds of poetry. And notwithstanding the failure of Dyer's own over-ambitious experiment, there was no reason why the greater ode should not reverse the general trend of indebtedness and make good, if perhaps rather more limited, use of topography.

Gray's *The Bard* is one example of such usage, but there is another and earlier ode, mentioned previously in a quite different connexion, which appears to choose itself as my next exhibit. Two years after the publication of Hill's *Paraphrase* and Dyer's ode version of *Grongar Hill*, one of the subscribers to the volume in which they appeared brought out *Ocean: An Ode* together with an introductory essay 'On Lyric Poetry'. The ode, addressed to George II by Edward Young, is little better than most other odes to Augustus, but it deserves our attention here both because Coleridge certainly knew it and the accompanying essay and be-cause it further illustrates how ode, Psalm and loco-descriptive poetry rubbed off on each other—if no more than that—during the hey-day of English neoclassicism.[34] *Ocean: An Ode* begins with a prospect which recalls Dyer and a posture which anticipates Coleridge:[35]

> Sweet rural scene!
> Of flocks and green!
> At careless ease my limbs are spread;
> All nature still,
> But yonder rill;
> And listening pines nod o'er my head:

> In prospect wide,
> The boundless tide!
> Waves cease to foam, and winds to roar;
> Without a breeze,
> The curling seas
> Dance on, in measure to the shore.

Though unmistakably a greater ode, *Ocean* deviates from normal English Pindaric practice in its tripping monostrophic form. Quite as much as anything else, this unfortunate choice defeats Young's sublime intent when, in the main body of the poem, he moves ambitiously out on the great Deep to celebrate its storms, its naval battles and its usefulness to British commerce. At last, after various digressions, with a sudden shift of mood and direction he returns to refuge ashore, concluding with a moralizing prayer.

It is tempting to say that *Ocean* can only have shown Coleridge how not to write an ode, and certainly I do not wish to suggest that he ever took this clumsy monster of a poem as his model. Yet the companion essay was one he read early and recalled on at least two occasions in later years, and some of Young's manœuvres in this ode might have struck him as poetic in conception even though pedestrian in execution. Above all he might have noticed the way

Young uses a rural landscape to introduce the convention of a prospect (on Nature, on Life, on Time) and eventually to frame the lyric action. Because the ocean is Young's theatre of the Sublime, he is careful in his description of the land to avoid any but those associations which belong to the aesthetic category of the Beautiful: sweet, still, safe. Coleridge, on the other hand, while relying on essentially the same aesthetic categories and stock associations (as of ocean with sublime), also describes solitary heights of land and invests them with the sublimity of the prospect they open out for him, reserving 'beautiful' qualities for the domestic cot, nest or bower to which he retires or at least longs to retire. This difference excepted, *France: An Ode* may be said to use landscape much as *Ocean* does.

In the Conversation poems and *Dejection*, however, Coleridge continues to draw on the same associative resources but develops a descriptive technique and structural use of landscape which are distinctively his own. Whereas Young's descriptions of the 'sweet rural scene' are as stereotyped as the aesthetic properties that attach to it, Coleridge's freshly observed particulars—that thatch smoking in the sun-thaw, the green light lingering in the west—persuade us that he has actually seen and felt something beautiful or sublime. Typically in these poems the lyric action does not begin with a 'prospect' (and thus differs markedly not only from *Ocean* but also from *Tintern Abbey*) but instead moves gradually outward and upward in memory and imagination, and frequently attains the climactic moment of spiritual contemplation or prophetic vision at the precise moment that the mental journey reaches the highest point of terrestrial elevation. This is less clear in *Dejection* than in *This Lime-Tree Bower My Prison* or *Frost at Midnight* because the former is more concerned with sky-scape and weather than with topography. But the mountain scenes that open *France: An Ode*, and the moment of most perfect spiritual calm is attained when the earth-bound poet is at last able to project his own watchful concern for the Lady onto the stars looking down upon her:

> May all the stars hang bright above her dwelling,
> Silent as though they watched the sleeping Earth!

In no other poem by Coleridge are the 'low' and the 'high' so distant from each other.

Distant too are *Dejection* and *Ocean* in poetic achievement. And yet, as I have suggested, Young's ode may have taught Coleridge in his apprenticeship something about the uses of landscape in lyric poetry that benefited the Conversation poems and *France: An Ode* and, through them, *Dejection* as well. At all events, Coleridge must certainly have been struck by Young's motto for *Ocean*: 'Let the sea make a noise, let the floods clap their hands.' For he had adapted the same verse from the Ninety-eighth Psalm in a passage in *Religious Musings* which I have already quoted as an epigraph to Chapter IV. I give the passage again because of its important associations with Addison, the Psalms, and Joy:

> The favoured good man in his lonely walk
> Perceives them, and his silent spirit drinks
> Strange bliss which he shall recognize in heaven.
> And such delights, such strange beatitudes
> Seize on my young anticipating heart
> When that blest future rushes on my view!
> For in his own and in his Father's might
> The Saviour comes! While as the Thousand Years
> Lead up their mystic dance, the Desert shouts!
> Old Ocean claps his hands!

Now *Religious Musings* is not an ode but a 'desultory poem' in Miltonic blank verse; it is of a kind with *Night Thoughts* rather than with *Ocean*. Yet the rhythm, theme and diction of the passage above would be highly suitable in an ode. For according to Renaissance theories of lyric poetry which were inherited by Addison and Young, and passed on by various hands to Coleridge and Wordsworth, the Psalms of David were the Hebrew equivalents of the odes of Pindar.[36] This is why Addison called his paraphrases of the Nineteenth and Twenty-third Psalms 'odes'; why Aaron Hill used the Cowleyan stanza for his paraphrase of the One-hundred-and-fourth Psalm; and also, I suspect, why 'vallies laugh' and 'floods of glory' drown Jones' sight in *The Muse Recalled*. To choose a motto from the Psalms was therefore an apt thing for an ode writer to do. But Young possibly had a further and more specific reason for thus prefacing a poem so centrally concerned with land and seascape: as Young's hero and sometime-mentor Addison had observed in a famous *Spectator* paper, 'The Psalmist has in several of his divine Poems celebrated those beautiful and agreeable Scenes which make the Heart glad, and produce in it that Vernal Delight which I have before taken notice of'. To be sure, the ocean in Young's poem inspires awe rather than vernal delight, but the one is the counterpart of the other here as in many passages of the Psalms which are concerned with God's terrible and delightful natural Creation.

Aims and assumptions which can in this way be inferred from eighteenth-century practice are stated with clarity in a theoretical work that Coleridge probably read in late 1796, Robert Lowth's once-famous *Lectures on the Sacred Poetry of the Hebrews* (1753).[37] Lowth follows earlier commentators in concluding that the Psalms are Hebrew odes and that the ode is the oldest kind of poetry: 'the origin of the ode may be traced into that of poetry itself, and appears to be coeval with the commencement of religion, or more properly the creation of man'.[38] Just as such influential later theorists as Jones and Hugh Blair were to do, he imagines that the first maker of odes was no less a personage than Adam.[39] The ode, he says,[40]

was the offspring of the most vivid, and the most agreeable passions of the mind, of love, joy, and admiration. If we consider man on his first creation, such as the Sacred Writings represent him; in perfect possession of reason and speech; neither ignorant of his own nor of the divine nature, but fully conscious of the goodness, majesty, and power of God; not an unobservant spectator of the beautiful fabric of the universe; is it not probable, that on the contemplation of these objects, his heart would glow with gratitude and love? And is it not probable, that the effect of such an emotion would be an effusion of praise to his Great Creator, accompanied with a suitable energy and exaltation of voice?

In Lowth's view, joy is one of the passions which is excited by and in turn creates sublimity:[41]

Joy is more elevated, and exults in a bolder strain. It produces great sentiments and conceptions, seizes upon the most splendid imagery, and adorns it with the most animated language; nor does it hesitate to risk the most daring and unusual figures . . . nothing can excel in this respect that noble exultation of general nature, in the Psalm which has been so often commended, where the whole animated and inanimate creation unite in the praises of their Maker. Poetry here seems to assume the highest tone of triumph and exultation, and to revel, if I may so express myself, in all the extravagance of joy. . . .

219

His quotations are from the Ninety-sixth and Ninety-eighth Psalms, from which I give the following extracts in Gregory's translation from Lowth's Latin:

Let the glorious Heavens rejoice,
The Hills exult with grateful voice;
Let Ocean tell the echoing shore,
And the hoarse waves with humble voice adore!
Let the verdant plains be glad!
The trees in blooming fragrance clad!
Smile with joy, ye desert lands,
And rushing torrents, clap your hands!
Let the whole earth with triumph ring. . . .

It is easy to see why Lowth concluded that 'Imagery from natural objects is peculiarly adapted to the ode; historical common-places may also be admitted, as well as descriptions lively but short, and (when it rises to any uncommon strain of sublimity) frequent personifications'.[42] Elsewhere citing the Ninety-eighth Psalm in illustration, he remarks that[43]

The parabolic style no less elegantly assigns a character and action to inanimate objects than to abstract ideas. The holy prophets, moved with just indignation against the ungrateful people of God, "obtest the Heavens and the Earth, and command universal Nature to be silent. They plead their cause before the Mountains, and the Hills listen to their voice." All is animated and informed with life, soul, and passion . . .

No student of Wordsworth and Coleridge can fail to observe how closely Lowth's comments on the origins of the ode parallel key passages on creativity in the 1802 Preface to *Lyrical Ballads*, and how clearly the ode as described by Lowth is related to the great poems of joy and dejection of the *annus mirabilis* and after. When Wordsworth wrote, "The cataracts blow their trumpets from the steep', he wrote in the vein of the Hebrew 'ode': 'All is animated and informed with life, soul, and passion'. Nature thus apprehended is not the nature of the loco-descriptive poem. On the other hand, neither is the 'particularized and usually . . . localized, outdoor setting' of the greater Romantic lyric the setting of a Psalm. In the early masterpieces of the greater Romantic lyric, the springtime joy of Adam animates, if only in bereaved recollection, the sunny prospects of eighteenth-century loco-descriptive poetry.

The precise route by which Coleridge arrived at the greater Romantic lyric can no longer be certainly retraced; and surely Coleridge himself could not have drawn a complete, accurate map. What I seek to do here is not to follow the step-by-step development of the kind, but only to identify several crucial aspects of eighteenth-century theory and practice which contributed to the eventual synthesis. My approach seems the more worthwhile because there is reason to believe that by the autumn of 1802 (and probably earlier) Coleridge himself came to understand his poetic aims and achievement in terms of the very theory and practice which I have been describing. In one of his most important letters (to Sotheby, 10 September 1802), he criticizes Bowles in words which might equally apply to the entire loco-descriptive tradition: [44]

There reigns thro' all the blank verse poems such a perpetual trick of *moralizing every thing*—which is very well, occasionally —but never to see or describe any interesting appearance in nature, without connecting it by dim analogies with the moral world, proves faintness of Impression. Nature has her proper interest; & he will know what it is, who believes & feels, that every Thing has a Life of it's own, & that we are all *one Life*. A Poet's *Heart* & *Intellect* should be *combined*, *intimately* combined & *unified*, with the great appearances in Nature—& not merely held in solution & loose mixture with them, in the shape of formal Similies—

He goes on to clinch his point about the joining of heart and intellect by (inaccurately) recalling Young's essay 'On Lyric Poetry': 'Young somewhere in one of his prose works remarks that there is as profound a Logic in the most daring & dithyrambic parts of Pindar, as in the ''Ορуανον of Aristotle—the remark is a valuable one'. And later in the same letter he returns to the idea of the 'one Life': [45]

Imagination, or the *modifying*, and *co-adunating* Faculty. This the Hebrew Poets appear to me to have possessed beyond all others —& next to them the English. In the Hebrew Poets each Thing has a Life of it's own, & yet they are all one Life. In God they move & live, & *have* their Being—not *had*, as the cold System of Newtonian Theology represents/ but *have*.

Though fragmentary and disconnected, in this letter cluster many of the ideas about creativity, form, theme and style which have been the subject of this and the previous chapter. One way of summarizing them is to say that, while Coleridge was revising *Dejection*, his poetic absolute and reference point was the joyous Hebrew 'ode' in which 'All is animated and informed with life, soul, and passion'. That this ideal preoccupied him during the labour of revision is suggested by the lines he added to the poem sometime between 19 July and 4 October 1802:

> Those sounds which oft have raised me, whilst they awed,
> And sent my soul abroad,
> Might now perhaps their wonted impulse give,
> Might startle this dull pain, and make it move and live!

As I have already pointed out, the allusion to the Pauline formula 'in him we live, and move, and have our being' connects these lines with 'the grand elementary principle of pleasure' in Wordsworth's Preface. In the present context we can see how the allusion also links them with the intimately joined ideals of pristine Joy and primitive ode.

In the ebullient mood of his letter to Sotheby, the ideals are transformed into a fantasy of achievement. He claims that he has recently poured forth, spontaneously, 'a Hymn in the manner of the Psalms'—which is to say, the *Hymn before Sun-rise, in the Vale of Chamouni*—which he had in fact translated and considerably expanded from Fredrika Brun's rhapsodic ode to Chamouny. Sadly, the reputation of the poem and our pleasure in reading it are inevitably shadowed by our knowledge that Coleridge misrepresents its origins both privately and publicly, and I am not sure that the shadow can ever be removed. Yet if Coleridge had simply footnoted his debt to Brun, nobody could have thought of the *Hymn* as anything but a very remarkable and original poem. Quite apart from the problematic claims to originality which any really successful poetic translation must have by virtue of the difficulty and rarity of the achievement, much of the poem certainly is his, not Brun's. However, my present concern is much less with the problems of personal and literary morality which the *Hymn* raises, or even with the value of the poem after various debits have been made, than it is with those aspects of literary theory and convention which it shares with *Dejection* and the Conversation poems. I do submit that the latter need to be fully understood before pronouncing judgment on the former.

Coleridge's debt to Brun confronted him with a problem not of morality in the first instance but of rhetorical strategy. As Coleridge and his readers knew (if they knew anything about poetry), primitivistic theorists like Lowth and Blair referred to what they supposed to be the earliest poems, hymns of praise like the Psalms, as 'effusions', and they and other theorists of the same persuasion (including Wordsworth) conceived of these effusions as spontaneous responses to an immediate vivid stimulus rather than to an experience recollected in tranquillity.[46] This theory, if taken to apply to modern imitations of such poems, left Coleridge's poem doubly compromised and inauthentic. For not only was it in part a deliberate copying from German into English rather than a fresh gush from an original spring, it was a poem written in response to a scene which he had experienced only at second hand. How serious was the dilemma?

Not very, we may answer, since Coleridge must have known that readers less gullible than Sotheby were in on the secret that the best modern poets often had to work hard and long to create a convincing air of improvisation, of the ink still drying on the first and only draft. For Coleridge, who had called a series of his early shorter poems 'effusions', that labour did not end with the text, title or explanatory notes but sometimes extended into his personal communications to friends. That many readers were taken in, and were meant to be, by such spurious precisions as 'composed and . . . first published on the last day of that year' is more than likely, but these fictions must also have been intended to promote, for more sophisticated readers, a willing suspension of disbelief in the spontaneity of the performance. For such readers as these an honest avowal of indebtedness to Brun might not have spoiled the *Hymn* entirely, but it must have weakened its rhetorical impact considerably. This explanation cannot meet the moral objections to plagiarism and is not meant to do so. But we must still inquire how serious the moral dilemma would have appeared to Coleridge.

Again the answer must be: not very. For he certainly knew then as later that both he and Brun were working within well-established conventions of an ancient literary kind, the morning hymn, which I have discussed earlier in connexion with the World Harmony tradition. Writing many years after he composed the *Hymn*, he gave an abbreviated and misleading but substantially correct account of the relationship between his poem and the other works belonging to the morning hymn tradition. He maintained that his *Hymn* differed 'from Milton's and Thomson's and from the Psalms, the source of all three, in the Author's addressing himself to *individual* Objects actually present to his Senses, while his great Predecessors apostrophize *classes* of Things, presented by the Memory and generalized by the understanding. . . .'[47] The touch of the illusionist is still to be discerned in his claim that the 'Objects' were 'actually present to his Senses', unless we concede that a first-hand experience at home in the Lake District inspired his paraphrase. At all events, Brun was certainly 'there' before him, while, on the other hand, his descriptions were more individualized, more concrete, than hers. What he might also have said for himself, had he been more candid about his borrowings from her, is that well before he had the linguistic skills to capitalize on her example he had known how to address himself to individual objects seemingly present to the senses in lyrics also radiant, like those of the Hebrew poets, with the certainty that each thing in nature has a life of its own and yet participates in the one Life. This describes not all but a large part of his original contribution to English poetry in the Conversation poems.

Not all, because the reforms of style, structure and poetic *persona* Coleridge and later Wordsworth introduced were not less essential to the creation of a new kind of extended epiphanic lyric in the Conversation poem. By creating a viable new model, they in their turn transmitted some of the ancient procedures of epiphanic poetry to later poets who by no means always shared either their strong sense of generic distinctions or their transforming experiences of divine immanence in nature. Arnold's *Dover Beach*, Hardy's *Beeny Cliff* and even Larkin's *Church-Going* are poems which could not have been written (or so it seems from the present perspective) without the example of the Conversation poems; but their epiphanies are Joycean, i.e. secular and psychological, rather than Joyous in character; what they reveal is that there is and can be no ultimate source or sanction 'from above'. *Beeny Cliff* and *Church-Going* may depart too far from Abrams' paradigm to be called greater Romantic lyrics, but *Dover Beach* conforms rather closely. It does so because Abrams' description emphasizes psychological process and 'insight' but does not mention any culminating moment of supermundane vision. Yet the omission from it of something so central to the Conversation poems as their moments of joyous vision does not mean that his paradigm is not helpful or accurate within its intended limits. For his purpose is to discover a common ground not merely between the early Romantics but between them and certain later poets; the secular bias is not his but that of later English poetry. After Coleridge, Wordsworth and Shelley, the greater Romantic lyric in England (but not necessarily in other English-speaking countries) is more often 'thoughtful' than epiphanic. And surely it is no coincidence that after enjoying a brief renascence alongside the Conversation poems and *Stanzas Written in Dejection*, with which they are so closely related in many crucial features, the Romantic versions of the greater ode also very nearly disappear from English poetry.

NOTES

1. Abrams, 'Structure and Style in the Greater Romantic Lyric', *From Sensibility to Romanticism*, ed. Hilles and Bloom (New York, 1965), 527–60. Abrams amplifies his discussion of *Dejection* as a greater Romantic lyric in *Natural Supernaturalism* (New York, 1971), 271–77.

2. Abrams, 'Structure and Style', 527–28.

3. Abrams, 'Structure and Style', 528.

4. For Coleridge, of course, the great traditional kinds included the ballad as imitated by Chatterton and the Shakespearian tragedy as imitated by Schiller.

5. The problem of *Dejection*'s generic identity is recognized by several critics, e.g. George Watson in *Coleridge the Poet* (London, 1966), 73–80. But the first real engagement with *Dejection* as an ode is A. Harris Fairbanks, 'The Form of Coleridge's Dejection Ode', *PMLA*, XC (October 1975), 874–84. Fairbanks' article is an excellent piece of formalistic criticism; my own discussion, although coinciding with his in a few particulars, has other emphases and is considerably wider in scope. The closest anticipation of my approach is in Max F. Schulz's fine *The Poetic Voices of Coleridge* (Detroit, 1963), 27–48.

6. 'On Poesy or Art', reprinted by Shawcross in *Biographia Literaria*, II, 262.

7. *Letters*, I, 289, dated 26 December 1796, to Poole: 'If it [*Ode to the Departing Year*] be found to possess that Impetuosity of Transition, and that Precipitation of Fancy and Feeling, which are the *essential* excellencies of the sublimer Ode, its deficiency in less important respects will be easily pardoned. . .'.

8. Blair, *Lectures on Rhetoric and Belles Lettres* (London, 1783), II, 355.

H

Coleridge read Blair between 29 January and 26 February 1798. (Whalley, 'Bristol Library Borrowings', 125.)

9. Young, 'An Ode to the King'. Anderson, X, 39.

10. Horace, Odes, IV, ii. The English version is from Christopher Smart's The Works of Horace (London, 1756), I, 221-3.

11. The most striking instance of which I am aware occurs in Pound's versions of Chinese poetry which Wai-lim Yip, in Ezra Pound's Cathay (Princeton, 1969), has shown to be closer to the originals than the prose translations of sinologist Ernest Fenollosa on which Pound based his 'translations'! The problems raised by Pound's 'mistranslations' are too complex to go into here.

12. Anderson, X, 216.

13. William Collins, Odes on Several Descriptive and Allegoric Subjects (London, dated 1747 but actually published 1746), 36-38. Ode to Evening was republished in a revised version in Dodsley's Collection 1748.

14. Anderson, V, 153 and 156.

15. Letters, I, to John Thelwall (17 December 1796), 279.

16. Eduard Fraenkel, Horace (Oxford, 1957), 40.

17. 'Studia Pindarica. II: The First Isthmian Ode', University of California Publications in Classical Philology, 18 (1962), 35.

18. R. W. B. Burton, Pindar's Pythian Odes: Essays in Interpretation (London, 1962), 2. For other examples of conventional artifice in Pindar's odes, see C. M. Bowra, Pindar (Oxford, 1964), 195-238.

19. Pindar perfected a lyric form which had been evolving over a long period. For an interesting speculative account of the origins of the ode in the ancient cult hymn, see Kurt Schlüter, Die Englische Ode (Bonn, 1964), Ch. 2. Useful on circularity, the prophetic element and prayer in Pindar's odes is Carol Maddison, Apollo and the Nine: A History of the Ode (Baltimore, 1960), 4, 10, 33, 170 and 235. Of course there are more specialized studies, such as those of Bundy and Burton, which the reader with Greek will wish to consult. My own discussion of Pindar derives largely from the works mentioned in this and the three preceding notes; it makes no claim to originality except the very modest one of abstracting ideas and information for use in a different scholarly context.

20. Anderson, XII, 314. For a good brief discussion of Nemean I, see Bowra, 306.

21. Pope, Essay on Criticism, lines 71 and 189. As for Pindaric imitations in English, there are many brief and a few lengthy scholarly treatments of this subject but none that is wholly satisfactory. George Shuster's The English Ode from Milton to Keats (New York, 1940) is informative but rather mechanically descriptive. Schlüter's archetypal approach is often revealing; but, besides being more selective than its title might lead one to expect, Die Englische Ode is excessively unhistorical. In many ways the best discussion remains Norman Maclean's excellent 'From Action to Image: Theories of the Lyric in the Eighteenth Century', in Critics and Criticism: Ancient and Modern, ed. R. S. Crane

(Chicago, 1952), 408–60. Its limitation is that it discusses particular odes briefly and then only in illustration of contemporary theories of the lyric.

22. 'A Discourse on the Pindarick Ode', *Letters and Documents of William Congreve*, ed. J. C. Hodges (New York, 1964), 213–19.

23. See Robert M. Myers, 'Neo-classical Criticism of the Ode for Music', *PMLA*, XLII (June 1947), 399–421. More recent are studies of the Cecilian odes by John Hollander in *The Untuning of the Sky* and 'Wordsworth and the Music of Sound'.

24. *Anderson*, X, 220. W. J. Bate has a useful note on the intimidating example of Milton for poets like Gray in *The Burden of the Past* (London, 1971), 77—a book which, although more concerned with theory than practice, is highly relevant to the present essay.

25. 'Extended epiphanic lyric' is a label I use reluctantly. But as my discussion moves into the late eighteenth century and more recent times, my need for a term both more and less limiting than 'ode' or even 'greater ode' becomes urgent. There are notable precedents for the use of 'epiphanic' rather than one of the several synonyms that come to mind. In *Anatomy of Criticism* (Princeton, 1957), 203, Northrop Frye defines 'point of epiphany' as 'the point at which the undisplaced apocalyptic world and the cyclical world of nature come into alignment'. For Kurt Schlüter the prototypical ode is a lyric with a point of epiphany. Following both Frye and Schlüter, Geoffrey Hartman describes the 'crisis-rhetoric' and 'epiphanic structure' of Pindaric odes and their progeny in 'Poem and Ideology: A Study of Keats' "To Autumn"', *Literary Theory and Structure: Essays in Honor of William K. Wimsatt*, ed. Frank Brady et al (New Haven, 1973), 307–27. Although my own approach to generic matters is deliberately more traditionalist than theirs, I am indebted to these scholars for something more than terminology. One reason for preferring 'epiphanic' to words like 'oracular' or 'visionary' or 'orphic' is that Joyce has familiarized 'epiphany' for modern usage without sacrificing its sense of sudden and extraordinary illumination associated with uncommon feeling. As I use it, however, 'epiphany' is never completely secularized. For epiphanies in Pindar, see Burton, 182–4.

26. Jones, *The Muse Recalled, An Ode* (Strawberry Hill, 1781).

27. Note printed at the end of Vol. I of *Lyrical Ballads* (2nd edn, London, 1800).

28. The most telling evidence of his admiration is his sonnet *To the Poet, John Dyer*.

29. *Miscellaneous Poems and Translations*, ed. Richard Savage (London, 1726), 36.

30. *Anderson*, V, 673.

31. The ode version of *Grongar Hill* was also published in the *Miscellaneous Poems and Translations*, 60–66.

32. *Anderson*, IX, 551.

33. Letter to Lady Beaumont, dated 20 November 1811. Quoted by R. C. Boys in his introduction to *Grongar Hill* (Baltimore, 1941), 42.

34. Coleridge quotes from Young's essay 'On Lyric Poetry', which invariably prefaced *Ocean: An Ode*, in *Notebooks*, I, 33–36 (1795); recalls it in *Letters*, II, 864 (10 September 1802); and paraphrases it in the wisdom attributed to Bowyer in the *Biographia*, I, 4: 'I learnt from him that Poetry, even that of the loftiest and, seemingly, that of the wildest odes, had a logic of its own, as severe as that of science'.

25. *Anderson*, X, 43.

36. Maddison, *Apollo and the Nine*, 128–29, 169–71. Shuster, *The English Ode*, 50–54. In his essay 'On Lyric Poetry', prefixed to *Ocean: An Ode*, Young classes Buchanan's paraphrase of the Psalms with Casimire's Pindaric odes as admirable examples of the modern ode.

37. In its Latin version of 1753, Lowth's book acquired a European celebrity. It was translated by G. Gregory and first published in English in 1787; this version was reprinted several times during the eighteenth and nineteenth centuries. I quote from the first edition. Coleridge read the Latin version between 16 and 22 September 1796. (Whalley, 'Bristol Library Borrowings', 123.)

38. Lowth, II, 192.

39. Blair, *Lectures on Rhetoric and Belles Lettres* (London, 1783), II, 311–23. Jones, 'Essay on the Arts Commonly Called Imitative', *Works* (London, 1807), X, 363–64. Jones' essay was first published in 1772.

40. Lowth, II, 190.

41. Lowth, I, 378–79.

42. Lowth, II, 198.

43. Lowth, I, 288.

44. *Letters*, II, 864. Abrams cites the same letter, but his use of it does not turn, as mine does, on Coleridge's references to Young and the Psalms.

45. *Letters*, II, 866.

46. Wordsworth, 'Appendix to the Preface' (1802), *Literary Criticism of William Wordsworth*, ed. Paul M. Zall (Lincoln, Neb., 1966), 63: 'The earliest Poets of all nations generally wrote from passion excited by real events; they wrote naturally, and as men: feeling powerfully as they did, their language was daring, and figurative'.

47. *Letters*, IV, to an unknown correspondent (November 1819), 974. My attention was called to this letter by Adrien Bonjour in *Coleridge's 'Hymn Before Sunrise'* (Lausanne, 1942), 117–19. Reeve Parker makes good use of this and other evidence in his excellent discussion of the *Hymn* in *Coleridge's Meditative Art* (Ithaca and London, 1975), 139–72. Professor Parker is also considerably more thoughtful than most critics about the relationship between Stanzas VI and VII of *Dejection* (*Coleridge's Meditative Art*, 194–208).

6

Dejection: An Ode

In previous chapters I have often been obliged to lose sight of *Dejection* for many pages at a time, and even when I have had it directly in view my focus has usually been on a single passage or aspect rather than on the poem as a whole. What is wanted now, I believe, is neither a digest of everything I have already said about *Dejection* itself nor yet additional commentary on obscure points, but rather a straightforward reading of the poem from start to finish. Of course I shall add some further glosses and also restate conclusions reached earlier, but my emphasis will be on the un-folding design and the artistic whole that emerge as we read the poem from epigraph to concluding prayer. Only by doing so can we begin to appreciate it as a major work of art as well as a major document in the history of Romanticism.

Coleridge's epigraph to *Dejection* consists of lines rearranged from the Percy version of *Sir Patrick Spence*:[1]

> Late, late yestreen I saw the new Moon,
> With the old Moon in her arms;
> And I fear, I fear, my Master dear!
> We shall have a deadly storm.

This ballad quatrain serves first of all as a graceful point of de-parture for a poem in which weather develops both as a series of external meteorological events and (fitfully and ambiguously) as a Wordsworthian 'corresponding . . . creative breeze' within. It also prepares for an ironic reversal at the end of the first stanza, since the 'deadly' storm which is feared in the epigraph is wished for in lines 15–20:

> And oh! that even now the gust were swelling,
> And the slant night-shower driving loud and fast!

> Those sounds which oft have raised me, whilst they awed,
> And sent my soul abroad,
> Might now perhaps their wonted impulse give,
> Might startle this dull pain, and make it move and live!

Aside from their role in the development of the mental and physical action—the poem is 'dramatic' in the specific sense that it is an *imitation* of such action—the lines from *Sir Patrick Spence* have a further prophetic function, which Coleridge calls attention to in his opening:

> Well! If the Bard was weather-wise, who made
> The grand old ballad of Sir Patrick Spence. . . .

He was weather-wise, of course, since the ancient Celtic as well as the ancient Greek poets were seers, in touch with the primitive powers of earth and air and potent to forecast the doom of men and things. The 'sign' which the Bard reads—'the new Moon, / With the old Moon in her arms'—is a most striking personification, a brilliant instance of the sort of creative interaction between man and nature which has become impossible for the poet of *Dejection*. In this ballad figure we observe the polar opposite of the sophisticated 'abstruse research' of Stanza VI. The same may be said of the balladic repetition, which registers a very 'unscientific' wonder before the powers both of nature and language:

> For lo! the New-moon winter-bright!
> And overspread with phantom light,
> (With swimming phantom light o'erspread
> But rimmed and circled by a silver thread)

No apostrophe or opening invocation sets the poem in motion, but as Donald Davie comments, an 'extraordinary sentence' which achieves in little all that the poem does':[2]

> Well! If the Bard was weather-wise, who made
> The grand old ballad of Sir Patrick Spence,
> This night, so tranquil now, will not go hence
> Unroused by winds, that ply a busier trade
> Than those which mould yon cloud in lazy flakes,
> Or the dull sobbing draft, that moans and rakes
> Upon the strings of this Æolian lute,
> Which better far were mute.

The sentence both prophesies and, in syntactical mime, rehearses the main action of the poem. Not with total fidelity, of course, since the passage functions not only as an epitome of the whole but also as the establisher of mood, time and weather *now*. So the double-negatived phrase 'will not go hence / Unroused by winds' refers to, but scarcely mimics, the explosive release of wind and emotion in Stanza VII. The sentence as a whole—which starts out conditionally and keeps going, compulsively, by sprouting one adjectival clause out of another—entirely lacks the volitional thrust of the traditional Pindaric invocation:[3]

> Awake, Æolian lyre, awake,
> And give to rapture all thy trembling strings....

In *Dejection* the problem is not to awaken but to induce the in-somniac lute to be still. Like the elegaic instruments of Orpheus, Sidney and Thomson, but with far mournfuler music, it plays on after the poet is dead.

Whereas Gray's 'lyre' is 'Æolian' only in the sense of being (figuratively) 'inspired', Coleridge's lute is an actual wind instrument subject to actual breezes. Precisely because it belongs to the world of Newtonian Mechanism it is, by Hartleyan extension, an apposite figure for the helplessly, exquisitely responsive sensibility of genius, registering each aerial tremor and nuance of internal pain. Clearly, Coleridge invites us initially to identify lute and poetic persona, though without sacrificing the lute's presence as a concrete quotidian object. And because the lute exists distinctly as both wind instrument and analogue for the suffering poetic sensibility, Coleridge's opening passage implicitly raises—what was buried in Gray's conventional Pindaric metaphors—the crucial problem of the relationship between matter and animating spirit in man and nature. The problem did not urgently concern Gray because he never supposed, as did the author of *The Nightingale*, that inspiration came to him from the green hills and marvellous evening sky. If the poet could no longer believe in that source, the Æolian lute figure would have to be abandoned or somehow trans-formed—as indeed happens in Stanza VII.

I suppose most readers of *Dejection* share my pleasure in the descriptive passages which fill the rest of Stanza I and much of Stanza II, and certainly it was Coleridge's strategy to make us feel some part of the beauty which he no longer could feel. How else should his declaration of loss carry conviction? And yet we probably respond more appreciatively than Coleridge intended to the poised, precise notation of

And those thin clouds above, in flakes and bars,
That give away their motion to the stars;
Those stars, that glide behind them or between,
Now sparkling, now bedimmed, but always seen:
Yon crescent Moon as fixed as if it grew
In its own cloudless, starless lake of blue;
I see them all so excellently fair,
I see, not feel how beautiful they are!

For in spite of his enthusiasm for the writings of the naturalist Bartram, he shared his contemporaries' low opinion of 'genre painting' in poetry. And that this verse is as well-written as prose would have pleased him, but not so much as it pleases us. That it is 'prosaic' particularly because of comparative sparseness of metaphor—which to us suggests a salutary respect for the otherness and uniqueness of the things described—would not have seemed a strong recommendation to one who, with Wordsworth, thought of the Poet as 'a man pleased with his own passions and volitions, and who rejoices more than other men in the spirit of life that is in him; delighting to contemplate similar volitions and passions as manifested in the goings-on of the Universe, and habitually impelled to create them where he does not find them'.[4] True, it is the doctrine of *Dejection* that the poet always does 'create' rather than 'find' those 'similar volitions and passions' in nature:

O Lady! we receive but what we give,
And in our life alone does nature live:
Ours is her wedding garment, ours her shroud!

Yet there is never any doubt that creating the 'life' of nature is vitally important to the man as to the poet. To express this felt life, these volitions and passions, the poet has a powerful figurative device, *prosopopeia* or personification. The Bard of *Sir Patrick Spence* used it memorably, as did Wordsworth of course and the ancient Hebrew poets whom Coleridge most admired; it was supposed to be the hallmark of the greater ode. Other kinds of poetry, neither odes nor much concerned with external nature, might use this figure sparingly or not at all—and be the better for it. But its general absence throughout Stanzas I, II and III can be taken as a sign of poetic failure: a sign which has this much validity: these stanzas do not live up to generic expectations and do not evidence the kind of relationship with nature which Coleridge desired. They are not bad or negligible poetry and were not meant to be, but they fall short of the occasion as that was understood by Coleridge and his contemporaries. Of course the 'failure' here contributes to the overall success of the poem; it is an essential preparation for the climactic reversal of Stanza VII.

At the other extreme, which is to say the stanzas written in praise of Joy (IV, V, and VIII), Coleridge not only attributes human qualities to nature, albeit with a phrasing which takes them back in the act of giving: 'Ours is her wedding garment, ours her shroud!' He also seems to attribute the powers and properties of external nature to man:

Joy is the sweet voice, Joy the luminous cloud—
We in ourselves rejoice!
And thence flows all that charms or ear or sight,
All melodies the echoes of that voice,
All colours a suffusion from that light.

But perception as such is not at issue. The 'new Earth and new Heaven' which (we are told) Joy gives us by 'wedding Nature to us' are new not because of any Lockean secondary qualities projected upon them—joyless Coleridge *sees* the 'peculiar tint of yellow green' in the western sky—but because they appear to us animated and informed by a transensory power of human but ultimately divine origin. The coupling of 'new Earth and new Heaven' helps us to understand what Coleridge is saying about the aesthetic and spiritual apprehension of nature. Heaven cannot be the object of human perception, but Earth can be. Therefore, if Heaven is to be felt as anything more than a stale abstraction, it must be through an experience within human reach, i.e. through a new experience of Earth which is sensory in the first instance (as it must be) but transensory too. Heaven reveals itself in and through Earth to the individual who brings to Earth both his senses and the animating spirit of Joy. Presumably, as it is spiritual as well, this must be the highest kind of aesthetic experience, but—to anticipate later developments in the poem—it cannot be the only kind. The imaginative experience of art, whether in the creation or appreciation of it, is an earthly analogue available to those who are not perfectly 'pure, and in their purest hour' but who can still bring feeling to it; while aesthetic pleasure is likewise analogue and echo of Joy.

In Coleridge's usage 'Joy' has religious connotations which derive from the Judeo-Christian tradition:[5] 'When the morning stars sang together, and all the sons of God shouted for Joy.' Joy is associated with the Creation, both as its consequence (e.g. in the passage from *Job* above) and as its cause (e.g. by such writers as Boehme and Akenside). By analogy, the Joyous man is most god-like, most creative: as Young and Wordsworth both joyously affirm. In turn, this analogy between Joyous Creator and creative person suggests something further about the role of Joy in our aesthetic and spiritual experience. Essentially, the Creation is an act which brings multiplicity out of unity; and yet it both leaves the original unity intact and separate, and *informs* the created world with unity. Joy in man is 'the spirit and the power' which allows us to create (or recreate) that unity, which *is* the divine life of man and nature:

> Joy lift her spirit, joy attune her voice:
> To her may all things live, from Pole to Pole,
> Their life the eddying of her living soul!

Coleridge's conception of Joy bringing unity out of multiplicity, identity out of diversity,

> And thence flows all that charms or ear or sight,
> All melodies the echoes of that voice,
> All colours a suffusion from that light

probably owes something to the Newtonian principle of structural analogy between colour, sound and planetary gravity, just as his conception of aesthetic psychology probably owes something to Addison's spiritualization of Locke. But fundamentally it is an attack on the mechanistic world-view of the New Philosophy, of Newton and his successors, as it is also an attack on the incipient pantheism of *The Eolian Harp* and *The Nightingale*. Betrayed by the latter and unsatisfied by the former, Coleridge here affirms a sophisticated post-Newtonian philosophy which promises to under-write the reality of the primitive world-views of *Job* and the Psalms and of Greek World Harmony. That reality, however lost to him, is still available to 'the pure, and in their purest hour' just as in the beginning when the morning stars sang together.

As we should expect, form and doctrine in *Dejection* are closely though complexly related. According to Edward Young, the ode, 'as it is the eldest kind of poetry, so it is more spiritous, and more remote from prose than any other, in sense, sound, expression, and conduct'.[6] In the first three stanzas of this ode, Coleridge's genial spirits fail and the verse is closer than usual in his poetry to good prose:

> My genial spirits fail,
> And what can these avail
> To lift the smothering weight from off my breast?
> It were a vain endeavour,
> Though I should gaze for ever
> On that green light that lingers in the west:
> I may not hope from outward forms to win
> The passion and the life, whose fountains are within.

The irregular Pindaric stanza, designed to express a wild 'spiritous' movement of thought and feeling, is an ironic shape (or 'outward form'!) for the paraphrasable substance and deliberate, metrically regular and end-stopped rhythm of these lines. In this context, the phrase 'genial spirits' evokes both Milton's Samson at his nadir and the Hebrew world of the Holy Spirit and the joyous Psalms of David—Psalms which were supposed to be the Hebrew equivalents of Pindar's odes, effusions inspired by the joy of the sons of God in nature and nature's God. Though the hills do not leap and old Ocean does not clap his hands in any part of *Dejection*, the 'unanimated' descriptions of Stanzas I, II and III are balanced by the paens to Joy of Stanzas IV and V, and, as we shall see, by the 'notable *prosopopeias*' of Stanza VII. *Dejection* is therefore an ode which both upsets and conforms to the expectations which Coleridge's contemporaries would have shared with him. But at no point does the upsetting of expectations degenerate—as easily and commonly happened—into a burlesque of the ode form and the author: the ironies operate quietly and with dignity, reaffirming the value of what has been lost without degrading the loser.

As in *Frost at Midnight* and *Tintern Abbey*, the persona of *Dejection* digresses from a carefully established present scene to a former time and contrasting situation, then back to the present before moving into the future vision of prayer. In *Dejection*, however, the time scheme is not based on a counterpoise of slowly, almost unnoticeably marching chronometric 'present' and fluid mental movement before and after, but on simultaneous and intersecting developments in time. Thus the present tense of Stanzas IV and V belongs to the static world of being, of the eternal verities, rather than to the world of action of the first three stanzas, but we are meant to imagine chronometric time swiftly advancing all the while he philosophizes about Joy and, in Stanza VI, regresses into the world of memory. Though the opening of Stanza VI

> There was a time when, though my path was rough,
> This joy within me dallied with distress,

owes its evocative force to Wordsworth, the stanza eventually builds to a moving climax in which the language becomes commensurate with the theme:

>   each visitation
> Suspends what nature gave me at my birth,
> My shaping spirit of Imagination.

Like the spirit of Imagination itself, time past is here suspended within, rather than superseded by, time present. Nothing very odd about that, but how strangely is time past robbed of its pastness in the remainder of the stanza:

> For not to think of what I needs must feel,
> But to be still and patient, all I can;
> And haply by abstruse research to steal
> From my own nature all the natural Man—
> This was my sole resource, my only plan:
> Till that which suits a part infects the whole,
> And now is almost grown the habit of my Soul.

The words in this passage are comparatively short and simple (and seem more so because of the swelling diction of the immediately preceding lines), but the syntax certainly is not. Only when we reach the fifth line do we discover that the 'plan' described in the first four lines '*was*' rather than '*is*'. Verbs in the sixth line which might have been in the past tense are in the present, and both the 'this' of the fifth line and the 'now' of the seventh are positioned to take an emphatic stress. Indeed, though describing a process which began sometime in the past, the entire passage is so insistently *present* in feeling that it appears to be self-referential: an enactment of the suicidal practice of 'abstruse research', which on this reading must mean (besides metaphysical or scientific enquiry) self-analysis and experimentation with his own reflexes. The 'habit' has become so ingrained that potentially redemptive reminiscence and confession—a 'natural outlet . . . [and] relief, / In word, or sigh, or tear'—slides compulsively and insidiously into yet another attempt to steal from his 'own nature all the natural Man'.

At this juncture Coleridge checks himself abruptly and makes a sudden transition back to the external scene:

> Hence, viper thoughts, that coil around my mind,
>   Reality's dark dream!
> I turn from you, and listen to the wind,
>   Which long has raved unnoticed.

This kind of shift—articulated by a dash or, as here, a gap between strophes—belongs to traditional Pindaric artifice, and occurs when the poet suddenly recognizes that he has been carried away by a (sometimes dangerous) digressive impulse. When the same device was employed in *Monody on the Death of Chatterton* ('Hence, gloomy thoughts!'), it signalized a recognition that, in meditating on Chatterton's fate, the author himself had fallen into a suicidal train of thought which had to be emphatically rejected. The parallel act of repudiation in *Dejection* is pivotal in that it is Coleridge's first active motion in the poem and is accompanied by an implicit repudiation of the passive lute/poet analogy:

>   What a scream
> Of agony by torture lengthened out
> That lute sent forth! Thou Wind, that rav'st without,
>   Bare crag, or mountain-tairn, or blasted tree,
>   Or pine grove whither woodman never clomb,
>   Or lonely house, long held the witches' home,
>   Methinks were fitter instruments for thee,
>   Mad lutanist!

What startles the poet's dull pain and makes it move and live in the wind and the figure of the wind/poet is not the external impulse of the storm sounds, but an internal shock of recognition. This act of recognition and reversal has a structural importance that cannot be easily exaggerated: without it the poem would be the bundle of fragments which it is sometimes supposed to be. Though the same reversal appears in the drafts of 1802,

Nay, wherefore did I let it haunt my Mind
The dark distressful Dream!
I turn from it, & listen to the Wind

the same recognition does not. The 'dark distressful Dream' in the verse letter is of Coleridge finding himself unable to attend Sara in her illness; while in the *Morning Post* version it has no antecedent, because the immediately preceding stanza is 'omitted'. If the dream were chiefly of Sara's rather than his own suffering, we should perhaps feel that he had won release, as he did before in *This Lime-Tree Bower My Prison* and as the Mariner did when he blessed the water-snakes. But the dream in the letter is only another bid for Sara's pity and his turning away from it another escape. The final revision, made sometime between late 1802 and 1817, therefore both dramatizes and results from an authentic act of self-discovery which places the blame squarely where it belongs.

Though it is true, as House maintained,[7] that 'Hence, viper thoughts' is awkward, and true too that the substitution later on of 'Otway's self' for 'Wordsworth's self' disturbs every knowledgeable reader, both late revisions seem calculated to remind us of the eighteenth-century literature of Sensibility. This often took its bearings from *L'Allegro* and *Il Penseroso*:[8]

Hence loathed Melancholy,
Of Cerberus and blackest Midnight born. . . .

and eventually transformed the poet himself into the chief hero and victim of ecstatic flights and plunges into despair:

By our own spirits are we deified:
We Poets in our youth begin in gladness;
But thereof comes in the end despondency & madness.

Merely to mention Otway's name was to summon up a host of other ill-fated literary geniuses ranging from Spenser and Collins to Chatterton and Burns. To this tradition of literary legend and actuality belong both *Dejection* and Wordsworth's 'answer' to Coleridge, *Resolution and Independence*. To know this tradition is to realize that Wordsworth's sane and firm-minded admonition deserves our respect and sympathy. Yet it can be answered in its own terms: the old Leech-Gatherer is very admirable in his way, but about all he shares with a literary genius like Burns is social and perhaps national background. In this poem at least, Words-

worth does not face up to the possibility that although too much
Sensibility destroys the man, too little might destroy the poet. So
long as feeling can be kept alive, something can be made of pain
and misfortune—as Otway made something in *The Orphan* or as
Milton did in *Samson Agonistes*. And through tragic art the poet
himself can achieve catharsis 'And calm of mind all passion
spent':

> Thou actor, perfect in all tragic sounds!
> Thou mighty Poet, e'en to Frenzy bold!
>   What tell'st thou now about?
>   'Tis of the Rushing of an Host in rout,
> With groans of trampled men, with smarting wounds—
> At once they groan with pain, and shudder with the cold!
> But hush! there is a pause of deepest silence!
>   And all that noise, as of a rushing crowd,
> With groans, and tremulous shudderings—all is over—
>   It tells another tale, with sounds less deep and loud!
>   A tale of less affright,
>   And tempered with delight,
>   As Otway's self had framed the tender lay,

The language here and at the end of Stanza I quite possibly echoes
Milton's restatement of Aristotle in the Preface to *Samson Agonistes*:[9] 'Tragedy, as it was anciently compos'd, hath been . . . said
by *Aristotle* to be of power, by raising pity and fear, or terror, to
purge the mind of those and such like passions, that is, to temper
and reduce them to just measure, with a kind of delight, stirred
up by reading or seeing those passions well imitated'. The catharsis of tragic art cannot restore the plenary Joy which is given only
to 'the pure, and in their purest hour'. But the experience of tragic
art mediates, so far as mediation is humanly possible, between
the polar extremes of feelingful Joy and feelingless Dejection.
Southey saved himself from Sensibility by rooting it out; Wordsworth, by willing himself to be stoic and strong. Coleridge, with
more faith in art and less in himself, takes the riskier course of
fighting fire with fire, or, as Milton has it, using 'sour against
sour, salt to remove salt humours'.

Just as the descriptive passages in Stanzas I and II probably
seem more valuable to us than they did to their own author, so,
I suspect, did the 'sublime' cadenza of Stanza VII mean more
to Coleridge and his contemporaries than it easily can to a twenti-

eth-century reader. If 'Hence, viper thoughts' annoys us, how shall we pass by 'whither woodman never clomb' or 'e'en to Frenzy bold' without a tasteful shudder? And the further the personification of the wind is extended, the more it is likely to seem, to us, to lose sensory contact: Coleridge feels, not hears, how the wind 'raves'. Wallace Stevens' 'inhuman' seascape—of 'meaningless plungings of water and the wind'—seems a salutary corrective to such greedy anthropomorphism.[10] Yet if we cannot wholly enjoy Coleridge's art in this stanza, we can readily perceive how certain apparent defects were part of his design in *Dejection*. One way to describe this design is to say that from the start the poem aspires to Pindaric heights, but reaches them only in Stanza VII. According to Robert Lowth,[11] 'Imagery from natural objects is peculiarly adapted to the ode . . . and (when it rises to any uncommon strain of sublimity) frequent personifications'. Just as Young said an entire ode should be, this single stanza is 'spiritous' in every possible way, and above all in the way Coleridge's 'shaping spirit' breathes human life into an April wind. So far as problems of diction are concerned, Young can again be appealed to for guidance: 'The Ode, as it is the eldest kind of poetry, so it is more spiritous, and more remote from prose than any other, in sense, sound, expression, and conduct'. Or another perilous Longinian counsel: 'this may be said, in general, that great subjects are above being nice; that dignity and spirit ever suffer from scrupulous exactness; and that the minuter cares effeminate a composition. Great masters of poetry, painting, and statuary, in their nobler works, have even affected the contrary: and justly; for a truly masculine air partakes more of the negligent, than of the neat, both in writings and in life'.[12] Though we may feel that he overplayed his hand, what Coleridge wanted and needed at this point was a striking contrast with the contained rhythms, the minute observations, and the chaste diction of the early stanzas. He required the air of almost defiantly poetic improvisation in, for instance, the rhyming of 'whither woodman never clomb' with 'witches' home'. The same may be said of the redundant 'groans' and 'shudderings' mid-stanza and of several poetical contractions ('rav'st', 'mak'st') which he might easily have weeded out—to its improvement, doubtless, as an isolated fragment of poetry, but maybe to its final disadvantage as part of the whole that is *Dejection: An Ode*.

That these minor stylistic blemishes or affectations were part of his larger design is corroborated, I believe, by the conclusion of Stanza VII:

It tells another tale, with sounds less deep and loud!
A tale of less affright,
And tempered with delight,
As Otway's self had framed the tender lay,
'Tis of a little child
Upon a lonesome wild,
Not far from home, but she hath lost her way:
And now moans low in bitter grief and fear,
And now screams loud, and hopes to make her mother hear.

Where his aim is pathos rather than passion, to be affecting rather than sublime, Coleridge follows the advice of (among others) Goldsmith, to spare the metaphor.[13] To be sure, the epithets 'tender' and 'bitter' are metaphorical, but so commonplace—though apt in a description of a lost child—as not to be at all striking. The risk that this unfigurative verse will seem the same as the equally unfigurative 'uninspired' verse of the earlier stanzas is a real one, and yet we can see that there is a difference: the subject and 'imaginative' mode of apprehending it demand an emotive language ('lonesome wild') quite different from the languages of objective description or intellectual analysis. Moreover, Coleridge takes advantage of one of the resources of the irregular Pindaric stanza here by making it imitate song measure. This effect, created by the shorter lines and more frequent recurrence of end-rhyme, is reinforced in the longer closing lines by partial rhyme ('home', 'low', 'loud') at the caesura. Altogether, this passage provides a suave modulation from the stormy Pindaric climax to the calm of the final stanza.

The closing prayer, again characteristic of the ode form, is a satisfying conclusion in many ways:

'Tis midnight, but small thoughts have I of sleep:
Full seldom may my friend such vigils keep!
Visit her, gentle Sleep! with wings of healing,
And may this storm be but a mountain-birth,
May all the stars hang bright above her dwelling,
Silent as though they watched the sleeping earth!
With light heart may she rise,
Gay fancy, cheerful eyes,
Joy lift her spirit, joy attune her voice:

241

To her may all things live, from Pole to Pole,
Their life the eddying of her living soul!
  O simple spirit, guided from above,
Dear Lady, friend devoutest of my choice,
Thus mayest thou ever, evermore rejoice.

The main themes and images of the preceding stanzas—Dejection and Joy, storm and sky, observation and creative vision—are gathered together here in a new yet familiar configuration. A minor emotional and artistic miracle has occurred, but not such as to give the poet a new Earth and new Heaven. The true measure of change, I believe, is the change in his description of the stars. Now they are animated with the spirit of his concern and watchfulness over the distant lady, and so become a bridge between himself and her. Thus far has he lifted himself out of the numb self-absorption of the opening stanzas and the self-fascinated yet morbidly detached 'abstruse research' of Stanza VI. As for the Lady, 'simple spirit' sums up her essential modesty and greatness with fine economy. To say that she is 'simple' is partly to say that she is unsophisticated and unpretentious, but it is also to liken her to an unmixed element: pure and perfect in its oneness, and consequently fit receptacle for the unifying power of Joy. 'Spirit' is a key word, meaning several things, in *Dejection*; and in this fifth and final usage it means those things and also something new. A 'simple spirit' is a being in whom the indwelling spirit is neither compounded with grosser elements—the blinding appetites of 'the sensual and the proud'—nor vulnerable to the destructive assays of abstruse research. It is a splendid tribute, idealizing but never sentimentalizing its object. And though less for this do we prize *Dejection* than for its wise, sad, and honest portrait of human imperfection and loss, Coleridge's tragic vision cannot be fully shared unless we also feel some sympathy for his and Wordsworth's vision of human Glory and Joy.

Attuned as we have become to the free verse rhythms and associative leaps of poets like H.D. and Lawrence, Pound and Bunting, we probably fail to register the 'discords' and 'irregularities' of *Dejection* quite as we should. That is, we do not immediately register them as departures from expected symmetry which nonetheless contribute to an ultimate *concordia discors*. Probably few of Coleridge's contemporary readers were familiar with the relationships between the *concordia discors* principle in art and the Neoplatonic doctrine of World Harmony or between the latter and the plenary creative Joy celebrated in Stanzas IV, V, and VIII, but they would have felt Coleridge's 'lapses' from stylistic decorum and formal pattern with something like their intended force. We, on the other hand, hopefully have the advantages of our deficiencies: we are perhaps less likely to be distressed by minor disturbances and so miss the final concordance of the whole.

I do not invoke *concordia discors* as an alchemical principle capable of answering every criticism of the poem. *Dejection* is a unified work of art, but no poem composed as it was could be free from defects. I have tried to show that the excesses—'e'en to Frenzy bold!'—of Stanza VII were intended to contribute to the overall design of the poem; whether Coleridge went too far is a question which each reader must answer for himself. But there are other and, as it seems to me, more substantial faults which cannot be argued away or shrugged off as minor problems of taste.

The most serious of these is that his terminology in Stanzas IV, V, and VI is sometimes very slippery and his meaning consequently obscure. 'Joy' demands much glossing if we are to reach a full and exact understanding, but its basic meaning seems to me intelligible without a learned commentary. On the other hand, 'Nature' seems to mean several things—Mother Nature, the non-human creation, general human nature and possibly individual 'genius'. Of course this ambiguity is implicit in his view of his subject; it might be said to *be* his subject. But it leads to inevitable confusion. At one point 'nature' is said to give the poet a shaping spirit of Imagination at his birth; at another, we are told, Joy is given to the pure, and in their purest hour, and Joy then weds 'Nature' to us and so gives in dower a new Earth and new Heaven. What Coleridge seems to be saying is that Imagination is an inborn human faculty belonging 'by nature' to us, but that Joy is a gift of God, given, if at all, to a few select spirits to whom alone Nature is 'wedded', and who may or may not be poets. But is the 'natural Man' of line 90 the unbaptized man of Imagination then, or the baptized man of joyous vision? Perhaps the lower case *n* of 'natural Man' indicates the former, sublunary identity; but I am not convinced that Coleridge does consistently employ initial caps to make such discriminations. How can we be certain? True, from what he provides us in these stanzas, we can infer a theology and theory of Imagination that will answer such questions. But

243

where so much is to be inferred from words that mean so many things, who can be sure what Coleridge meant or that Coleridge himself knew? Let us be candid: though *Dejection* is never empty or incoherent, there are dozens of Renascence and medieval poems which handle philosophical concepts with greater ease, clarity and precision. *Dejection* is not a philosophical poem primarily but a poem which registers the shattering effect, when proven on the quick of individual experience, of allegiance to false philosophical ideals. As such it is moving and often powerful even where its exact meaning is in doubt. But we have to remember that certain poets whom Coleridge admired, such as Greville and Donne, sometimes wrote as movingly as he did here, and also with philosophical exactitude.

The sheer formal achievement of *Dejection* is astonishing, both in the local excellence of its writing and in the complex unfolding of its design. Our astonishment is the greater because of what we know or can guess about the history of its composition, and if a few imperfections persist as reminders of that history, well, they can be borne with for the sake of the whole; or they can be sentimentally treasured. I believe they are to be borne with, and can be so only because of the general success of Coleridge's stern labour of revision.

Effective as the final stanza mostly is, surely it is a weakness that there is no preparation whatever for our discovery there that the Lady too has been ill, though not with the disease of spirit that afflicts the poet. Other revelations and reversals in the poem are carefully, even elaborately anticipated, and I can only suppose that a prayer for the recovery of the Lady (or Wordsworth or Sara) was not part of the original plan of the poem. In the verse letter, the issue of Sara's illness does not arise before line 116 and virtually disappears after a prayer for her recovery in lines 216–25 (corresponding to lines 126–33 of the ode), while the brief concluding prayer of the letter (like the nearly identical closing six lines of the ode) refers not at all to her illness. By conflating the two prayers from the letter, Coleridge extended what otherwise must have seemed a very hasty exit. The gain doubtless outweighs the loss, but must it not be accounted a defect that a new circumstance is suddenly obtruded at this stage of the poem's development?

These weaknesses in *Dejection* are not incidental, and they make the poem less great than it might have been. But a great poem it is, and great precisely because its corresponding strengths are far more prevalent and far more remarkable. I know of no other English Romantic poem which achieves so much in so few lines; which offers so much variety in a brief compass without loss of unity; which epitomizes the experience of so many poets without ever seeming merely 'literary' or 'representative'; and which in its formal qualities and thematic concerns looks so far before and after. Though I have said that it is not a philosophical poem, its intellectual substance is rich and wise, and as adequate to the emotional occasion as perhaps was possible at that place and time. Truly, in the fullest sense of Arnold's phrase, it is a criticism of life. We should be right to describe *Dejection* as an instance of the greater Romantic lyric, but there is more to be said: in it, better than in any other poem I know, we can perceive how that kind originated in the eighteenth-century ode and loco-descriptive poem, and how the fragmentary symbolist poem of Whitman and the last Romantics did likewise. Other poems by Coleridge, notably *Kubla Khan* and *The Ancient Mariner*, are relatively unprecedented and thus more uniquely Coleridgean than *Dejection*; other poems by other Romantic poets are more perfectly achieved or greater in scope. But where in the whole range of Romantic poetry do you find a poem so urgently and immediately personal and yet so generously alive to the joys and dejections, innovations and traditions, of poetic generations then dead or unborn?

NOTES

1. The lines which Coleridge conflated are these:

   'O say na sae, my master deir
      For I feir a deadlie storm.

   Late, late yestreen I saw the new moone,
      Wi' the auld moone in hir arme,
   And I feir, I feir, my deir master,
      That we will cum to harme.'

2. *Purity of Diction in English Verse* (2nd edn, London, 1967), 129.
3. Thomas Gray, *The Progress of Poesy: a Pindaric Ode. Anderson*, **X**, 218. Anderson duly notes the parallel between these lines and the Psalm: 'Awake, my glory: awake, lute and harp'.

4. Wordsworth, Preface to the *Lyrical Ballads* (1802), 48–49.
5. *Job*, 38:7.
6. 'On Lyric Poetry', *Anderson*, X, 41.
7. House, *Coleridge*, 134.
8. *Anderson*, V, 153.
9. *Anderson*, V, 125.
10. 'The Idea of Order at Key West', *Collected Poems of Wallace Stevens* (New York, 1955), 129.
11. Lowth, II, 198.
12. *Anderson*, X, 41, 43.
13. Davie, *Purity of Diction*, 18–19. I am generally indebted to Professor Davie's fine discussion of Coleridge's diction, though we differ fairly widely about the diction of *Dejection*.

Appendix

DEJECTION: AN ODE

AND THE VERSE LETTER TO SARA HUTCHINSON

Coleridge frequently quoted brief passages from *Dejection* in his letters and criticisms, but the few negligible variants that appear in these quotations do not properly belong to the genetic history of the text. To follow that history closely, one would have to compare all of the surviving complete or nearly complete transcriptions and printings that the poem received during the author's lifetime:

letter to Sara Hutchinson	4 April 1802
transcription for William Sotheby (*Soth.*)	19 July 1802
publication in the *Morning Post* (*MP*)	4 October 1802
transcription for the Beaumonts (*Beau.*)	13 August 1803
publication in *Sibylline Leaves* (*SL*)	1817
publication in *The Poetical Works of S. T. Coleridge*	1828, 1829, 1834

An exhaustive collation of these texts would sacrifice ease of comparison for completeness, and, in omitting the variants that appear in two of them (*Soth.* and *Beau.*), I believe I have left out nothing essential either for tracing the textual development of the poem or for deciding which text(s) should be taken as definitive for critical comment. The reader who wishes to supply what is missing here may of course do so by consulting Vol. II of the *Letters*.

The verse letter to Sara survives in a unique holograph which is unmistakably a fair copy very lightly revised in the course of transcription. Was this the text exactly or very nearly as it was transmitted to Sara soon after 4 April, or was it the text of the verses 'repeated' to William and Dorothy Wordsworth on 21 April? The manuscript supplies no answers to such questions.

The text that Coleridge transcribed for Sotheby is of a poem in transition from one state to another, and its configuration is more readily described here than reproduced in the lists of variants given below. The poem is now addressed to Wordsworth and, with a few minor exceptions, is made up of lines that survive in its later avatars. However, these are grouped together in what amount to three fragments corresponding to (1) Stanza VI, (2) Stanzas I–V and VIII, and (3) Stanza VII of the final version(s).

The *Morning Post* text, addressed to Wordsworth under the pseudonym of 'Edmund', omits the seven lines beginning 'For not to think of what I needs must feel'; but its arrangement of parts is the final one. The lines corresponding to 17–20 of later versions are new and the only significant additions. The poem in its final form is now substantially achieved.

Again addressed to Wordsworth, the text transcribed for Sir George and Lady Beaumont breaks off after 'My shaping spirit of Imagination' and is described by Coleridge himself as 'imperfect'. I have recorded one variant, corresponding to line 67 of subsequent versions, because it introduces a Neoplatonic image ('Joy, effluent & mysterious') which Coleridge developed in a new line (68) added in 1817 and revised in 1828.

From *Sibylline Leaves* onwards the variants are few and minor indeed, and, so long as these are recorded, it cannot make much difference which version is chosen as the copy text. There is at least a possibility that Coleridge's nephew Henry Nelson Coleridge may have been responsible for the several unimportant (but in my opinion injudicious) changes of punctuation that appear in the 1834 text. There is no doubt that Coleridge himself was responsible for the decision to change the 1817 wording of line 68 to what appears in the 1828 and later versions. The text of *Dejection* printed in 1829 corrects one obvious compositor's error but is otherwise typographically identical with that of 1828. A strong case can be made for choosing the 1834 version as copy text, but, for the reasons suggested, I have decided to reproduce that of 1829 as the text which probably conforms most closely to the author's final intentions.

Since nearly ninety percent of the variants recorded in my collation derive from the *Morning Post* version, it would be uneconomical and perhaps obfuscating to affix the 'MP' label to all that do. I have therefore identified the sources of the other variants listed and specified *MP* as a source only when not to do so would be confusing.

I should add that the explanatory note to line 100 first appeared in the *Morning Post*. The 'is' of the first and the 'and' of the last clauses were added in *Sibylline Leaves*, whilst 'Storm-wind' was substituted for 'wind' in 1828.

A final comment: although a parallel text presentation of the verse letter and *Dejection: An Ode* is attractive in principle, it is feasible only through line 46 of the ode (51 of the letter), and so I have followed the usual practice of printing the two texts in tandem, leaving the reader to perform his own collation of the letter with later versions.

N.B. The recently discovered manuscript mentioned in the Introduction belonged to an extraordinary cache of Wordsworth–Coleridge MSS. put up for auction by Sotheby's (London) on 6 July 1977—i.e. shortly after this book had gone to press. I was able to inspect the MS. closely, but not to undertake a full collation, before it was sold. Transcribed by Mary Hutchinson, this version of the poem is untitled and undated. But it is addressed to Sara, and although its variant phrasings are numerous (adding up to as many as eighty-five words by Sotheby's count), it is substantially the same poem as the verse letter. The Sotheby's catalogue places this draft (which I shall refer to as *MH*) after the verse letter but before *Soth.*, i.e. between 4 April and 19 July 1802, and this dating may well be correct. What appear as verse paragraphs in the letter are numbered here and therefore are much more recognizable as Pindaric strophes. It is reasonable to suppose that the more formal version copied by Sara's sister is also the relatively more public and later one. Moreover, a few of the variants in *MH* seem more 'advanced': e.g. 'mountain Pond' of the letter is 'Tairn' in *MH*, and 'mountain Tairn' in *Soth.* and later versions. However, some of the evidence points in the opposite direction. For in several instances the letter is more 'advanced' and the *MH* variants must be considered either temporary second thoughts or earlier phrasings: e.g. 'Ere I was wedded' in *MH* reads 'There was a time when' in all other known versions of the poem. The biographical and manuscript evidence (e.g. a watermark date of 1798) appears equally inconclusive. My own hypothesis is that *MH* is not a revision of the letter or *vice versa*, but that both are experimental copies, i.e. copies in which variant wordings are being tried out, of a version X which has not survived. Thus *MH* might well be the later draft and yet still preserve some readings (including strophe numbers) that antedate those of the letter. In any case, I can find nothing in *MH* that undermines the argument of Chapter One; on the contrary, a variant like 'Ere I was wedded' (or 'suffus'd' instead of 'overspread') might be construed to reinforce it. I should add that *MH* was sold to a bookseller and, at the time of writing, has yet to find a home in a public repository and be made available for publication in full.

A Letter to——
April 4, 1802.—Sunday Evening.

Well! if the Bard was weatherwise, who made
The grand old Ballad of Sir Patrick Spence,
This Night, so tranquil now, will not go hence
Unrous'd by winds, that ply a busier trade
Than that, which moulds yon clouds in lazy flakes,   5
Or the dull sobbing Draft, that drones & rakes
Upon the Strings of this Eolian Lute,
Which better far were mute.

For, lo! the New Moon, winter-bright!
And overspread with phantom Light,   10
(With swimming phantom Light o'erspread
But rimm'd & circled with a silver Thread)
I see the Old Moon in her Lap, foretelling
The coming-on of Rain & squally Blast—
O! Sara! that the Gust ev'n now were swelling,   15
And the slant Night-shower driving loud & fast!
A Grief without a pang, void, dark, & drear,
A stifling, drowsy, unimpassion'd Grief
That finds no natural Outlet, no Relief

In word, or sigh, or tear—   20

This, Sara! well thou know'st,
Is that sore Evil, which I dread the most,
And oft'nest suffer! In this heartless Mood,
To other thoughts by yonder Throstle woo'd,
That pipes within the Larch tree, not unseen,   25
(The Larch, which pushes out in tassels green
It's bundled Leafits) woo'd to mild Delights
By all the tender Sounds & gentle Sights

Of this sweet Primrose-mouth—& *vainly* woo'd
O dearest Sara! in this heartless Mood
All this long Eve, so balmy & serene,
Have I been gazing on the western Sky 30
And it's peculiar Tint of Yellow Green—
And still I gaze—— with how blank an eye!
And those thin Clouds above, in flakes & bars,
That give away their Motion to the Stars;
Those Stars, that glide behind them, or between, 35
Now sparkling, now bedimm'd, but always seen;
Yon crescent Moon, as fix'd as if it grew
In it's own cloudless, starless Lake of Blue—
A boat becalm'd! dear William's Sky Canoe!
—I see them all, so excellently fair! 40
I see, not feel, how beautiful they are.
    My genial Spirits fail—
      And what can these avail
To lift the smoth'ring Weight from off my Breast?
    It were a vain Endeavor, 45
      Tho' I should gaze for ever
On that Green Light which lingers in the West!
I may not hope from outward Forms to win
The Passion & the Life whose Fountains are within!
These lifeless Shapes, around, below, Above, 50
    O what can they impart?
When even the gentle Thought, that thou, my Love!
    Art gazing now, like me,
    And see'st the Heaven, I see— 55
Sweet Thought it is—yet feebly stirs my Heart!

    Feebly! O feebly!—Yet
      (I well remember it)
In my first Dawn of Youth that Fancy stole
With many secret Yearnings on my Soul. 60
At eve, sky-gazing in 'ecstatic fit'
(Alas! for cloister'd in a city School
The Sky was all, I knew, of Beautiful)
At the barr'd window often did I sit,
And oft upon the leaded School-roof lay, 65
    And to myself would say—
There does not live the Man so stripp'd of good affections
As not to love to see a Maiden's quiet Eyes
Uprais'd, and linking on sweet Dreams by dim Connections 70

To Moon, or Evening Star, or glorious western Skies—
While yet a Boy, this Thought would so pursue me
That often it became a kind of Vision to me!   75

Sweet Thought! and dear of old
To Hearts of finer Mould!
Ten thousand times by Friends & Lovers blest!
    I spake with rash Despair,
    And ere I was aware,
The Weight was somewhat lifted from my Breast!   80
O Sara! in the weather-fended Wood,
Thy lov'd haunt! where the Stock-doves coo at Noon,
    I guess, that thou hast stood
And watch'd yon Crescent, & it's ghost-like Moon.
And yet, far rather in my present mood   85
I would, that thou'dst been sitting all this while
Upon the sod-built Seat of Camomile—
And tho' thy Robin may have ceas'd to sing,
Yet needs for *my* sake must thou love to hear
The Bee-hive murmuring near,   90
That ever-busy & most quiet Thing
Which I have heard at Midnight murmuring.

    I feel my spirit moved—
    And wheresoe'er thou be,
    O Sister! O Beloved!   95
    Those dear mild Eyes, that see
    Even now the Heaven, *I see*—
There is a Prayer in them! It is for *me*—
And I, dear Sara—*I* am blessing *thee*!

It was as calm as this, that happy night   100
When Mary, thou, & I together were,
The low decaying Fire our only Light,
And listen'd to the Stillness of the Air!
O that affectionate & blameless Maid,
Dear Mary! on her Lap my head she lay'd—   105
    Her Hand was on my Brow,
    Even as my own is now;
And on my Cheek I felt thy eye-lash play.
Such Joy I had, that I may truly say,
My Spirit was awe-stricken with the Excess   110
And trance-like Depth of it's brief Happiness.

Ah fair Remembrances, that so revive
The Heart, & fill it with a living Power,
Where were they, Sara?—or did I not strive
To win them to me?—on the fretting Hour
Then when I wrote thee that complaining Scroll   115
Which even to bodily Sickness bruis'd thy Soul!
And yet thou blam'st thyself alone! And yet
    Forbidd'st me all Regret!

And must I not regret, that I distress'd
Thee, best belov'd! who lovest me the best?   120
My better mind had fled, I know not whither,
For O! was this an Absent Friend's Employ
To send from far both Pain & Sorrow thither
    Where still his Blessings should have call'd down Joy!
I read thy guileless Letter o'er again—   125
I hear thee of thy blameless Self complain—
And only this I learn—& this, alas! I know—
That thou art weak & pale with Sickness, Grief, & Pain—
    And I—I made thee so!

O for my own sake I regret perforce   130
Whatever turns thee, Sara! from the Course
Of calm Well-being & a Heart at rest!
When thou, & with thee those, whom thou lov'st best,
Shall dwell together in one happy Home,
One House, the dear *abiding* Home of All,   135
I too will crown me with a Coronal—
Nor shall this Heart in idle Wishes roam
    Morbidly soft!
No! let me trust, that I shall wear away
In no inglorious Toils the manly Day,   140
And only now & then, & not too oft,
Some dear & memorable Eve will bless
Dreaming of all your Loves & Quietness.

Be happy, & I need thee not in sight.
Peace in thy Heart, & Quiet in thy Dwelling,   145
Health in thy Limbs, & in thine Eyes the Light
Of Love, & Hope, & honorable Feeling—
Where e'er I am, I shall be well content!
Not near thee, haply shall be more content!
To all things I prefer the Permanent.   150

And better seems it for a heart, like mine,
Always to *know*, than sometimes to behold,
    Their Happiness & thine—
For Change doth trouble me with pangs untold!
To see thee, hear thee, feel thee—then to part   155
    Oh! it weighs down the Heart!
To *visit* those, I love, as I love thee,
Mary, & William, & dear Dorothy,
It is but a temptation to repine—
The transientness is Poison in the Wine,   160
Eats out the pith of Joy, makes all Joy hollow,
All Pleasure a dim Dream of Pain to follow!
My own peculiar Lot, my house-hold Life
It is, & will remain, Indifference or Strife—
While *ye* are *well & happy*, 'twould but wrong you   165
If I should fondly yearn to be among you—
Wherefore, O wherefore! should I wish to be
A wither'd branch upon a blossoming Tree?

But (let me say it! for I vainly strive
To beat away the Thought) but if thou pin'd,   170
Whate'er the Cause, in body or in mind,
I were the miserablest Man alive
To know it & be absent! Thy Delights
Far off, or near, alike I may partake—
But O! to mourn for thee, & to forsake   175
All power, all hope of giving comfort to thee—
To know that thou art weak & worn with pain,
And not to hear thee, Sara! not to view thee—
    Not sit beside thy Bed,
    Not press thy aching Head,   180
    Not bring thee Health again—
        At least to hope, to try—
By this Voice, which thou lov'st, & by this earnest Eye—

Nay, wherefore did I let it haunt my Mind
    The dark distressful Dream!   185
I turn from it, & listen to the Wind
Which long has rav'd unnotic'd! What a Scream
Of agony by Torture lengthen'd out
That Lute sent forth! O thou wild Storm without!
Jagg'd Rock, or mountain Pond, or blasted Tree,   190
Or Pine-Grove, whither Woodman never clomb,
Or lonely House, long held the Witches' Home,

Methinks were fitter Instruments for Thee,
Mad Lutanist! that in this month of Showers,
Of dark brown Gardens, & of peeping Flowers,
Mak'st Devil's Yule, with worse than wintry Song
The Blossoms, Buds, and timorous Leaves among!
Thou Actor, perfect in all tragic Sounds!   195
Thou mighty Poet, even to frenzy bold!
    What tell'st thou now about?
'Tis of the Rushing of an Host in Rout—
And many Groans from men with smarting Wounds—
At once they groan with smart, and shudder with Cold!   200
'Tis hush'd! there is a Trance of deepest Silence,
Again! but all that Sound, as of a rushing Crow'd,
And Groans & tremulous Shudderings, all are over—
And it has other Sounds, and all less deep, less loud!
    A Tale of less Affright,   205
    And temper'd with Delight,
As William's Self had made the tender Lay—
    'Tis of a little Child
    Upon a heathy Wild,
Not far from home—but it has lost it's way—   210
And now moans low in utter grief & fear—
And now screams loud, & hopes to make it's Mother hear!

'Tis Midnight! and small Thoughts have I of Sleep—
Full seldom may my Friend such Vigils keep—
O breathe She softly in her gentle Sleep!   215
Cover her, gentle Sleep! with wings of Healing.
And be this Tempest but a Mountain Birth!
May all the Stars hang bright about her Dwelling,
Silent, as tho' they watch'd the sleeping Earth!
Healthful & light, my Darling! may'st thou rise   220
    With clear & chearful Eyes—
And of the same good Tidings to me send!
    For, oh! beloved Friend!
I am not the buoyant Thing, I was of yore—
When, like an own Child, I to Joy belong'd;   225
For others mourning oft, myself oft sorely wrong'd,
Yet bearing all things then, as if I nothing bore!

    Yes, dearest Sara! Yes!
There was a time when tho' my path was rough,
The Joy within me dallied with Distress;   230
And all Misfortunes were but as the Stuff

255

Whence Fancy made me Dreams of Happiness:
For Hope grew round me, like the climbing Vine,
And Leaves & Fruitage, not my own, seem'd mine!
But now Ill Tidings bow me down to earth—
Nor care I, that they rob me of my Mirth—   235
    But oh! each Visitation
Suspends what Nature gave me at my Birth,
    My shaping Spirit of Imagination!   240

I speak not now of those habitual Ills
That wear out Life, when two unequal Minds
Meet in one House, & two discordant Wills—
    This leave me, where it finds,   245
Past cure, & past Complaint—a fate austere
Too fix'd & hopeless to partake of Fear!

But thou, dear Sara! (dear indeed thou art,
My Comforter! A Heart within my Heart!)
Thou, & the Few, we love, tho' few ye be,   250
Make up a world of Hopes & Fears for me.
And if Affliction, or distemp'ring Pain,
Or wayward Chance befall you, I complain
Not that I mourn—O Friends, most dear! most true!
    Methinks to weep with you   255
Were better far than to rejoice alone—
But that my coarse domestic Life has known
No Habits of heart-nursing Sympathy,
No Griefs, but such as dull and deaden me,
No mutual mild Enjoyments of it's own,   260
No Hopes of its own Vintage, None, O! none—
Whence when I mourn'd for you, my Heart might borrow
Fair forms & living Motions for it's Sorrow.
For not to think of what I needs must feel,
But to be still & patient all I can;   265
And haply by abstruse Research to steal
From my own Nature all the Natural Man—
This was my sole Resource, my wisest plan!
And that, which suits a part, infects the whole,
And now is almost grown the Temper of my Soul.   270

    My little Children are a Joy, a Love,
    A good Gift from above!
But what is Bliss, that still calls up a Woe,

And makes it doubly keen

Compelling me to *feel*, as well as KNOW, 275
What a most blessed Lot mine might have been.
Those little Angel Children (woe is me!)
There have been hours, when feeling how they bind
And pluck out the Wing-feathers of my Mind, 280
Turning my Error to Necessity,
I have half-wish'd, they never had been born!
That seldom! But sad Thoughts they always bring,
And like the Poet's Philomel, I sing
My Love-song, with my breast against a Thorn. 285

With no unthankful Spirit I confess,
This clinging Grief too, in it's turn, awakes
That Love, and Father's Joy; but O! it makes
The Love the greater, & the Joy far less.
These Mountains too, these Vales, these Woods, these Lakes, 290
Scenes full of Beauty & of Loftiness
Where all my Life I fondly hop'd to live—
I were sunk low indeed, did they *no* solace give;
But oft I seem to feel, & evermore I fear,
They are not to me now the Things, which once they were. 295

O Sara! we receive but what we give,
And in *our* Life alone does Nature live.
Our's is her Wedding Garment, our's her Shroud—
And would we aught behold of higher Worth
Than that inanimate cold World allow'd 300
To the poor loveless ever-anxious Crowd,
Ah! from the Soul itself must issue forth
A Light, a Glory, and a luminous Cloud
Enveloping the Earth!
And from the Soul itself must there be sent 305
A sweet & potent Voice, of it's own Birth,
Of all sweet Sounds the Life & Element.

O pure of Heart! thou need'st not ask of me
What this strong music in the Soul may be,
What, & wherein it doth exist, 310
This Light, this Glory, this fair luminous Mist,
This beautiful & beauty-making Power!
Joy, innocent Sara! Joy, that ne'er was given
Save to the Pure, & in their purest Hour,
Joy, Sara! is the Spirit & the Power, 315

That wedding Nature to us gives in Dower
A new Earth & new Heaven
Undreamt of by the Sensual & the Proud!
Joy is that strong Voice, Joy that luminous Cloud—
    We, we ourselves rejoice!
And thence flows all that charms or ear or sight,
All melodies the Echoes of that Voice,
All Colors a Suffusion of that Light.   320

Sister & Friend of my devoutest Choice!
Thou being innocent & full of love,
And nested with the Darlings of thy Love,
And feeling in thy Soul, Heart, Lips, & Arms   325
Even what the conjugal & mother Dove
That borrows genial Warmth from those, she warms,
Feels in her thrill'd wings, blessedly outspread—
Thou free'd awhile from Cares & human Dread   330

By the Immenseness of the Good & Fair
    Which thou see'st every where—
Thus, thus should'st thou rejoice!
To thee would all Things live from Pole to Pole,   335
Their Life the Eddying of thy living Soul—
O dear! O Innocent! O full of Love!
A very Friend! A Sister of my Choice—
O dear, as Light & Impulse from above,
Thus may'st thou ever, evermore rejoice!   340

                   S. T. C.

DEJECTION:

AN ODE.

———

I.

Well! if the Bard was weather-wise, who made
The grand old ballad of Sir Patrick Spence,
This night, so tranquil now, will not go hence
Unroused by winds, that ply a busier trade
Than those which mould yon cloud in lazy flakes,
Late, late yestreen I saw the new Moon,
With the old Moon in her arms;
And I fear, I fear, my Master dear!
We shall have a deadly storm.
        BALLAD OF SIR PATRICK SPENCE.

Than those which mould yon cloud in lazy flakes,
Or the dull sobbing draft, that moans and rakes
    Upon the strings of this Æolian lute,
    Which better far were mute.
For lo! the New-moon winter-bright!
And overspread with phantom light,
    (With swimming phantom light o'erspread
    But rimmed and circled by a silver thread)
I see the old Moon in her lap, foretelling
    The coming on of rain and squally blast.
And oh! that even now the gust were swelling,
    And the slant night-shower driving loud and fast!
Those sounds which oft have raised me, whilst they awed,
    And sent my soul abroad,
Might now perhaps their wonted impulse give,
Might startle this dull pain, and make it move and live!

II.

A grief without a pang, void, dark, and drear,
A stifled, drowsy, unimpassioned grief,
Which finds no natural outlet, no relief,
    In word, or sigh, or tear—
O Lady! in this wan and heartless mood,
To other thoughts by yonder throstle woo'd,
    All this long eve, so balmy and serene,
Have I been gazing on the western sky,
    And its peculiar tint of yellow green:
And still I gaze—and with how blank an eye!
And those thin clouds above, in flakes and bars,
That give away their motion to the stars;
Those stars, that glide behind them or between,
Now sparkling, now bedimmed, but always seen:
Yon crescent Moon as fixed as if it grew
In its own cloudless, starless lake of blue;
I see them all so excellently fair,
I see, not feel how beautiful they are!

III.

My genial spirits fail,
    And what can these avail
To lift the smothering weight from off my breast?
    It were a vain endeavour,
    Though I should gaze for ever

On that green light that lingers in the west: 45
I may not hope from outward forms to win
The passion and the life, whose fountains are within.

IV.

O Lady! we receive but what we give,
And in our life alone does nature live:
Ours is her wedding-garment, ours her shroud!
And would we aught behold, of higher worth, 50
Than that inanimate cold world allowed
To the poor loveless ever-anxious crowd,
Ah! from the soul itself must issue forth,
A light, a glory, a fair luminous cloud
  Enveloping the Earth— 55
And from the soul itself must there be sent
  A sweet and potent voice, of its own birth,
Of all sweet sounds the life and element!

V.

O pure of heart! thou need'st not ask of me
What this strong music in the soul may be! 60
What, and wherein it doth exist,
This light, this glory, this fair luminous mist,
This beautiful and beauty-making power.
  Joy, virtuous Lady! Joy that ne'er was given,
Save to the pure, and in their purest hour, 65
Life, and Life's Effluence, Cloud at once and Shower,
Joy, Lady! is the spirit and the power,
Which wedding Nature to us gives in dower
  A new Earth and new Heaven,
Undreamt of by the sensual and the proud— 70
Joy is sweet voice, Joy the luminous cloud—
  We in ourselves rejoice!
And thence flows all that charms or ear or sight,
  All melodies the echoes of that voice,
All colours a suffusion from that light. 75

VI.

There was a time when, though my path was rough,
This joy within me dallied with distress,
And all misfortunes were but as the stuff
Whence Fancy made me dreams of happiness:

For hope grew round me, like the twining vine,
And fruits, and foliage, not my own, seemed mine.
But now afflictions bow me down to earth:
Nor care I that they rob me of my mirth,
    But oh! each visitation 85
Suspends what nature gave me at my birth,
    My shaping spirit of Imagination.
For not to think of what I needs must feel,
    But to be still and patient, all I can;
And haply by abstruse research to steal 90
From my own nature all the natural Man—
    This was my sole resource, my only plan:
Till that which suits a part infects the whole,
And now is almost grown the habit of my Soul.

VII.

Hence, viper thoughts, that coil around my mind,
    Reality's dark dream!
I turn from you, and listen to the wind, 95
    Which long has raved unnoticed. What a scream
Of agony by torture lengthened out
That lute sent forth! Thou Wind, that ravest without,
    Bare crag, or mountain-tairn,* or blasted tree, 100
    Or pine-grove whither woodman never clomb,
    Or lonely house, long held the witches' home,
      Methinks were fitter instruments for thee,
Mad Lutanist! who in this month of showers,
Of dark brown gardens, and of peeping flowers, 105
    Mak'st Devils' yule, with worse than wintry song,
The blossoms, buds, and timorous leaves among.
      Thou Actor, perfect in all tragic sounds!
      Thou mighty Poet, e'en to Frenzy bold!
        What tell'st thou now about? 110
    'Tis of the Rushing of an Host in rout,
With groans of trampled men, with smarting wounds—
At once they groan with pain, and shudder with the cold!
But hush! there is a pause of deepest silence!

* Tairn is a small lake, generally if not always applied to
the lakes up in the mountains, and which are the feeders of
those in the vallies. This address to the Storm-wind will not
appear extravagant to those who have heard it at night, and
in a mountainous country.

And all that noise, as of a rushing crowd,
With groans, and tremulous shudderings—all is over—
It tells another tale, with sounds less deep and loud!   115
    A tale of less affright,
    And tempered with delight,
As Otway's self had framed the tender lay,   120
    'Tis of a little child
    Upon a lonesome wild,
Not far from home, but she hath lost her way:
And now moans low in bitter grief and fear,
And now screams loud, and hopes to make her mother hear.   125

VIII.

'Tis midnight, but small thoughts have I of sleep:
Full seldom may my friend such vigils keep!
Visit her, gentle Sleep! with wings of healing,
    And may this storm be but a mountain-birth,
May all the stars hang bright above her dwelling,   130
Silent as though they watched the sleeping Earth!
    With light heart may she rise,
    Gay fancy, cheerful eyes,
Joy lift her spirit, joy attune her voice:
To her may all things live, from Pole to Pole,   135
Their life the eddying of her living soul!
    O simple spirit, guided from above,
Dear Lady! friend devoutest of my choice,
Thus mayest thou ever, evermore rejoice.

NOTES

[N.B. The author's editorial comments are italicized; Coleridge's original italicized words are underlined.]

title: Dejection. An Ode, Written April 4, 1802.
epigraph: Late] LATE

2   The grand Old Ballad of SIR PATRICK SPENCE,
4   Unroused] Unrous'd MP, SL.
5   those] those,   cloud] clouds MP, SL.
6   Or this dull sobbing draft, that drones and rakes
7   Æolian] Eolian 1834.
9   New-moon] New Moon
12 rimmed] rimm'd MP, SL.
13 old] Old
14 blast:] blast:
       old] Old
       dear] dear,

15   oh] O

16   night-shower] night-show'r

17   raised] rais'd   awed] aw'd

22   unimpassioned] unimpassion'd *MP, SL.*

23   no natural outlet, no relief,] no nat'ral outlet, no relief

25   O Lady] O EDMUND

28   western] Western

29   its] it's *SL.*   yellow green] yellow-green

33   them or] them, or

34   bedimmed] bedimm'd *MP, SL.*   seen:] seen; *MP, SL.*

35   Moon] moon, *MP.* Moon, *SL*   fixed] fix'd, *MP, SL*   grew] grew,

36   blue;] blue,

after line 36: A boat becalm'd, a lovely sky-canoe]

37   all] all,   fair,] fair—

38   I *see,* not *feel,* how beautiful they are]

39   fail,] fail; *MP, 1834.*

40   avail] avail,

41   smothering] smoth'ring *MP, SL.*

42   endeavour] endeavor *SL.*

43   Though] Tho'

47   O Lady] O EDMUND

48   our] *our*   nature] Nature

51   world allowed] world, *allow'd* MP. world *allow'd SL.*

53   Ah!] Ah

59–75 *included in Stanza IV of MP.*

60   be!] be?

63   beautiful] beautiful, *SL.*   power,] power?

64   Joy, virtuous Lady] JOY, virtuous EDMUND

66   *This line does not appear before SL.*

      Life, and life's effulgence, cloud at once and shower, *SL.*

      Life, and life's effulgence, cloud at once and shower, *1834.*

67   Lady] EDMUND   power] pow'r

      Joy, effluent & mysterious, is the Power *Beau.*

68   dower] dow'r *MP, SL.* dower, *1834.*

69   Earth] earth

70   Undreamt] Undream'd

71   Joy . . . Joy] JOY . . . JOY

72   We in] We, we

76   *The new stanza is numbered V in MP and opens:*

      Yes, dearest EDMUND, yes]

      There was a time when, tho' my path was rough,

79   Fancy] fancy

81   seemed] seem'd *MP, SL.*

83   I] I,

84   oh] O

86   Imagination] imagination

87–93 *omitted in MP with this note in their place:*

      [The sixth and seventh Stanzas omitted.]

90 Man] man 1834.
93 Soul] soul 1834.
94–95 *The new stanza is numbered VIII in MP and begins:*
    O wherefore did I let it haunt my mind,
      This dark distressful dream?
96 you] it
97 raved unnoticed] rav'd unnotic'd MP, SL.
    wind,] wind
98 Of agony, by torture, lengthen'd out, MP
99 Thou Wind] O wind   lengthen'd SL
    ravest] rav'st MP, SL.
100 crag] craig 1834
101 pine-grove] pine-grove,
104 who] who,   showers] show'rs MP, SL.
105 dark brown] dark-brown   flowers] flow'rs MP, SL.
106 Devils] devil's   wintry] wint'ry SL.
107 timorous] tim'rous MP, SL.
109 e'en] ev'n   Frenzy] frenzy MP, 1834.
111 Rushing of an Host] rushing of an host MP. rushing of a host 1834.
112 With many groans of men with smarting wounds—
116 groans,] groans   over—] over!
117 loud!] loud—
119 tempered] temper'd MP, SL.
120 As EDMUND'S self had fram'd the tender lay— MP.   fram'd SL.
121 child,] child.
123 home,] home;   hath lost her way:] has lost her way—
124 low,] low,
125 hear,] hear!   fear,] fear;
126 but] and   sleep:] sleep;
128 her] him   Sleep!] Sleep,
129 mountain-birth] mountain birth
130 her] his
131 Silent, as tho' they watch'd MP   watch'd SL.
132 she] he

After 133 in MP the following lines appear:
And sing his lofty song, and teach me to rejoice!
O EDMUND, friend of my devoutest choice,
O rais'd from anxious dread and busy care,
By the immenseness of the good and fair
Which thou see'st ev'ry where,
Joy lifts thy spirit, joy attunes thy voice,

134 voice:] voice; 1834.
135 To thee do all things live from pole to pole, MP.   pole to pole 1834.
136 her] thy
138 O lofty Poet, full of life and love,
    Brother and friend of my devoutest choice,
139 mayest] may'st MP, SL.   ever] ever   rejoice.]rejoice!   MP. rejoice,
    1828.

MP is signed ΕΣΤΗΣΕ.

Index